Big Men, Little People

Alec Russell

Big Men, Little People

Encounters in Africa

MACMILLAN

First published 1999 by Macmillan
an imprint of Macmillan Publishers Ltd
25 Eccleston Place, London SW1W 9NF
Basingstoke and Oxford
Associated companies throughout the world
www.macmillan.co.uk

ISBN 0 333 75359 3 (Hardback)
ISBN 0 333 75360 7 (Trade Paperback)

A CIP catalogue record for this book is available from
the British Library.

Typeset by SetSystems Ltd, Saffron Walden, Essex
Printed and bound in Great Britain by
Mackays of Chatham plc, Chatham, Kent

For my parents

Contents

Contents

List of Illustrations

Section Two

Eugene Terre'Blanche, leader of South Africa's neo-Nazi AWB movement, in full apocalyptic flow in 1994 shortly before the collapse of the extreme Right-wing. *Jan Kopec, Camera Press*

Chief Mangosuthu Buthelezi, leader of South Africa's mainly Zulu Inkatha Freedom Party, at the annual Reed Dance with his nephew, King Goodwill Zwelithini. *Ian Berry, Magnum Photos*

A Zulu induna (headman) addresses an impi of Zulu men at a rally of the Inkatha Freedom party for the 1994 election. *Tiddy Maitland Titterton*

Detective Superintendent Douglas Campbell and Detective Inspector Jim Marshall of Scotland Yard in the Botswana village of Mochudi, on a mission to investigate a ritual killing. *Graeme Williams*

King Mswati of Swaziland, Africa's last absolute monarch, during an interview with the author in 1996. *Lori Waselchuk*

King Mswati in his traditional warrior costume at his enthronement ceremony. *Andrzej Sawa, Camera Press*

Huddled in a blanket and headscarf the Rain Queen, Modjadji V, of South Africa, cuts an obtrusive figure during an interview with the author in 1997. *Graeme Williams*

President Nelson Mandela in a trademark jazzy shirt. *Camera Press*

Winnie Madikizela-Mandela at an ANC rally in 1994. *Tiddy Maitland Titterton*

President Jerry Rawlings of Ghana in a characteristic intense pose. *Joshua Amartey, Camera Press*

Thabo Mbeki, President of the ANC and President Mandela's chosen successor. *Camera Press*

Yoweri Museveni of Uganda. *Alfred Pucciano, Camera Press*

Acknowledgements

Many people helped in writing and researching this book. Pursuing Africa's Big Men would have been impossible without the help of journalists all over the continent. In South Africa I owe a particular debt to Lourens Ackermann, Abbey Makoe, Christopher Munnion, Joy and Ian Brady, Peter Nkomo, and Dorah Mafifi for her care and constant good cheer.

As a foreign correspondent I owe much to my colleagues and editors in London. Max Hastings, the former editor of the *Daily Telegraph*, posted me to Johannesburg in the first place and Charles Moore, his successor, kept me there and then gave me four months off to write this book. Their foreign editors, Nigel Wade, Patrick Bishop and Stephen Robinson, and Will Ellsworth Jones of the *Telegraph Magazine* encouraged me to travel across Africa. On the foreign desk, Frank Taylor, Pat Prentice, Robin Gedye, Michael Kallenbach, Paul Hill, Patsy Dryden and Theresa Jeffrey offered stalwart support and advice. Thanks also to the switchboard for tracking me down so often in remote locations and the copy-takers for taking down my words usually on the most atrocious telephone lines. Michael Hill, the veteran Africa correspondents Sam Kiley and Chris McGreal, Hugh Dellios, John Balzar, Allan Little, George Alagiah, Steve Scott, Mary Braid, Inigo Gilmore and many other colleagues, enlivened the long days on the road.

Catherine Whitaker encouraged me to write the book and then offered invaluable advice on the manuscript. Peter Nkomo hunted down arcane references in Johannesburg as I sat writing in

Acknowledgements

Shepherd's Bush, six thousand miles to the north. The *Telegraph* library filled in the gaps. Fred Bridgland, Justice Malala, Khaba Mkhize, Musa Ndlangamandla, Louise Tunbridge and David Nthengwe pointed out flaws in particular chapters. Christopher Munnion, Roger Matthews and Lourens Ackermann cast their critical eyes over early drafts. Sophie, my wife, had the harder task of tackling chapters as they emerged even as Mungo burst into our life – if he hadn't learned to sleep through the night at three months, this would never have been written.

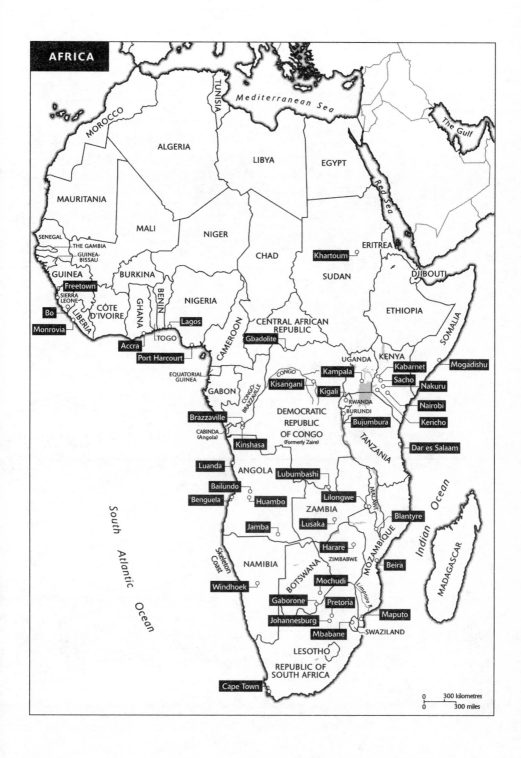

AFRICA

Mediterranean Sea

The Gulf

MOROCCO

TUNISIA

ALGERIA

LIBYA

EGYPT

Red Sea

MAURITANIA

MALI

NIGER

CHAD

SUDAN

ERITREA

DJIBOUTI

SENEGAL
THE GAMBIA
GUINEA-BISSAU

GUINEA

BURKINA

NIGERIA

KhartoumÂ·

ETHIOPIA

SOMALIA

SIERRA
LEONE

Freetown

BoÂ·

Monrovia

LIBERIA

CÔTE
D'IVOIRE

GHANA

BENIN

TOGO

Lagos

Accra

Port Harcourt

EQUATORIAL
GUINEA

CAMEROON

CENTRAL AFRICAN
REPUBLIC

Gbadolite

GABON

CONGO

CONGO-
BRAZZAVILLE

Brazzaville

CABINDA
(Angola)

Kinshasa

DEMOCRATIC
REPUBLIC
OF CONGO
(Formerly Zaire)

Kisangani

Kigali

UGANDA

Kampala

RWANDA

BURUNDI

Bujumbura

TANZANIA

KENYA

Kabarnet

Sacho

Nairobi

Nakuru

Kericho

Mogadishu

Dar es Salaam

Luanda

ANGOLA

Lubumbashi

Bailundo

Benguela

Huambo

Jamba

ZAMBIA

Lusaka

Lilongwe

MALAWI

Blantyre

Indian
Ocean

South
Atlantic
Ocean

Harare

ZIMBABWE

MOZAMBIQUE

Beira

Limpopo R.

MADAGASCAR

Skeleton
Coast

NAMIBIA

BOTSWANA

Mochudi

Windhoek

Gaborone

Johannesburg

Pretoria

Mbabane

SWAZILAND

Maputo

LESOTHO

REPUBLIC OF
SOUTH AFRICA

Cape Town

0   300 kilometres
0   300 miles

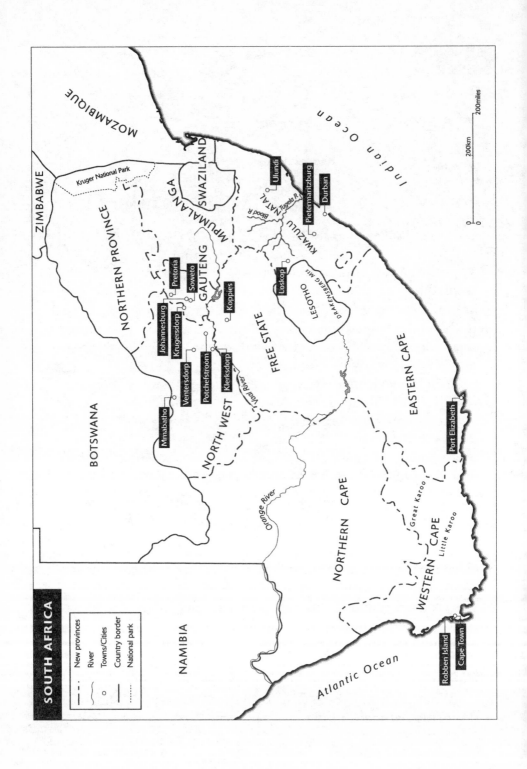

Introduction

Rhodes or Renaissance?

We were almost at the airport when they sprang the trap. There were thirty of them in pressed charcoal-grey uniforms with bright pink chevrons. A giant road-side poster proclaiming 'Jesus is our Commando' framed their oil-drum barricade. One of the ringleaders, a police inspector, swaggered towards us. With an exaggerated civility he shook our hands.

'You are welcome,' he said, before adding sternly: 'This is a mobile court.' Reuben, our driver, motioned us to keep silent. Swearing under our breath we pulled over, fearing we could be detained for hours. But it took only a moment to understand the workings of the mobile court: the police were prosecutor, jury and judge in one; there was no defence. We all knew the only issue was the size of the bribe, but the policeman doggedly maintained the pretence that his 'court' was a recognized arm of the law.

'No fire extinguisher?' he frowned when he opened our boot. 'That's very serious. You will have to come with me to the courtroom.' Reuben's protestations were not to be heard. He was escorted round the nearest corner to the 'judge', the senior police officer, to negotiate the appropriate fee.

Behind us, other 'judges' fanned out across the road. A lanky driver in a garish robe was shaking with rage. He yanked his hands up and down, remonstrating with an inscrutable sergeant.

'What do you mean, an explanation?' the driver shouted. 'You stopped me! I'm the one who needs an explanation.' But of course there was nothing he could do; to drive in Nigeria, under the late dictator General Sani Abacha, was to run an endless obstacle course. One day there was a purge on wind-screen wipers, the next on bumpers, the next on tyres. The only way to survive was to lower your gaze and pay the fee. The policeman shook our hands once Reuben had paid the fine.

'You are free to go,' he said solemnly. 'The court is over.' Quivering with the pent-up humiliation of years of such affronts, Reuben accelerated away through the back-streets of Port Harcourt, Nigeria's southern oil town. A devout Catholic, he had been a policeman at independence in 1960 and through the bloody Biafran war of 1967–70, when up to a million Nigerians died in an abortive attempt at secession by the Ibo tribe.

'We would never have behaved in this way,' Reuben said. 'We had pride in our work. But these guys, they do anything.' We drove on in silence to the airport.

♦♦♦♦

I heard Reuben's lament for the independence era many times when travelling in sub-Saharan Africa in the late Nineties. The Sixties were a heady time for Africans: all over the continent colonial flags were being struck; Africans were at last to be free; a glittering future beckoned. But for most of the continent the last forty years have been a shattering experience. Since inde-pendence Africans have been terribly betrayed.

They have been betrayed by the European powers, which abandoned their colonies in unseemly haste, leaving them with a handful of graduates to try to forge and then govern new nation states. They have been betrayed by the superpowers, who used Africa as a battlefield in the fight for global domina-tion, and sanctioned corruption and tyranny as long as their interests were served. Most of all they have been betrayed by their own leaders, who have done little but bask in personality cults, fill foreign bank accounts and beggar their people.

Independence was never going to be easy. A largely pre-literate society was being thrust headlong into the modern world. But the Big Men, as the independence leaders became known, made the task far harder. Under their misrule, Africa has plunged relentlessly downhill. The 'Toad Kings', as Wole Soyinka, Nigeria's dissident writer, dubbed them, pandered to the most grotesque caricatures of Third World dictators: courts were suborned; opponents were jailed; treasuries were pillaged; rival tribes were excluded from power. All the while the state media lauded their idiosyncrasies as the mark of genius.

From time to time a new optimistic gospel has done the rounds. In the Eighties the talk was of 'structural adjustment', a rigorous programme of free-market reform. Earnest World Bank and International Monetary Fund consultants toured the continent's capitals claiming they had the medicine for Africa's economic woes. But the austerity programmes that were essential if the reform was to work have proved all but impossible to sustain in Africa's impoverished and demoralized states. Then came the Nineties, billed as the decade of democracy following the end of the Cold War. But this too has had limited success. The euphoria over a wave of multi-party elections in the early Nineties soon waned as many of the new democrats have proved themselves cut from the Big Men's autocratic cloth.

Even Nelson Mandela's inauguration as South Africa's president in 1994, which was hailed as a new African dawn, has had limited impact on the rest of the continent. As Afrikaner fighter pilots flew over their new black president to mark the end of white rule, 2,000 miles to the north Rwandans were hacking down fellow Rwandans with machetes and hoes in a genocide that was to claim up to a million lives.

Now, at the end of the twentieth century, Africa is stumbling into another new era: the age of the Big Men is drawing to a close. The 'Great Helmsman' of Zaire, Mobutu Sese Seko; General Sani Abacha, the most brutal and corrupt in a sequence of venal Nigerian leaders; Malawi's Dr Hastings Banda, best known for his ban on long hair, mini-skirts and jeans – all died within eight months of each other. Zambia's Kenneth Kaunda has retired from the fray. A few ageing autocrats cling on to power in the same self-serving ways, notably Kenya's Daniel arap Moi and Zimbabwe's Robert Mugabe. But the independence generation is all but extinct. The key question is – inevitably – what happens next?

Can a new generation of leaders turn the tide? Have they learned from their predecessors' mistakes to fuel a renaissance? Or are the pessimists who predict more trouble ahead merely daring to face up to the truth? Is Africa doomed to more decades of turmoil? Will the twenty-first century see it slip off the edge of the world's economic map? Are the neo-colonialists right? Is it that African society is somehow unequipped to adapt to the modern world and needs outsiders to give it a helping hand?

The stories of nine very different African leaders attempt to assess these questions. It is not a comprehensive picture: more than half the leaders come from southern Africa. But it does try to show there are currents coursing through the continent which never make the news and yet which suggest that Africa's journey into the new millennium, while unsteady, is not irredeemably bleak.

I begin in the steamy heart of the Congo, the proverbial Heart of Darkness, where the twentieth century opened amid international hand-wringing over atrocities by Belgian rubber planters and closed in a depressingly similar way with outrage over massacres and mass graves. Straddling these two eras was the long rule of Mobutu, the 'King of Kleptocracy', under whom everything and everyone had a price.

Mobutu was a preposterous figure. Sustained by Cold War politics, his avarice was legendary even among other Big Men. His subjects were playthings to be exploited at will, and yet as he gazed defiantly over his palace grounds on his last public appearance, resplendent in a turquoise and gold tunic, it was easy to understand how he dazzled his people back in the Sixties when he took power. The last days of his regime shone a ray of light into the rapacity of Big Man rule and the corruption that is Africa's curse. The speed with which his successor, Laurent Kabila, imposed his own cult and forfeited

international sympathy is a sobering introduction to the difficulties Africa faces in finishing with Big Men once and for all.

My second Big Man, Dr Banda of Malawi, was, like Mobutu,
defiant to the last. As he sat in his quarters in the old British
governor's residence, a few months short of his ninety-eighth
birthday, he insisted as he always had that Malawians were like
children and could not govern themselves. His extraordinary
career from being a successful GP in North London to Life
President highlights the ease with which dictators can take
power and the difficulties would-be democrats face. Shrivelled
like a dried-up prune, he cackled to himself, muttering that
Julius Caesar was his role model because he knew how to be
'tough'.

Moi, who still rules Kenya after thirty years in the inner
circle, completes the opening trio of old-style Big Men. Moi has
been canny enough to reform just enough to stay in power.
When I finally wheedled my way into his presence he gave me
a sombre lecture on the dangers of tribalism. The bloodstained
record of Kenya's neighbours underlines his case, but Moi is, of
course, like all Big Men, a pastmaster at playing the tribal card
and indeed just about anything else that will ensure his survival.

My encounters with Mobutu, Banda and Moi leave little
doubt that the 'Four Horsemen of the Apocalypse' are not
suddenly going to retire from their favourite stamping ground;
corruption, dictatorship and tribal bloodshed will continue to
dominate Africa's political agenda. But the three leaders' bewilderment and frustration with the changing face of world politics
did also shed light on one of the positive developments of the
last decade. For more than a century Africa has been a proxy
battlefield, first for Europe's feuding colonialists and then for
the superpowers. Now the end of the Cold War has left Big
Men scrambling for support, even if one of the dangers of the
new millennium is that the superpowers' disengagement is
fuelling a weariness with Africa and a drying up of the investment it so badly needs.

The Angolan rebel leader Jonas Savimbi, now in his fourth

decade as a bush-fighter, is proof that you do not need backers to survive. He is the Frankenstein's monster of the Cold War: sustained for years by the CIA, he has now outgrown his handlers. After months underground, which sparked rumours that he was wounded or dead, he finally emerged from his bush hideaway in a dark Mercedes, wearing a cream jacket, waving an ebony cane, and oozing mystery and power. He looked like a black-marketeer, which in a sense he was – Angola's long-running war testifies to the cynicism of superpower meddling and also to Africa's bane, its vast mineral wealth. With a few exceptions, it is a sad but fundamental rule of Africa that where there are minerals there is war.

The news from Africak, however, is not all gloom. When I arrived in Johannesburg, fresh from reporting the war in Bosnia, there was talk of South Africa going the same way as the former Yugoslavia. A few years later, however, the sight of a doughty Boer farmer bumping along the road north to find a new plot in the Zambian bush was tangible proof that change is sweeping through southern Africa. The end of the Cold War paved the way for the end of apartheid, opening up South Africa, the continent's superpower, to engage with the rest of Africa. For Afrikaners it is a faltering process personified by F.W. De Klerk, Africa's last white president: they are African and yet were raised to look down on Africa. Many will stay in the *laager*; Cape Town may become the last white refuge. Others, however, are learning to engage with their continent, suggesting that Afrikaners are free at last to play a more co-operative role.

With the West losing interest in Africa, it may indeed be that whites will end up playing the same supervisory and interventionist role as their forebears in the last century, whether as individuals, corporations, or in mercenary bands. The belligerent caperings of Eugene Terre'Blanche, the white extremist, came to naught. My last sight of him was in a court in a small South African town slumped in the dock after he was sentenced to six years in prison for attempting to kill a black employee. But white militarism is on the resurgence. Swaths of the continent are on the brink of returning to the buccaneering days of Cecil Rhodes, the mining magnate and imperialist visionary, who carved an empire out of the continent. One of my most extraordinary encounters was with an Afrikaner mercenary colonel, or rather 'business consultant', in Sierra Leone. He had renamed a local hill after the Voortrekker Monument, Afrikanerdom's most hallowed memorial, as he provided security for his partners to exploit the local diamond mine. But he was adored by thousands of locals who were overjoyed that someone was compensating for the failure of their government by protecting their village.

There is, however, an Africa beyond the television images of famine and war. Most strikingly, there is a new realism among African intellectuals and politicians which hints that the psychological trauma of colonialism may be wearing off. Pinning the blame on the white man is no longer the trump card it once was. All over the continent there are people willing to say publicly that Africa has failed and that Africans themselves have to take a share of the blame. As Africa searches for a way to reconcile the medieval with the modern, Christianity and Islam with animism and tradition, many are also starting to appreciate that the continent has to find an accommodation between traditional and Western values.

Chief Mangosuthu Buthelezi, the Zulu leader, is the very image of the new-age tribal chief. He uses ethnicity and fealty to maintain his position and yet in his government office in Cape Town he is the quintessential modern man. He manipulated chiefs ruthlessly to bolster his power, but his story shows how Africa may have to find a place for the tribal chiefs who held sway before the arrival of the colonists and who still play the role of father-confessor-cum-robber baron in large tracts of the continent.

The boyish King Mswati III of Swaziland more than any other African leader understands the complexity of tradition. He made a welcome change from the pitiless politicians of central Africa. It is easy to mock Africa's last absolute monarchy with its arcane rituals and ways. The chief of police preceded me into the king's presence on his hands and knees. But the fissures that threaten Mswati's monarchy reflect the divisions at the heart of African communities, between town and country, reason and superstition, reaction and reform.

If there was one man who could bring purpose and hope to this confused and turbulent continent it was the living embodiment of reconciliation, Nelson Mandela. He is of course the great exception among independence leaders. Far from closing down streets ahead of his motorcade as is *de rigueur* for Big Men, he arrived for a lunch I was hosting without a single outrider. He is one of a handful of African heads of state to have had the interests of his people at heart. He acts as a bridge between the old and the new schools of leadership. His reconciliatory vision was imbued with African *ubuntu* (humanity) and inspired the world to hope that the continent really could throw off its troubled past. But his saintly halo slipped a little during his term in office. Even the 'Mandela magic' had limits, it seemed.

And so it is hardly surprising that South Africa's leaders faced scepticism when they talked of an 'African Renaissance'. As the millennium approaches, the future looks depressingly familiar: of Africa's four giants, only South Africa is stable; Nigeria is hazarding its umpteenth attempt at democracy; the Congo is in turmoil; the Sudan is racked by famine and war. In much of Africa minerals and might are all that count.

If Mandela's dream of a rebirth is to be realized, much depends on his successor, Thabo Mbeki, and Africa's 'new' leaders, pragmatic autocrats like Ghana's President Jerry Rawlings and Uganda's President Yoweri Museveni. The three can be roughly labelled as the democrat, the reluctant democrat and the anti-democrat. None of the three are Big Men. All indeed have vociferously condemned corruption and cults. Their challenge is stark: a relapse to the days of Rhodes, or Renaissance.

1

The King of Kleptocracy

Mobutu Sese Seko – The Curse of Corruption

For a tantalizing moment the mêlée cleared. After a stifling two-hour wait in the market which masqueraded as the arrivals hall at Kinshasa's N'djili Airport I had had my passport stamped. I had also dispensed a hundred US dollars to sundry officials, including a colonel in a band-master's uniform who bore a marked similarity to General Noriega, the pineapple-faced ex-leader of Panama. Unfortunately the 'system' had not yet finished with me. Just when it looked as though I could head for the exit and start the next battle for a taxi into town, a willowy teenager in a baggy gown ran up to me waving his arms. My 'protocol', the local euphemism for airport pimp, who had fastened on to me the moment I had left the reassuring safety of the South African Airways jet, had returned.

'There is one more thing, monsieur. The *chef*, you have to see the *chef*.' Leading me through a side-door at a canter into a maze of back-corridors, my guide explained we were bound for the head of the airport police. Enervated by my long wait and mindful of the many horror stories that criss-cross Africa about the hazards of alienating Zairean officials, I opted for a policy of beaming acquiescence. It was, in hindsight, a mistake.

A life-size portrait of President Mobutu Sese Seko hung on the *chef*'s back wall. It was the only object in the room that was not close to collapse. The wooden desk, like the walls, was visibly rotting in the tropical heat. A sidekick lounged in the far corner. His shirt was frayed at the cuffs and collar, and badly

9

needed a wash. The *chef*, however, did not have a hair out of place. Greeting me in immaculate English, he shook my hand and ushered me to the only chair. He was a senior agent of SNIP (National Police Intelligence Service), Mobutu's ubiquitous and feared secret police. He tutted when he saw my laptop computer.

'Do you have a permit? Customs duties on these are very expensive,' he said with an intake of breath. 'But fortunately I like journalists. So there is no charge.' It was a masterly act but it was all too obvious what was coming. 'I think this calls for a *petit cadeau.*'

In the dying days of Mobutu's regime N'djili Airport had the dubious accolade of Africa's most unpopular destination. That was quite an achievement in a continent where at any one time it can be guaranteed there are half a dozen small wars, but as I sat and sweated before the *chef* it was easy to appreciate why. While I never ascertained what right he had to his title, what he may have lacked in validity he made up in menace. I emerged from my ten-minute audience minus another hundred dollars. My temper was not improved when my taxi stopped on Kinshasa's outskirts and the driver said he would take me back to the airport unless I paid twice the agreed fare.

A Nigerian colleague met me in the lobby of the Intercontinental Hotel with a wry smile. On his way out of the airport a soldier had put a gun to his head, juggled a grenade, and demanded $500.

'Nigerians are children compared to this,' he said. 'You wait. Press accreditation is $700 not counting the unofficial bribes. And if you want to go to the front . . .'

More than a thousand miles to the east, Laurent Kabila, the leader of a little-known rebel group, the Alliance of Democratic Forces, had just announced he would overthrow Mobutu. Over the next six months, as the rebellion gathered momentum, I learned the old hands' tricks to soften the shock of arrival at N'djili. The Intercontinental's resident spook would for a fee pay off the enforcers and meet me at the gate. I stashed notes of different denominations in different pockets to 'satisfy' the various officials I might confront. I learned the body language of the protocols and so knew when to grovel and when to bluff.

Inevitably the tales of the Zairean frontier became a stock motif for correspondents on the long evenings before May 1997 when the rebels reached the gates of Kinshasa and Mobutu fled into exile. They pandered to the West's caricature vision of an African banana republic and fitted the Heart of Darkness clichés about the Congo. The absurdity seemed complete at another border crossing, when, to my surprise, a Zairean colonel handed back to me a bribe which a subordinate had just extracted and gave him a loud public lecture about the need for honesty. Assuming I had chanced on the one upright officer in the army, I headed on my way, thanking him profusely, only to be overtaken by the very lackey he had just abused.

'The colonel says you did not give enough,' he whispered. 'You must give us double.'

For the forty million Zaireans, however, there was nothing comic about this daily routine. Over time, I came to appreciate that the most important lesson of the airport was that, far from revelling in their power, many of the officials – although not, I suspect, the *chef* – were mortified by the state to which they had been reduced. I struck up a friendship with a young SNIP agent at the airport who went by the *nom de guerre* of Mr King. He explained that none of his colleagues had been paid for months. If they were to feed and clothe their families, let alone pay for schooling and medicines, their only option was to follow the lead of their president and sully themselves.

Zaireans called the system 'co-operation'. You had to give co-operation to get anything from a driving licence to a good school report. Expatriates called it daylight robbery. In the same week as my first harum scarum arrival at N'djili, South Africa sent a consignment of medical aid supplies. The ambassador, Jan van Deventer, a giant of an Afrikaner who understood the realities of Zaire far better than most of his more urbane European peers, had to intervene when officials started demanding 'samples' of each package. 'I drew the line at the microscope,' he recalled. 'I said you can't have a sample of that. It is all or nothing. And they backed down saying "Of course Monsieur . . . We are just doing our job." '

The result was just as Mobutu had hoped. Everyone was compromised. Over the years Africa has bred more brutal and bloodthirsty tyrants, but no one has so comprehensively pillaged a state. He was, in the words of one advisor, the 'King of Kleptocracy'. By the end of his rule Zaire had become a parody of a state where everyone and everything could be bought for the right *cadeau*.

⋔⋔⋔

For a chilling insight into how the scientific developments of the early twentieth century can be run in reverse there can be few better laboratories than Kisangani. Zaire's third largest town is 800 miles of dense rain-forest east of Kinshasa. Since the Victorian explorer and journalist Henry Stanley hacked his way there in the 1870s, slaughtering natives in his path and losing more than half his 250-strong party to disease, starvation and war, it has had a ghoulish reputation for cruelty and despair. Joseph Conrad's Kurtz was to be found there at the end of Marlow's journey to the 'Inner Station'. A Kinshasan friend had warned me that there were only three diversions in Kisangani – drinking Primus, the local beer, swatting mosquitoes and watching the soupy waters of the river Congo, or Zaire as it was renamed by Mobutu. I soon understood why. Given the cloying heat, the constant threats and intimidation from drunken soldiers, and the collapse of the infrastructure, even to move from my hotel was an almost impossible task.

I learned my lesson the hard way. I had been told the British Honorary Consul, a Belgian businessman named François Séneque, had one of the shrewdest heads in town. His residence was three miles from the centre of town and yet it took the best part of an hour to get there. The roads – if you could call them roads – had crevasses that could swallow a car, so my taxi driver had to spend much of the time ploughing through the undergrowth, which was busily reclaiming the streets. A street lamp, which amazingly was still lit, peered out of one particularly dense bush, like a monument to a bygone age. I appreciated at last an old Zairean joke. A Zairean is giving a foreigner a few driving tips. 'Which do you prefer, a pothole with water or one without?' Answer: 'The full one' because at least you know it has a bottom.'

Since independence from Belgium in 1960 the state had in all but name ceased to exist. More than four-fifths of the estimated 80,000 miles of roads had been reclaimed by the bush, as had most of the railway. Or so at least it was presumed; years had passed since anyone had travelled the roads to check. The telephone cables had long since been uprooted. The only ways to Kisangani were by air – an impossible expense for all but the élite – or a pestilential cruise up-river from Kinshasa. Locals relied on pirogues (dug-out canoes) just as they had in Stanley's day. Rule by chaos was one of Mobutu's cardinal tenets. Legend has it that when a fellow dictator telephoned him in despair to say a rebel army was at his gates, he replied, 'I told you not to build any roads.' But the collapse of the infrastructure owed as much to greed as to tactics. It was estimated in the late Seventies that more than two-thirds of the government's budget never reached its destination. By the Nineties, central funding had effectively ceased. Despatched to the extremities of the vast country, which was the size of Western Europe, provincial governors had a free hand to pillage and extort as if they were running independent states, although if Mobutu deemed one of his proconsuls had become too powerful, he swiftly summoned him back to Kinshasa and cut him down to size.

With his florid face and clipped moustache, Monsieur Séneque lent himself to a caricature of a Belgian *colon*. Kisangani was a far cry from British Leyland, where he had once worked. Two rusting sports cars in his drive testified to his long tenure in the former Stanleyville. They lacked wheels, parts of the chassis and key components of their engines and yet there they were, like their owner, waiting against the odds for better times. I half-expected to settle into a pink gin and a long tirade against Zaire. From the moment he answered his intercom service and ushered me into an air-conditioned salon I realized I could not have been more wrong.

To survive, let alone thrive, as a white businessman in Zaire has always required a touch of the diplomat, a touch of the trader and a heavy dose of the gambler. But the game had become even more complicated in the early Seventies when Mobutu introduced *authenticité*, his far-reaching Africanization programme. Officially the aim was to purge the colonial past by Zaireanizing the state. In good revolutionary style, *Monsieur* and *Madame* gave way to *Citoyen* and *Citoyenne*, the necktie to the loose African shirt, and the river Congo, like the country, was renamed Zaire. In practice it became clear to all but the most star-struck or self-interested Mobutuists that *authenticité*, like everything else Mobutu did, was about making money and entrenching his position and cult. Foreigners were among the first to understand. Overnight, party *cadres* took over their businesses 'in the interests of Zaire'.

When I arrived at Séneque's door, Kisangani was on the brink of another of its periodic convulsions. Flushed with victory, Laurent Kabila, the rebel leader, was pushing out from the eastern Kivu region where his revolt had started, and was naming Kisangani, 700 miles to the west, as his next target. M. Séneque rolled his eyes at the idea. He was adamant that the rebellion would dissipate in the jungle as had its many predecessors. Local politics may have coloured his opinions. The over-riding concern of men like Séneque was to remain on good terms with Kisangani's governor, who ran the city like a feudal fief and was wont to unleash his soldiers to remind the citizens who was in charge. But it was a credible line shared by most Zaire-watchers, as over the years Mobutu had survived many a rebellion. After a brisk lime and soda I was on my way out of his oasis into the tropical heat, convinced he was probably right and that Mobutu's misrule – or rather chaos, since even the word misrule implied an element of order – was set to continue.

My driver took me back via a tumbledown Catholic church on the edge of town where a fledgling human rights group was taking a grim record of the latest abuses by Mobutu's rabble of an army. During the previous week the soldiers had been their usual freebooting selves. Many had retreated from the battle-front and were taking out their frustrations on their own communities as they fled. Incident by incident, *Les Amis de Nelson Mandela* went through the reports, which detailed anything from soldiers entering a church during a wedding service and opening fire, to the looting of mattresses for makeshift beds. After corroboration by several witnesses the reports were entered longhand in a battered old ledger.

It was a humbling sight. None of the members had been out of Kisangani, let alone Zaire, yet there they were trying to lead their society down a new moral path inspired by Mandela's example. For an hour they quizzed me on life outside Zaire, the world's reaction to their country's crisis, and, most of all, insights into their hero, the South African president. They gave me a report to be sent on to human rights groups in the free world. I handed over a copy of *Gulliver's Travels*, whose satirical comments on man seemed all too apt. Robert Numbi, their boyish president, looked at me with a wan smile. 'Little by little our people are beginning to understand what is really happening . . .'

By then we were relying on candle-light. With the sun the dimmest of blurs it was time to return to my hotel. As a parting shot I asked for their explanation as to why Zaire had gone so terribly wrong, how an entire state could be up for sale. Numbi looked at me in surprise and – was it my imagination? – with a twinkle in his eyes.

'The chief learned his lessons well from you [whites].'

✦✦✦✦

A century after the 'Scramble for Africa' the argument about the motives and intentions of the colonists and their political masters is still bubbling, but it has lost the partisanship of the independence days. Old imperialists are prepared to concede that there was a shabby side to the Livingstonian ethos of 'civilization, Christianity and commerce', which could be rephrased 'capitalism, conquest and continental rivalry'. In

Africa itself the larceny and anarchy of the independence years have put the colonists in context. Indigenous historians accept there were romantic idealists who genuinely believed, however arrogant it now seems, that they had a role and duty to uplift the native from a state of primitive backwardness and who earnestly and honestly did their best in pursuit of this goal.

There are, however, some absolutes in this debate. One of these is that nowhere was the depredation more brazen and brutal than the Belgian Congo, the predecessor of Mobutu's Zaire. His administrators had to look back just fifty years for a case study in exploitation. Indeed it could even be argued that King Leopold II of Belgium, the founder of the Congo and the driving force behind the 'Scramble', was a role model for Mobutu.

Just as the reports of the massacres that accompanied the rebellion against Mobutu were to trickle out of the jungle in a blur of rumour and unconfirmed reports, so too the excesses of the Belgian rubber planters at the turn of the century took a long time to emerge. From his palace at Laeken King Leopold ran a masterful public relations exercise which painted his venture in the Congo as a noble humanitarian enterprise. His propaganda suggested the central African region was to become a model state. In reality the territory, which was eighty times the size of Belgium, was a giant sweat-shop which he ran as a private estate.

In the last days of Mobutu, the best sources of information for the course of the fighting in the interior were the Catholic missionaries, whose network extended across the country. Only at the end of the rebellion did I appreciate the value of their information and I made a daily trek down Kinshasa's potholed central boulevard to glean the latest. I should have read my history books more closely: missionaries had provided the bulk of the evidence against the Belgian rubber planters. For several years their horrific accounts were dismissed as hearsay until the Foreign Office finally despatched its consul, Roger Casement, to investigate. Brimming with the same ardour that was to lead him to a firing squad after his part in the Dublin uprising of 1916, his findings shocked the world.

Revelling in the soaring price of rubber, Leopold's planters treated the workers like wild animals. For most there was no pay. If they failed to deliver their quotas, they risked execution or torture. Soldiers collected baskets of severed hands, apparently to prove they had not wasted ammunition. Ears too were frequently forfeit. The abuses were ended only in 1908 when the embarrassed Belgian government formally took over responsibility for the Congo from King Leopold.

To their shock the Belgian authorities also discovered a massive discrepancy in the books. Millions of pounds of revenue had not been accounted for – a phenomenon which was to prove all too familiar to the World Bank and International Monetary Fund officials who attempted to unravel Mobutu's accounts during his long rule. Disgraced and disgruntled, King Leopold spent many of his last months in his estate at Cap Ferrat, in the south of France, just down from the villa where Mobutu was to spend much of his last year trying to keep his prostate cancer at bay. Shamed by outrage in America and Britain and indeed among their own subjects, the Belgian government remedied some of Leopold's worst abuses, but the Congo remained nothing more than a cash cow which they milked at will. With the discovery of copper and cobalt deposits and diamonds and gold, it proved even richer than Leopold had hoped when he first sponsored Stanley to chart the region. While the Belgians built roads and railways and spacious colonial towns which stocked French cheese and vintage champagne, the Africans received a minimal wage. There is even a story of a Congolese seaman jumping ship in Europe and being forbidden by the Belgians to return lest he fired up his countrymen with reports of what freedom really meant.[1]

When the wind of change blew through Africa in the 1950s there were only a handful of Congolese with an education. After riots in 1959 in Leopoldville, the colonial capital that was to be renamed Kinshasa, the Belgians panicked. They set a date for elections and independence and, just eighteen months after the disturbances, scuttled out with all they could carry. Such was their legacy to Zaire.

ᚦᚦᚦᚦ

Mobutu proved a star pupil. He once told a party congress, 'If you steal, do not steal too much at a time. You may be arrested. Steal cleverly, little by little,' but this was advice he clearly felt no need to follow. Eschewing the more underhand techniques of the élites in Nigeria and Kenya, by a narrow margin Zaire's understudies in corruption, he shamelessly flaunted the proceeds he had stolen from the state. In 1984 he went so far as to boast to American television on *60 Minutes* that he was the second richest man in the world. In his heyday his fortune was estimated at between two and five billion pounds.

His property constellation included a vineyard in Portugal, a thirty-two-room mansion in Switzerland, a castle in Spain and a magnificent first-floor apartment in Paris close to the Arc de Triomphe and within easy walking distance of the furrier who made his leopard-skin hats. The *pièce de resistance* was his pink marble palace in his home village, Gbadolite. In time-honoured Big Man style, on taking power in 1965 he set about transforming his birthplace, then a tiny jungle settlement, to be on a par with Western capitals. Four-lane highways linked his palace to the airport. The runway was specially lengthened to accommodate the Concorde which he chartered from Air France to take him to his dentist in France. In the late Eighties he sent a government-owned DC8 to Venezuela thirty-two times to pick up 5,000 sheep of a rare long-haired breed for a private ranch. 'I know my people. They like grandeur,'[2] Mobutu once said. 'They want us to have respect abroad in the eyes of foreign countries.'

'Versailles in the Jungle' operated to the very end as a parody of a Western capital. Fred Raké, the European Union ambassador, a maverick Dutchman with a keen eye for the absurd, was summoned there for a meeting in the last month of Mobutu's long rule. He was met at Gbadolite airstrip by Honore Ngbanda,

Mobutu's security advisor, in a flowing pink silk suit, at the head of a fleet of limousines which swept him to his audience.

'It was completely ridiculous,' he recalled when he was returned safely to the Intercontinental. 'Everyone was springing to attention and jumping around and saying "Yes Monsieur Ambassador. This way, Monsieur Ambassador." But it was all a façade. You have ordinary states, weak states, strong states, welfare states and then you have pretend states . . .'

Mobutu's technique was childishly simple: Zaire was his personal bank account to be debited at will. His favourite source of revenue was Zaire's fabulous mineral reserves. At one stage he was estimated to have pillaged more than a hundred million pounds a year from the copper mines alone. A Zairean banker explained to me that when Mobutu ran short of ready cash he would send a minion with a chit to the Bank of Zaire. 'Mobutu would ask for such and such a sum of dollars, the minion would take his cut by raising the amount on the slip, the bank manager would do the same, and so on until the bank had dished out more than twice the original amount.'

The difficulties that Mobutu's élite faced in managing their financial affairs once they had fled to exile showed just how easy life had been for those in his clique. Several of his generals fled to South Africa with a fortune in cobalt in their suitcases. Soon after arriving, General Baramoto Kpama, one of Mobutu's right-hand men, telephoned a prominent Zairean émigré with a sheepish request. 'He was terribly embarrassed,' Dennis Kadima, a Zairean academic in Johannesburg, told me. 'He was looking for a stockbroker but he did not know how to go about it. He had never needed to invest anything before.'

Mobutuists trotted out a weary old defence and claimed that their Western critics did not understand Zaire. One of Mobutu's close allies from his early days, Kithima bin Ramazani, a former secretary general of the ruling Movement for the Popular Revolution, lived two floors above my room in the Intercontinental Hotel. Every day he stomped through the hotel coffee shop, Zaire's political and financial nerve centre, in a tailored charcoal-grey suit, barking at the waitresses and moaning about the service. He invited me to his suite and defended his master's record with the inevitable non sequiturs. 'In the village we have one chief, only one. We have big differences, us as black men and you as white men, and we have to respect the chief. I've known President Mobutu for many years. He's a generous man. He's a good man.'

There was a time when most Zaireans lapped up such vapourings. After the exploitation of the Belgians and the confusion of independence, when the Congo was riven by civil war, the people were desperate for a father-figure who would restore hope and pride. The 'Great Helmsman', as Mobutu – then the dashing army commander – later styled himself, brilliantly read the prevailing mood. He would lead them from the abyss, and, initially at least, he did by restoring peace with the aid of his Western allies, and then kindling a national spirit with his *authenticité* drive. But it was no coincidence that Kithima seldom set foot outside the hotel. If he had dared to broadcast his views in the bustling *Cité*, the heart of Kinshasa, where thousands of unemployed youths lounged on the street corners, he would have been lynched. Years of official exploitation and disdain have bred an anger and despair in the capital that just need a spark to explode.

By the mid-Seventies it had become all too apparent that the country was spiralling relentlessly downhill. World Bank figures show that by the mid-Nineties the economy had shrunk to its pre-independence level, while in the same period the population had tripled to more than forty million. The figures also suggested that if the country had sustained its pre-independence growth rate the GDP would have been about $1400 a head. As it was, by the end of Mobutu's reign the figure was about $100. It came as no surprise to hear that even the Belgians were remembered with star-struck eyes.

Martin Ilunga, who was born in 1934, the same year as Mobutu, spent twenty years at UTEX Africa, one of Zaire's largest cloth emporiums, cutting the material adorned with his president's face which was worn by everyone from aides to street vendors. Much of that time Ilunga had accepted without question that the chief deserved a special lifestyle. But on the eve of Mobutu's return from his French villa, where he was convalescing from cancer treatment, Ilunga could barely curb his disdain for the presidential cloth.

'No one is buying this now. And let me tell you, none of us will be out there when he comes in the streets. We will stay at home and block our ears and shut our doors.' He followed me to the car. His lined face was shaking with rage and also, I suspect, with the agony of having to admit what he was about to say. 'It is a sick joke. We had everything under the Belgians. Now we have nothing.'

As the rebels quickened their advance, the West became more strident in its calls for Mobutu to step down. A spokesman for the White House called him 'a creature of history'. Even Belgium disowned its old ally. The official statements brimmed with outrage and disdain. Chagrin, however, would have been more appropriate. For years the West funded Mobutu as its Cold War ally to stop Soviet expansion in Africa, even when it was clear that all but a fraction of the aid was going into his pocket. Mobutu may personify the follies of the independence leaders, but so, too, was his Zaire a monument to the superpowers' selfishness in the world's poorest continent.

ﾊﾊﾊ

One of the more redundant expatriates in Kinshasa in the closing days of Mobutu's rule was a charming Bulgarian United Nations official called Gabriel Milev. We met on the Intercontinental tennis court on one of the dog days of the conflict when the rebels were bogged down in the jungle. He could be found on the court most evenings, and as I came to know him better I began to wonder why he was not out there swinging his racket on mornings and afternoons too.

Milev was a high-flier from the UN's head office in New York, charged with helping to organize the elections which had been scheduled in a political programme negotiated by the West with Mobutu. There was just one problem: Mobutu had no intention of keeping to his word. Foreign donors had promised to put $100 million into an election fund provided Zaire contributed the same amount. To the surprise of no one in Kinshasa, Zaire's contribution somehow never appeared.

Unlike some of the European diplomats who were earnestly talking up his undertaking, Milev understood the absurdity of his mission. 'I know, I know, I was a journalist once. Elections in Zaire go on to the comics page.' But New York's bureaucracy was, as ever, running at its own pace and with its own agenda, and seemingly no one was listening to their man in Africa. Election was the buzzword and reality was ignored. The only consolation was that the world had finally learned its lesson and Mobutu was not, for once, allowed to dip his hand in the pot.

The history of Zaire is one of the worst possible advertisments for foreign aid. Money was showered on Mobutu throughout the Seventies from the West, the World Bank and the International Monetary Fund with minimal preconditions and no forethought. Even as living conditions plummeted year after year, the bonanza continued, encouraging Mobutu to ever greater excesses.

Inevitably he fell prey to 'Big Dam' syndrome; dictators revel in engineering projects, the bigger the better. Not only are they symbols of prestige, but they also require massive amounts of foreign capital, creating endless opportunities for kickbacks. A classic case was the Turkwel Gorge Dam in Kenya, whose construction was eagerly promoted by the government of President Daniel arap Moi despite an environmental outcry and allegations of massive corruption. Mobutu was no better. Ever ambitious for glory and money, he commissioned two giant dams and a double-level suspension bridge over the Congo – one level of which was for a railway that did not exist. By 1980 Zaire's foreign debt was estimated at four billion dollars, but the state had nothing but fripperies to show for it.

America was the most willing accomplice. In the late Seventies Zaire received nearly half President Carter's aid budget for black Africa. The bonanza peaked in the Eighties when foreign powers funded 90 per cent of Mobutu's army. As one American diplomat explained later with a wry smile, 'It was one big freebie.' At one stage, on paper at least, the army resembled a unit of the United Nations. In a mark of Mobutu's political genius, America, Belgium, France, Italy, Germany, Israel, China and North Korea were all financing different units. And yet all this largesse was despite clear evidence of systematic embezzlement by the Zairean government.

The most damning testimony came in September 1981 when Nguza Karl I Bond, a former prime minister and foreign minister, testified in Washington against his old master. He charged that Hercules C-130 transport planes given by America were routinely used by state black-marketeers, pointing out that the air force, like everything else in Zaire, was used by Mobutu and his relatives as a private company. One C-130 crashed, the committee heard, when landing at an airport in the interior because it carried an excessive cargo of rice for officers.[3] In the last days of Mobutu's rule the *Financial Times* revealed that the loans continued despite a warning from a senior IMF official to Western powers that Zaire was endemically corrupt. It is estimated that Zaire was loaned nearly four billion dollars between 1982 and 1991 when Mobutu finally fell from grace.

The West justified its disbursements, if only to itself, with Cold War *realpolitik*. Ever the opportunist, Mobutu brilliantly played on America's fears of Soviet expansionism in Africa. As the world's most important non-Soviet supplier of cobalt he was a valued client. He also provided a conduit for the CIA to smuggle arms to its principal African puppet, Jonas Savimbi, the Angolan rebel leader. In the Eighties, when the Angolan war was at its height, the American embassy in Kinshasa was one of the largest CIA stations in the world.

For the Zaireans, however, the Cold War merely prolonged the agony of life under Mobutu. Half-hearted attempts in the Eighties to tighten up the conditions for loans did nothing to improve the lot of the suffering people. In December 1988 Belgian newspapers indicated that the £70 million of aid given to Zaire each year was embezzled by Mobutu. As Mobutu feigned outrage and announced he was halting repayments on his massive debt to Belgium, Brussels declared it would stop funding development projects in its former colony. It was a moment of truth, but in the time-honoured tradition of Western governments towards their old protégés, Belgium failed to stand up for its principles; commerce came first. In July 1989 Belgium agreed to cancel Zaire's public debt. Mobutu had won again.

For Mobutu and his acolytes, Western aid was a tap which occasionally needed a refit but would never be turned off. It was, in their deluded minds, a divine right. Whenever a loan was withheld Mobutu fulminated about Western neo-colonialism. In a telling indication of how accustomed his aides were to duping the West, long after the eastern provinces of Zaire had been lost to Kabila's rebel alliance, the EU was petitioned to help uplift the region with agricultural grants. A month before the fall of Kinshasa, the prime minister, General Likulia Bolongo, summoned Raké, the EU ambassador, to an urgent meeting.

'I thought, this is it,' Raké said. 'He is finally seeing sense. He wants to discuss a way out of the crisis. He sat me down and said: "I have something very important to ask you." And I nodded and said, "Yes, Monsieur Premier Ministre . . ." But I should have known better. All he wanted was a grant to help chlorinate Kinshasa's water supply . . .'

The West's gullibility and culpability in Zaire are echoed across sub-Saharan Africa where tyrants have been indulged with billions of pounds of aid. But this of course does not excuse the kleptocratic king and his court, who went on pilfering the tattered remains of the economy to the very end.

†††††

Alexis Thambwe, Minister of Public Works, former ambassador in Rome, and veteran of four Mobutu cabinets, was clearly not used to being interrupted. He gazed through his billowing silk curtains over the garden of his residence as his butler scuttled in and out serving drinks. Vivaldi's *Four Seasons* tinkled in the background from the latest Japanese hi-fi. Glasses of pink

Laurent Perrier sparkled on the blue marble coffee table. Naive Zairean art depicting idyllic African sunsets and heroic peasants lined the pillars on either side of the doorway leading to the swimming pool. After a suitable pause and a muttered aside to the business partner against whom he had just played a needle game of tennis, the minister resumed his discussion on the 'new' Zaire.

Smooth, sycophantic and utterly implausible, not to say loathsome, Thambwe was one of the hundred-odd toadies who danced attendance on Mobutu to secure a place in the government. His record in office was dismal even by the standards of Zaire. Barely a road in Kinshasa was not potholed, barely a sewer was not suppurating. The stench of palm oil cloaked the air. On our way to Thambwe's villa we passed several freelance road-workers who were filling holes in return for tips from drivers. Thambwe, however, was calmly convinced the rebels would need him in the next era. He would, he said on reflection, be willing to offer his services.

Kinshasa in the last months of Mobutu's regime brought to mind accounts of the Roman Republic in its dying days, as senators talked precedent and procedure over their fishponds even as the old order fell apart. One evening, as the rebels were encircling Kisangani, I attended a soiree in the Salon Zaire, the Intercontinental's banquet hall. The party was in full swing by the time I arrived, a sweaty swirl of dinner jackets, flowing West African gowns and shiny faces. Waiters in royal blue tunics with black trousers handed round trays of champagne, bottles of Beaujolais and chilled Belgian beer. Models paraded along a catwalk in the latest French collections. Madame Diallo Djeinabu, the organizer, was handing out pink raffle tickets at the entrance. In her shimmering ball gown she could have been the hostess of a London charity dance.

At $25 a head, hundreds of thick-jowled bankers, government officials, diplomats and other luminaries had come to raise funds for refugees displaced by the fighting in the east. The army was in headlong retreat, but the war was still half a continent away from Kinshasa, and barely a distraction from the social whirl. A Zairean journalist was hovering outside, unwilling to disturb the élite at play. I muttered that the fall of Kisangani would shatter their complacency. He looked at me as if I were mad. 'You don't understand. The government is planning a counter-offensive. We have mercenaries. We will drive the rebels back. You'll see.'

A few days later I listened to the prime minister, Kengo wa Dondo, making a ringing speech in which he claimed Kisangani *'ne tombera pas'*. The city fell, as widely expected, three days later. I left Kengo's press conference imagining the prime minister would return home that night chuckling at his attempt to bamboozle us. But on reflection I suspect I was wrong. The oligarchs of the inner circle were trapped in a fantasy world and none more so than Mobutu himself.

No one should ever underestimate a dictator's powers of self-delusion. To an outsider the shambolic state of Camp Tshatshi, Mobutu's Kinshasa residence, was a mirror of Zaire's decay. The stone perimeter walls were moss-covered and crumbling. Scruffily dressed soldiers scoured the grounds for kindling and the early evening smoke from their campfires wreathed the rear entrance. Brambles poked through the railings as at a long-abandoned country house. But from his balcony Mobutu saw only what he wanted to see. His sentries wore plumed helmets and green liveried uniforms. Peacocks strutted in his front garden. Behind them, through the spray of a magnificent stone fountain, the Congo boiled through a series of rapids on its way to the Atlantic Ocean.

Reassured by the apparent normality of his surroundings, Mobutu summoned his commanders and moved non-existent armies on the map. He had, after all, always managed to buy or blackmail his way out of trouble before. The last time I saw him in the flesh was in the Tshatshi grounds as the rebels closed on the capital. He was wearing a glorious turquoise and gold jacket buttoned to the neck, his usual thick-rimmed square glasses and his leopard-skin hat. He could have been at the height of his powers. The only indication that he was aware of the gravity of the situation was that he had decided to forgo the enigmatic silence which he traditionally used to wrongfoot his opponents.

'I am Mobutu,' he declared, jabbing his finger over our heads as if to say, 'Do you know who I am?' A few minutes later he waved us away and stepped back inside. After all, was he not Mobutu Sese Seko Koko Ngbendu wa za Banga? The official translation is 'the all-powerful warrior who, because of his endurance and inflexible will to win, will go from conquest to conquest leaving fire in his wake'. But Zairean wags interpret it more loosely as the 'cockerel who squires all the chickens'.

All the most successful Big Men collected preposterous titles. Partly this was to entrance and mystify their largely uneducated subjects, partly this was for childish fun and partly it reflected the cultural confusion of the post-colonial age. Few carried off the act with the élan of Mobutu.

⚔⚔⚔

I was at N'djili when he returned to Kinshasa for the last time from the Riviera villa where he was recovering from treatment for his prostate cancer. More than a hundred dignitaries, including Prime Minister Kengo and the army high command, were waiting on the runway when his rented DC8 jet touched down. A red carpet was rolled out of the tumbledown terminal. A black stretch limousine drew up beside the stairwell. Five, ten, fifteen minutes passed. Then an aide appeared at the gangplank, summoned an official and suddenly secret policemen were everywhere ordering everyone to leave. The 'Guide' did not want to be seen.

Such was the mêlée, the guard of honour nearly knocked over Kengo and a troop of flower girls. I was driving back through the bustling back-streets, debating furiously with a colleague whether Mobutu could be on his deathbed, when by chance we drew level with the Mobutu motorcade, which had come a different way. The weight of people in the road had forced it to a crawl. No one seemed to know whether to cheer or boo. Then the smoked-glass side window slid down and a hand emerged waving Mobutu's distinctive wooden cane. It was a masterstroke. A cheer went up followed by loud applause. Within moments the city was buzzing with rumours that he was back and in charge.

Mobutu had come a long way from his impoverished childhood as the son of a maid and a cook. He is believed to have arrived in Leopoldville from his native Equateur province with only five pounds to his name.[4] Even then he was displaying the traits which would serve him so well. According to a Zairean historian who lived in exile during the dictatorship, Mobutu was expelled aged nineteen from mission school for 'his adventurous character, his proclivity for delinquency and his burglary of the mission library'.[5]

The CIA knew a shrewd operator when they saw one. Lawrence Devlin, a young operative who met Mobutu in the pre-independence years when he was a journalist, is widely credited with masterminding his rise through the turbulence of the early Sixties. In the late Sixties, Devlin took breakfast with Mobutu on most mornings to plot the next move. More than three decades later as the rebels closed on Kinshasa, diplomats charged with negotiating a peaceful settlement frantically tried to contact Devlin as one of the few voices Mobutu might heed. But it was far too late.

When the foreign aid dried up after the end of the Cold War, the soldiers stopped being paid, let alone trained. Mobutu had always believed that by running down his army he had insulated himself from the threat of a coup, but instead he had hastened his end. As the rebels advanced, so his soldiers melted away, and the 'war' became little more than a route march. Mobutu's Chinese-trained tank division, which could have changed the course of the last battle for Kinshasa, languished a hundred miles away lacking crucial spare parts.

In the final irony, in the ultimate burglar's nightmare and in a sober lesson for his thieving imitators, Mobutu ran out of things to steal – not that he recognized this until far too late. He put some of his foreign properties on the market and his aides had one last pillage of state resources. 'They are all busily back-dating letters of credit,' the British ambassador explained wearily, clearly expecting nothing less after several years' experience in the posting. Many of Mobutu's properties in Europe had already been mortgaged to raise instant cash for relatives, many of whom had learned all too well from the 'chief' and defrauded him as readily as he did the state. Diplomats said at the end he barely had enough money to fuel the personal jet he leased to fly him to Europe for his cancer treatment, let alone to fight a war.

Mobutu had long vowed that he would die in office. After years of watching him weave his magic, some Zaireans were convinced his prostate cancer would claim him as the rebels arrived. But he could not hold the rebels off long enough to achieve his goal. He fled, like the Belgians, with what he could carry. A friend of the family told me later that he suddenly panicked. 'It was terrible. No one had seen the old man lose his nerve before. He just did not know what to do. So his wife took charge and told everyone to pack their bags.' Such was Mobutu's haste that he left half his luggage on the runway.

The morning after his flight, I shared the Intercontinental Hotel lift down to the ground floor with a young woman in hip-hugging suede trousers and with waist-length plaited hair who was struggling with two huge suitcases. She was also clutching a plastic bag brimming with cardboard folders and a shoulder bag with a teddy bear sticking out. I offered to carry her largest case to the foyer. 'Books?' I hazarded. 'No. My clothes and my studies,' she said. She was, I learned later, a niece of Mobutu.

For three hours she sat amid a pile of Gucci suitcases before she was evacuated across the river to Brazzaville, the capital of the neighbouring Republic of Congo, escorted by Mobutu's most hated son, Kongolo, whose nickname was Saddam Hussein. His final act before fleeing was to fire two rocket grenades at the façade of the Bank of Zaire, the institution he and his kind had debased for so long. It was a fittingly petty way for the last of the Mobutus to leave Zaire.

Barely twenty-four hours later, the Intercontinental lobby was again humming with activity. But this time there were no designer labels. The rebels' suitcases were shabby and battered, as befitted a movement that had moved headquarters dozens of times and travelled more than a thousand miles in the previous six months. The low-key luggage was a hopeful sign that a new guard was in charge that would lead Zaire into an honest future – but no one was holding their breath.

🚶🚶

The fall of Mobutu was tentatively hailed as a turning point for Africa. For years Zaire had been a 'black hole' the size of Western Europe. Everyone and everything that came into contact with it suffered – with the exception of government officials and foreign companies extracting its mineral riches. Its vast interior provided hideaways for half a dozen guerrilla movements to destabilize its neighbours. When in 1995 there was news of a rare outbreak of the deadly flesh-eating Ebola virus it seemed grimly apt that it should have emerged in Zaire.

With Mobutu ousted, there were grounds for hope that the regional monolith might at last play a more positive role in the continent. Optimists compared his downfall with the end of apartheid as a signpost for a brighter future. There was talk of the Congo cementing a central African trade bloc, opening up the continent and ensuring security from the Atlantic to the Indian Ocean. In the second city, Lubumbashi, Congolese businessmen and administrators were overheard in bars discussing the changing world order and hailing Tony Blair, who had just been elected in Britain, Thabo Mbeki, then Mandela's heir apparent, and Laurent Kabila in the same breath as leaders of a brave new world.

For his regional supporters the victory of Kabila's alliance was a triumph. The initial impetus for his rebellion came from the Banyamulenge, Zairean Tutsis whose rights had for years been abused by Mobutu. They were backed by the Tutsi-led army of neighbouring Rwanda, Uganda, the wily regional supremo, and also Angola. Kabila initially seemed little more than their frontman. He was a Luba with a long record of opposing Mobutu and so was a convenient riposte to the dictator's claims that he had been attacked by Tutsis. Kabila's political career had last flourished more than three decades earlier in the early chaotic months of independence as an ally of the independence prime minister, Patrice Lumumba. When Lumumba was murdered in 1961, Kabila fled into the bush and began a thirty-year odyssey in the political wilderness. As leader of a Maoist guerrilla band he waged a desultory jungle war. He was best known for dabbling in gold smuggling and hit the headlines only briefly when in 1975 his men kidnapped three American students and a Dutch researcher. But as the rebels advanced so he became a manifestation of Zaireans' despair. Drawing on financial and logistical backing from Angola and slipping through Zambia to accelerate their advance, the rebels easily outmanoeuvred Mobutu's forces. Within six months the war was over after one of Africa's most whirlwind military campaigns. On some fronts they were even able to advance by train.

Overnight the political map of central, southern and eastern Africa was transformed. Angola's UNITA (National Union for the Total Independence of Angola) rebels, who had for years used Zaire as a conduit for arms and a market for diamonds (their principal source of revenue), had lost their most important backer. Mobutu's overthrow also dealt a wounding blow to Rwanda's former Hutu extremist government, many of whose supporters had fled to Zaire in 1994 after organizing the genocide of up to a million Tutsis and moderate Hutus. Since then their forces had regrouped and launched raids against the new Tutsi-led Rwandan government. But Kabila's alliance drove many of their units more than a thousand miles from their homeland. Uganda's President Museveni, too, was delighted, as the way was clear for him to attack the bases of two rebel groups.

Even more strikingly, the downfall of Mobutu threatened to redraw the century-old division between francophone and anglophone Africa. With 40 million people, Mobutu's Zaire had been a jewel in *la Francophonie*, the network of French-speaking former colonies. For several years the first stages of a linguistic revolution had been filtering through Kinshasa as Zaireans realized they were as likely to do business with South Africa, the continent's powerhouse, as Belgium or France. Its currents even washed against the thick stone walls of the Lycée Molière, one of Kinshasa's top schools. The lycée was the lodestar of French culture, where Zaireans were raised to become little Frenchmen or Belgians. But since the mid-Nineties, the headmaster explained with an air of resignation, English was becoming increasingly popular.

With a frenzy bordering on paranoia, French officials saw Kabila's rebellion as a direct assault on the French-speaking world by the English-speaking governments of Uganda and Rwanda. In an entertaining throwback to the Anglo-French rivalry of the colonial era, the French and American embassies were barely on speaking terms. A French diplomat who had close links to the Elysée Palace spelled out to me in hushed tones how President Clinton and John Major were charting the rebels' every move. He was a colourful character who drove around Kinshasa in a sports car. You had to treat Mobutu 'like a woman', he insisted, and of course 'only the French' knew how.

While far from planning Kabila's uprising, as Mobutuists claimed, America was delighted to see Mobutu fall. First, he was an embarrassing reminder of America's old African policies. Second, Washington made no secret in the Nineties of its disdain for France's neo-colonial African policies. French troops had intervened in francophone Africa more than twenty times since the Sixties, most controversially in 1994 when they set up a buffer zone in south-west Rwanda, enabling many of the Hutu extremists to escape. Third, America welcomed the commercial and political advantages which they looked set to enjoy following the departure of Mobutu. Even before Mobutu was ousted, the rebels awarded a Texas-based mining firm a multi-million-dollar mining contract in recognition of the directors' buccaneering foresight in lending Kabila a private jet to ferry him around his newly won territories. Infuriated in part by the very

French diplomat who briefed me in Kinshasa, Kabila promised to withdraw from the association of francophone countries.

Coming barely two months after the death of Jacques Foccart, the enigmatic architect of France's Africa policy from the early Sixties, the downfall of Mobutu signalled a crossroads for France. Foccart had acted as an intermediary between African heads of state and French presidents – he once boasted that he had had 3,000 one-on-one meetings with de Gaulle – and was particularly close to Mobutu. The departure of two giants from the old francophone stage enabled liberals in Paris to push for a less paternalist approach to Africa; in 1999 British and French ministers toured the continent together and even talked of sharing embassies.

However, it soon became clear that France's loss was not to be America's, still less the Congo's, gain. By the end of Mobutu's rule his self-justification that he alone had kept together 200 tribes in one of the clumsiest creations of the colonial carve-up had long since lost its validity. Such was his corrosive influence that it was open to question whether the integrity of Zaire was worth keeping, and anyway Zaire was effectively functioning as several separate countries. But it did not take long for his catchphrase *'après moi le déluge'* to return to haunt his people. Kabila had hardly arrived in Kinshasa before he was behaving like his predecessor. In a sequence sadly familiar from elsewhere in the continent Congo found it was easier to get rid of a Big Man than it was to end Big Man rule.

Che Guevara, the Third World's revolutionary icon, briefly supported Kabila in the Sixties during a tour of Africa to foment the anti-colonial fight. Struck by his charisma Che backed him with a hundred soldiers. But he was soon disillusioned by Kabila's record of wining and whoring in Dar es Salaam. 'Nothing leads me to believe he is the man of the hour,' he wrote in a memoir. 'He is too addicted to drink and women.'[6]

Sadly for the Congolese, old bush-fighters, it seemed, could not learn new tricks. When Kabila flew to Angola's capital, Luanda, before the last abortive round of negotiations with

Mobutu, he went on a drinking binge and, according to one diplomat, had to be plucked from a bar by his Angolan backers to attend the talks.

'Zaire is like a hooker,' Guillaume Ngefa, the head of a human rights organization, told me. 'If you don't have any money, you go with the first man who comes along.'

♦♦♦♦

They had been waiting since dawn, huddled in cliques outside their headquarters seeking instructions from the new guard in town. In their shabby suits they looked like the tens of thousands of civil servants thronging ministries all over Kinshasa as they awaited their new masters. Their white-washed villa set back from the street had a pleasingly shambolic air. It could have been the arts ministry or a cultural centre. But under Mobutu no taxi would take you there, for it was there that SNIP enforced the dictator's will, sending out agents across his vast nation to intimidate his subjects.

Now, however, it was their turn to tremble. Paul Kabongo, the security chief of the new order, was inside issuing instructions. Some of the agents were clearly embarrassed by my presence. One of their main responsibilities had been harassing the press, and they hid behind their wraparound sunglasses. But as the morning wore on, so they relaxed. Any unease at my presence vanished when Mr King, my old friend and adversary from the airport days, bounded up to me with a warm smile.

'We are free. We were afraid our jobs were not secure. But they are okay. What we want more than anything now is to look after the security of our new country. Security should be strong. There should be all available means for that.'

Albert Kimongo, a counter-espionage agent, butted in enthusiastically to outline his hopes for a new streamlined service. 'We deserve cars and a higher salary because they need us to make this place work. In the past most of SNIP's money went to people in Mobutu's tribe. It killed the service. We had no motivation. But now we will give it a go.'

Intrigued, I followed them into their headquarters. M.

Kabongo was announcing that SNIP was to be renamed the National Agency of Information, a suitably bland yet sinister name for a secret police, when I caught his eye. 'Some things remain a secret,' he yelled. 'Get out of here.' It was the third day of Kabila's government and the old secret policemen were back on the streets with redoubled energies.

A few of Kabila's ministers took office genuinely believing the talk of a new era and determined to cleanse the taint of the past. They set up an 'anti-corruption centre' to eliminate graft. They even spruced up the airport – painting the walls, banning the protocols, and sweeping the floors.

Within a week of Mobutu's flight, passengers were queuing at the airport check-in desk, unheard of in the anarchic old days. A stern official examined my papers. There was no sign of the protocols nor the *chef*. Nor was there a question of my proffering a '*cadeau*'. The official handed me a receipt for my exit stamp – and wished me a *bon voyage*.

But the fervour soon faded, as Kabila's talk of democracy and freedom proved as illusory as so many previous Congolese dreams, and his alliance fell apart. When he took over, there was speculation he would form a coalition with Etienne Tshisekedi, Mobutu's long-standing political rival. But within days 'Tshi Tshi' was enduring the same harassment he had faced in the old days. After a night in prison he was forced into internal exile. The 'Sphinx', as Tshisekedi was known, was a pompous and uninspiring figure, but he had a genuine following and could have assisted Kabila to fuse the old with the new. His treatment reinforced the impression that all that had changed was the presidential headgear – Kabila favoured a floppy cowboy hat.

So jittery was Kabila's high command that when one of his generals moved into the villa where Thambwe had entertained me with Vivaldi and champagne, he dug up the flower beds in case of an ambush. He also excavated the swimming pool to look for buried gold – there was none. In such an atmosphere of paranoia and conspiracy there was no chance of justice. Hundreds of suspected Mobutuists were shot dead or lynched in the first fortnight of Kabila's government.

Even his sternest critics, however, were startled at the speed with which he managed to squander the international goodwill the Congo so desperately needed. As Kabila consolidated his position, he proved more interested in revisiting the old ideological battles of the Sixties than in forging new friendships. He seemed obsessed by the turn of events the last time he had been in Kinshasa in 1961, when America was on Mobutu's side and the CIA is thought to have approved the murder of his mentor, Lumumba, whose overtures to the Soviet Union had been rather too fulsome for the men from Langley. Within a year of taking power he was back in the bosom of *la Francophonie*, proving that French and Congolese diplomacy was as calculating as ever.

Any remaining hopes that Kabila might be a positive influence on the region vanished when he refused to co-operate with the United Nations over their attempts to investigate the massacres of thousands of Rwandan Hutus who had been killed by his army on their march through the interior. The refugees included some of the organizers and perpetrators of the 1994 genocide, but many of the victims were innocent women and children. The UN was eventually allowed to send a commission of enquiry to Kinshasa, but its members were never given permission to move into the interior, and were left whiling away their days in frustration at the Intercontinental, in the footsteps of so many thwarted delegations in Mobutu's era. The more the West criticized Kabila, the more he dug in his heels and insisted the commission was a vestige of neo-colonialism.

Unsurprisingly, African countries rallied to Kabila's defence, arguing it was hypocritical of the West to be hostile to Kabila after its long years of support for Mobutu. President Mandela himself spoke out for Kabila, partly for African solidarity and partly for reasons of trade. There was a wearying sense of *déjà vu* about his remarks. Africa has a long and ignoble tradition of turning a blind eye to the abuses of its fellow leaders – or at least its fellow black leaders. When a rebellion broke out against Kabila in 1998 – led by, among others, none other than Alexis Thambwe, the tennis-playing minister, who was once again proving his versatility – Zimbabwe, Namibia and Angola sent soldiers, tanks and planes to protect him. Their forces drove back the rebels from the gates of Kinshasa, entrenching a partition between the east and the west and south which may in time become a fixture, further undermining the Organization of African Unity's insistence on the inviolability of frontiers. But there was no principle in the so-called southern African solidarity, only politics and money. Kabila had mortgaged his country (or at least its minerals) to the hilt before taking power. Angola had invested millions in Kabila's takeover and feared the Congolese rebels might succour UNITA. Zimbabwe's President Robert Mugabe saw the foreign adventure as a convenient distraction from his parlous domestic record. He also had a pressing financial interest in Kabila's survival as his nephew, Leo Mugabe, and several top Zimbabwean businessmen were engaged in lucrative contracts with Kabila's regime.

The intervention coincided with the annual Non-Aligned Summit in Durban. Kabila flew down to the Indian Ocean port to put his case before retiring to his hotel room with two bottles of Chivas Regal. He had not, it seemed, changed since Che's day.

I sent an e-mail to a Malawian friend to bemoan the Congo's fate. 'It is simple,' he wrote back. 'This will stop only when our leaders stop being greedy.'

♦♦♦♦

In the arid heat of Botswana, many miles to the south of Kinshasa's rotting humidity and rotten political culture, a taciturn former British detective was hard at work in the mid-Nineties, convinced that the people of Africa did not have to give up hope of emerging from the stranglehold of the continent's corrupt élites. Graham Stockwell served for many years in a crack anti-corruption unit in Hong Kong. He opened a directorate run on similar lines in Botswana in late 1994 and, after a year of building up a team sponsored by the government and British aid money, launched a high-profile advertising campaign. The message was rammed home from car-stickers and road-side posters, by radio and television and even at school: 'Bribery – Heads you lose. Tails you lose. Either way you lose' and 'A corrupt country is like a country with lung disease. It has no future.'

His message, and his steadfast confidence, made a rare and reassuring sight in Africa. Economists estimate that over the last two decades $15 billion a year have been siphoned out of the continent, more than its annual allocation of foreign aid. Corruption is, of course, not unique to Africa. Dollar for dollar there are plenty of Asian and central American dictators who have embezzled as freely as Mobutu. Hurt by their reputation as the frontrunners in graft, Africans point to the record of Italy and other Western states. But its effect has proved far more destructive in Africa than elsewhere. Its economies have not just been undermined by graft, they have been devastated by it. The 'dash', the West African word for bribe, is a way of life all over the Third World. It oils the wheels in societies that lack a fully functioning state and so, it can be argued, often supplements rather than subverts. But in too many African states the élites have graduated from deploying the 'dash' to selling off the state. Mobutu was the most infamous embezzler, but he was not alone.

Successive Nigerian governments, military and civilian, have siphoned off billions of dollars of oil revenue which should have propelled the continent's most populous and vibrant nation into becoming a world leader. The looting peaked between 1993 and 1998 under the repressive military regime of General Abacha, who is estimated to have stolen more than three billion dollars. Kenya's Moi bestrides a system that is rapidly degenerating down similar lines. Moi is less ostentatious than Mobutu and Abacha. But, despite his many pledges to eliminate corruption, many of the worst offenders remain in his circle. While little is known about Moi's holdings, he is believed to control a vast property and business empire, a charge his supporters inevitably deny.

With its population of barely two million and its post-independence history of democratic elections – virtually unique in sub-Saharan Africa – Botswana was a far cry from the bedlam of Kenya and Zaire. In his nondescript office on the edge of the capital, Gaborone, Mr Stockwell acknowledged that it would be far, far harder to tackle many of the societies to the north and even south.

Even South Africa, which likes to regard itself as the continent's leader in ethics, as well as politics, is under threat. The white minority government wrapped itself in a mantle of probity and contended that the culture of bribes stopped at the Limpopo. It was true that the bureaucracy for the most part functioned without palm-greasing. But behind the scenes, the corporate values were as suspect as those in many a state to the north. The giant Afrikaner conglomerates that dominate the economy were born and flourished through white-collar crime. Under Mandela the same culture thrived much as before.

Stockwell's message is simple. If the government is genuinely committed to stamping out corruption, then a society, however diseased by the cancer of bribes, can be cured, but it has to start from the top. Stung by claims that they were as corrupt as the Nationalists, Mandela's government set up an anti-corruption commission. After General Abacha died of a heart attack in 1998, his reformist successor, General Abdulsalami Abubakar, tried to redress the financial mismanagement that marked his tenure. Abacha's family handed back to the government more than $750 million, but it was widely regarded as only a fraction of what Abacha had amassed. Since taking office Moi has regularly promised to tackle corruption, but his weary opponents concede that nothing can be done until he leaves office and even that will be only the start of a long road. Even Mandela's commission was widely criticized as a 'talking shop'.

Attempts by the West in the mid-Nineties to impose more stringent conditions on aid and loans have helped to limit the funds pouring into dictators' pockets. But the swiftness with which corruption scandals tarnished the new democratically elected governments in Malawi and Zambia, after their Big Men rulers were ousted in the early Nineties, have highlighted the difficulties of ushering in a new moral code. For centuries politics in Africa have been a route to riches. The independence leaders merely refined the lessons of history. Asked by an American delegation in the late Eighties about the reports of his fabulous wealth, Mobutu said: 'Yes, I have a fair amount of money. However, I would estimate it to total less than $50 million. What is that after twenty-two years as head of state of such a big country?'[7]

I was in South Africa when Mobutu died, still searching for a permanent exile. I discussed his career with a young student friend who was keen to learn about the rest of his continent.

'I would like to be a lawyer or set up my own business,' he mused. 'But maybe I should go into politics to make lots of money.'

Three months later he was given another object lesson in Big Man rule when the obituaries were written for Malawi's Dr Hastings Banda. With his Victorian pieties Banda was less destructive a leader than Mobutu. But his logic was the same: 'little people' were playthings to be despised; and his cackle was as sinister as anything I heard in the Congo.

2

The Last Days of a North London Doctor

Dr Hastings Banda – Dictators and Democracy

The Ngwazi's beady eyes peered at me out of his tiny shrivelled body. For a moment the 'chief of chiefs' appeared nonplussed. Dr Hastings Kamuzu Banda, Africa's first but sadly not last president for life, glanced for reassurance to his 'official hostess', Cecilia 'Mama' Kadzamira, his long-time nurse, companion and business partner. I was briefly reminded of long-forgotten schoolday nightmares of being summoned before a headmaster. In years past this would have been the cue for a flick of the fly-whisk with which Banda used to belabour importunate questioners. Instead he cackled and settled into his chair. And thus the Church of Scotland elder and African nationalist guru turned puritanical despot proceeded to belittle the traditions of his fellow Africans, the very people on whose behalf he had plotted the end of white rule in a Soho basement more than half a century before.

During the Ngwazi's thirty years as absolute ruler of Malawi his infrequent interviews were gruelling affairs. For years he banned foreign correspondents. When he did grant an audience he liked to berate his interlocutor before a gallery of fawning *mbumba*, the garishly clad women with whom he surrounded himself on official tours. If he was wearing his sunglasses you knew you were in for a tirade. When I saw him, in August 1995, however, the chorus had long since been disbanded. Only the glamorous 'Mama' was left. She sat a discreet few feet away, the model of courteous charm, controlling his hearing aid, prompting the odd answer and rephrasing questions. This was his first interview with a British correspondent for many years. It was also to be his last. Not only was Banda no longer master of Malawi's destiny, he was not even master of his own.

Inside his Mudi House residence, the governor general's quarters in the colonial era, time had stood still. His British lawyer, Clive Stanbrook, a top London QC, who secured my interview, called him 'Your Excellency' as if nothing had changed. But the brickwork on the walls was crumbling; footsteps were muffled and the flower beds were overgrown. Dustsheets covered the furniture and his Scots memorabilia. Even his famed tiger heads were obscured from view.

I saw Banda a year after elections had brought down the curtain on his long rule. Overshadowed by President Mandela's inauguration in South Africa, Malawi's first democratic elections in late May 1994 had attracted little attention in the outside world. But they, too, were an important signpost for the continent. The election of President Bakili Muluzi marked the end of one of Africa's longest-serving tyrants. Banda was the last of the old guard of post-colonial nationalists to remain in office. A new wind of democracy and accountability seemed to be blowing through southern Africa. There were even hopes it could waft further north.

For Banda the turning of the tables could not have been more complete. When I saw him he was under house arrest charged with conspiring to murder four politicians, including three cabinet ministers. They had been bludgeoned to death by the police with sledgehammers in 1983 after daring to voice dissent. Malawians had little doubt the orders came from the top: so personalized was Banda's rule, he was even reputed to sign most of the government cheques. The difficulty was to prove in a court of law that he sanctioned the murders.

Physically too the Ngwazi was a shadow of his bouncy old self. Banda was as old as the twentieth century. While his official birth date was 1906, independent estimates reckoned he was born in 1898. His voice was hardly a quaver. It seemed at times as if it would shatter the delicate bronze parchment which was his skin. His frame was eggshell-thin. The giant hearing aid attached to a Heath Robinson-esque contraption heightened the impression that he was near his end.

But the self-confidence was authentic Banda. For three decades he interfered in every aspect of life in his impoverished central African nation. He banned long hair, tight jeans and mini-skirts. He even prohibited the Simon and Garfunkel hit 'Cecilia' on the grounds that it was disrespectful of 'Mama'. It was classic tin-pot stuff, but these eccentricities were merely a quixotic façade. The man who once boasted that his enemies were 'food for crocodiles' was, when challenged, as ruthless, thieving and selfish as any of his more conventional despotic peers. His regime passed the three 'c's African Big Man test with ease – corruption, crackdown and cult. Millions of pounds were embezzled from state funds. Hundreds were killed by his security forces. He was worshipped like a God. As he sat bolt upright in his standard charcoal-grey pinstriped suit with a handkerchief protruding just so, it required little imagination to believe those days continued.

His contemporaries, Kwame Nkrumah, the father of African nationalism, who led the Gold Coast to independence as Ghana in 1957, and Jomo Kenyatta, the independence leader of Kenya, had long since left the stage. Tanzania's Julius Nyerere and Zambia's Kenneth Kaunda, whose idiosyncratic and idiotic economic policies wrecked their countries, were indulgently humoured as Africa's sages. But only with the greatest reluctance would the Lion of Malawi concede that he too had roared his last. 'I am not doing politics,' he declared as if retirement had been his choice. 'I am just resting now.'

Much of my interview was a history lesson. It was like delving into the long-forgotten archives of a dusty museum. One moment Banda was under the *kachere* tree whose branches shaded his first lessons in the bush, the next he was fulminating against Sir Roy Welensky, the Rhodesian leader of the short-lived white-led central African federation which he replaced.

For Banda this was also a last chance to air one of his favourite obsessions. 'African history . . . I have to admit there is not very much of that. The Africans were not an educated people . . .'

Banda was at least more honest than many of his fellow despots who despised their people in private but praised them in public. 'That is the trouble in Africa today – too many ignorant people who do not know anything about history,' he once told Malawi's parliament. 'And if they do know anything about it they do not know how to interpret and apply it. That is why Africa is in a mess. That is the tragedy of Africa: too many ignorant people are in a position of power and responsibility.'[1]

The irony is that, as the twenty-first century dawns with new hopes once again, it is the story of the Ngwazi and his rise to power more than anything that needs ramming home to Malawians. Banda was among the more astute Big Men. He was one of the few to appreciate that it was in his interests to limit his exploitation. He also genuinely seems to have had an understanding of the requirements and rhythms of his people's rural life. But his story shows all too clearly how easy it is for dictators to take office on a wave of popular support, a vital lesson for Africa as it dreams of democratic rule.

ᴪᴪᴪ

The rutted dirt-track snaking off from Malawi's main highway could be anywhere in Africa. For twenty miles a first-time visitor would be convinced he was on the wrong road. All around is featureless bush. Then without any warning, the potholes give way to smooth tarmac. An arch and wrought-iron gates come into view. Suddenly the visitor is in another world. The neat red-brick buildings visible through the railings of a smart front gate could be lifted from the grounds of a nineteenth-century British boarding school. There is a library – home to a dictionary signed by Ronald Reagan – a golf course and, of course, a rugby field. The pupils wear green blazers topped by straw boaters and learn Latin and Greek. Only one subject is strictly forbidden – the local language, Chichewa.

Welcome to the Kamuzu Academy, known far and wide as the Eton of Africa. From its foundation in the early Eighties, every year primary schools all over Malawi submitted candidates to compete for about seventy places. The lucky ones were plucked from rural poverty to a life of academic excellence – and also unfamiliar and anachronistic public school ways. With an expatriate staff and grounds which lacked for nothing, Banda's aides boasted it was a rare institution of excellence in a continent of mediocrity. They also claimed it was the old man's gift to the nation. He was said to fund the estimated £6,000 annual cost for each pupil. Such, at least, was the myth. In reality, after he lost power it emerged that the funds had come from the national purse at a time when the government spent about seven pounds a year on the average school-child.

The academy was the ultimate white elephant – an idiom which would almost certainly have delighted Banda's childish sense of humour. His obsessive attempt to transplant elements of Victorian society into Africa was a potent reflection of the identity crisis affecting the continent at the end of white rule. Banda's life story mirrors the end of colonialism. He stood for and espoused many of the colonists' precepts, in particular their muscular Christianity and patronizing disregard for the IQ of the native African. Like a mad scientist he blended that with a dose of spurious African lore and tradition to justify his personal rule. It was to prove a dangerous combination.

The disengagement of the colonial powers in the twentieth century had as seismic an effect as their arrival had had less than a century before. Between 1880 and the First World War, some ten million square miles with about 110 million subjects were taken over by the European nations. Less than two generations later, most of them had gone. Dragged in many cases out of the Iron Age, the new African states had been coated with a veneer of modernity and then left to cope with the complexities and confusions of the new order and the twentieth century as best they could. In some cases the colonists had barely set up administrations before they were preparing to leave. Many only started to train up their successors as they packed their bags.

When the Union flag was hauled down in Bechuanaland in 1966 the new-born Botswana was the third poorest country in the world, with twenty graduates and less than five miles of tarred road.

With a mixture of fear, indifference, anger and fascination, Africans had been exposed to a range of new ideas and aspirations. And yet, suddenly, they were free as new nations, and, inevitably, in thrall to a massive cultural trauma and schizophrenia. Banda was the archetypal product of his age. He was Western Europe without the liberalism. He was Africa without the communal values. For the people of Malawi it was the worst of both worlds.

Banda's long and confused relationship with the colonial world began at an early age. Like so many of the first generation of African statesmen he was educated by missionaries. Indeed, he took Hastings as his Christian name from the surname of one of his early Scots tutors. But as a teenager he suffered a humiliation which would have alienated many Africans from the white man for good. He failed his first round of teaching exams, because, he later claimed, he was so small that he had to stand up and so was accused of cheating and disqualified. And yet, far from retiring to his village, he set off towards southern Rhodesia in search of an education. It was to be an extraordinary odyssey through southern Africa, America and Britain which was to last nearly fifty years.

Banda's experiences on the way would have tested the most tolerant of Africans. After working on a Johannesburg mine under a bullying Afrikaner overseer, with the help of American missionaries he travelled to America to complete his studies. In Tennessee in the Twenties he witnessed a mob lynching a black man. Even after he qualified as a doctor and set up practice in Britain, the prejudices of his era stood in his way. His longstanding ambition to be a medical missionary in his homeland for the Church of Scotland was thwarted in the early 1940s when a group of white nurses in Nyasaland, as Malawi was then known, wrote to their Edinburgh headquarters to say they would not serve under an African doctor. Further insults were to come when Banda applied for a post with the Nyasaland government. After a long argument over whether he should be paid as much as a European, where he should live and whether he could use the swimming pool at Zomba, the colonial capital, he was offered a job as a medical officer. But according to some accounts there was a final twist. He received a letter from the Colonial Office informing him he must not seek social contact with white doctors. Banda turned down the offer.

And yet despite these setbacks and insults the influence of Banda's missionary upbringing endured. He remained if anything more Presbyterian than his tutors. He is said to have been appalled by the number of pubs in Glasgow when he docked there in 1937 after twelve years in America. He was also shocked that in Edinburgh, 'the very Mecca of the Church of Scotland', couples touched each other when ballroom dancing. Years later he contrasted this unfavourably with the 'propriety' of African traditional dances where men and women danced without body contact.

The influence lingered until his final day and, within the unstructured haze of his reminiscences, was a recurring theme in my interview. Long after the British had left he liked to see himself as the ultimate paternalist and 'civilizer of natives'. At first I thought his ramblings had a whiff of Dr Arnold's stern Victorian values. Then the voice of Banda's Scots mentors became clearer.

'Discipline. Unity. Hard work,' he insisted when I asked if he had a message to his people. 'I do not want stagnation. And of course dress is important. When I came here people were naked. I didn't like this. I told them we must be on good relations with the rest of the world. We must be presentable.'

Banda's life was undoubtedly the most varied of the independence leaders. It spawned a range of bizarre theories about his psyche. It has also inspired endless curiosity about his career. How, it has been asked time and again, did a doctor trained in the West and seemingly comfortably settled in its society metamorphose into a ruthless dictator? And how could the man who advised Nkrumah on how to take power prove so disdainful of

Africans that he employed only expatriates in his favourite hospital and school?

For those looking for the seeds of his dictatorial future he was a slow starter. He settled down to practice as a GP in the north of England in 1938 before moving to Harlesden, and thence to Brondesbury Park, archetypal London suburbs where he led a classic British middle-class existence. It was a remarkable achievement for an African of his generation. He sported a black Homburg and a rolled-up umbrella. He had a car and a secretary. Such was his reputation that young trainee colonial officers were sent to have briefings with him before taking up their posts.

Simultaneously he was a leading light in the liberal salons where talk of decolonization was all the rage. Drawing on his vast and varied experience he advised the fledgling independence movement in Nyasaland and leading African nationalists. He is said to have told Nkrumah that the Gold Coast was the best place to begin the drive for independence on the grounds that the mosquitoes were so virulent there that the British would be the easiest to dislodge. But Banda's was hardly a revolutionary existence. He was the height of respectability until his secretary's husband, a Major French, filed for divorce citing him as co-respondent. Shortly afterwards he closed down his practice and moved to Ghana, where he was joined a year later by Mrs French. Both almost certainly expected to retire.

Banda was at his lowest ebb. Not only was his domestic life in tatters but his dreams for his homeland had also come to naught. He had been working with the fledgling Nyasaland African Congress, which, like other nascent African nationalist movements, was formulating its pitch for independence. But in 1953 Nyasaland was joined in a federation with north and south Rhodesia, under Sir Roy Welensky, a burly ex-train driver, a development which Banda feared would leave them for ever under the yoke of the Rhodesian colonists. As a final blow his professional life had also suffered a setback. He was suspended as a doctor in Ghana in late 1957 because, it is thought, he had offended the authorities by running an illegal abortion clinic.

And yet this same man was hailed as a hero the following year when he returned to his homeland, aged sixty, to lead it to independence. For the Congress he was Nyasaland's most distinguished son: he had worked his way abroad and triumphed in the white man's world. For Britain, too, despite the opposition of Welensky, he was an obvious leader. When in 1964, as prime minister of one year's standing, he presided over the independence ceremony, hopes were high. His rhetoric was restrained and it was assumed his advanced years had encouraged a prudence and conservatism that would spare his people the radicalism of 'firebrands' like Nkrumah.

But in fact that was just about that for Malawi's dreams of freedom. In a sequence that was to become depressingly familiar in the rest of the continent, he rapidly began to believe his own propaganda. He was soon hailed as the country's Messiah and Moses. At the first whiff of serious criticism, political opponents were drummed out of sight. To get anywhere in life, Malawians had to carry party cards. In 1971 Banda became president for life. His 'Young Pioneers', which were founded as a boy scout movement, metamorphosed into a thuggish party youth wing which kept the people in line. It was a blueprint for Big Man rule.

For psychoanalysts the metamorphosis from middle-class London GP to African dictator is rich fare. Critics have had a field day trying to find a link between the two stages. A favourite theory is that he broke down and had a personality change during his three years in Ghana. There are even historians who claim that the Banda who returned to Malawi was not the man who had left all those years earlier. They attest his policy of speaking only English in public and relying on an interpreter. It was striking that he never slipped into his own tongue, not even when addressing peasantry, few of whom would have understood English. His biographer, Philip Short, however, gives the argument short shrift. He says Banda had not forgotten his local language, but it was rusty and archaic, and it was in keeping with the persona of a supreme leader to speak through an intermediary. Far from diminishing Banda's appeal,

Short concludes that speaking English would have enhanced it by placing him on a par with the Europeans.[2]

The most authentic witnesses, the Malawians, concur that there is little to explain. He was a clever man who was in the right place at the right time. With his education and experiences he had a headstart on most of his fellow countrymen. He arrived back home with three suits and little else. The temptation to improve on this wardrobe was clearly irresistible. He was overseeing an uneducated population who were hungry for a new message. In short he had a free rein for his foibles and fancies. He had his own country and he could do as he wanted.

'I want to be blunt,' he told his people soon after taking office. 'As long as I am here and you say I must be your president, you have to do what I want, what I like and not what you like, what you want . . . Kamuzu is in charge. That is my way.'[3]

He could hardly have been more direct – and yet there were voices, some partisan, some patronizing and others merely pragmatic, who argued his dictatorship was not all bad.

✦✦✦✦

Of all the many colourful episodes in Banda's rise to power, few are more absurd than the tale of 'the bruising of Miss Phombeya's toe'. She was a young woman whose foot was stamped on in a scuffle with colonial police officers and whose case for no particular reason caused a rumpus in Westminster. It is by most reckonings a footnote in the story of decolonization. It is literally little more than a footnote in Hansard. But the story helped to prime a belief in Europe, and particularly Britain, that Malawi was a comic opera society. It was a theory which was willingly bolstered by Banda to back his case that he was a benign dictator, a dangerously misleading argument.

The bruising occurred in 1960 outside Ryall's Hotel in Blantyre where Harold Macmillan was lunching on the homeward leg of his famous 'wind of change' tour. A crowd had gathered outside to protest at the imprisonment of Banda and other local leaders by the federation government. A cloudburst soon put a stop to trouble between the police and the crowd. It was more of a jostle than a riot, and would soon have been forgotten were it not for the prime ministerial press pack, whose prose in the next morning's newspapers in London was so purple that the affair reached the House of Commons and led to the appointment of a commission of enquiry.

The one-man commission duly met and concluded memorably:

> It does not appear that the amount of blood that was shed would be sufficient to test the capacity of an ordinary mustard spoon. Contemplating the measure of the injuries sustained by the demonstrators one cannot avoid the reflection that when the face of Helen launched a thousand ships and brought Agamemnon and the great Achilles to the shores of Phrygia it hardly achieved as much as Miss Phombeya's toe when it brought the paladins of Fleet Street in the aerial argosies of our day across two continents to appear before your Commissioner in the remote highlands of Middle Africa.

The simplistic portrayal of brutal colonial policemen and oppressed black protestors undoubtedly intensified pressure on London to undercut the federation and to grant full independence. Banda himself was later to remark that the over-reaction of the British press and government was the 'best turn the British ever did for me'. But by allowing her toe to be stamped on Miss Phombeya did her fellow countrymen a bad service, as the story also inadvertently fuelled the idea that Malawi was a cuddly teddy bear that played to different rules from the rest of the continent.

I heard this point of view many times in Blantyre as I underwent a long and elaborate courtship to see the Ngwazi. First I had to submit myself to preliminary interviews with bigwigs from Banda's Malawi Congress Party. Then I had to secure the permission of a range of government officials, from the head of police and the commissioner of prisons to the director of state protocol. Finally I needed the go-ahead of Clive

Stanbrook, the British QC who had been flown out to defend him. If I had stopped to think amid the form-filling, I would have paid my respects to him at the outset. I should have guessed that Banda would trust only a Briton as the gate-keeper to his presence. But as it was, I played the game by the book, so I had plenty of time on my hands.

The Mt Soche Hotel where I was staying had seen better days. The waiters sat in the shadows like museum curators. The service was as threadbare as their ancient stained tunics. Their buffet always looked as if it had been put out the previous day. Most evenings I retired across the road to a Chinese restaurant, the pride of the town with its plastic chairs and cheap Christmas lights. There, amid rows of empty tables, the years would roll back as a British couple who had 'stayed on' recalled happy memories of the days when floral print dresses were the rage and Banda kept Malawi in line.

The couple were among the last of a breed of white settlers. Raised in Rhodesia, they had been marooned by the post-colonial upheavals. Zimbabwe was out of bounds because of the husband's record in its independence war. Britain was alien and unfamiliar and anyway expensive to reach. The 'new' Malawi, too, did not feel like home, although it was at least Africa. There was plenty of time to talk, as the menu – like the Mt Soche's – was all form and no substance. Day by day their old life was crumbling. They were too honest to grumble. Instead they wistfully recalled the Banda era when Malawians knew where they stood. 'He was in many ways just the sort of leader that Malawians wanted. They are a friendly lot . . . but they need a father figure to keep them in line . . .'

As with all but the most brutal Big Men, there were arguments that could be marshalled in Banda's defence. Malawi was stable at a time when much of the continent was beset by coups and civil war. The economy grew at an average of more than 5 per cent a year in the late Sixties and Seventies. Banda was also a solitary voice at the foundation of the Organization of African Unity (OAU) to dare to question its unswerving commitment to the Soviet bloc and to argue for an independent line.

But the logic of personal rule soon took its toll. As Malawi became poorer, so Banda's bank balance grew. Tyranny is tyranny whatever its form and wherever it is. There are massive cultural and social differences between Europe and Africa, but there are also some absolutes. Africans have to – and indeed for the most part want to – be judged on the same terms as the rest of the world. Subservience and apathy should not be mistaken for consent. Witness the overwhelming vote which ousted Banda and other African dictators in first-time multi-party elections. To indulge African dictators is reverse racism. It also plays brilliantly into their hands.

As my companions at the Chinese restaurant chattered away, I recalled a meeting the previous day with a Malawian lawyer in a crumbling villa on the outskirts of Blantyre. Dr Vera Chirwa had for many years been an outspoken critic of Banda. Her husband Orton had been one of the early activists pushing for independence. Their relationship with Banda dated back to his London days when he had paid for Orton's living expenses at a post-colonial conference. But the Chirwas had grown increasingly disillusioned after independence. They were imprisoned in 1981 after they were kidnapped from exile in neighbouring Zambia. For the first four years Vera was held in leg-irons. She was released only in January 1993 as Malawi moved towards democracy under pressure from the foreign aid donors on whom its economy relied. Her husband had died mysteriously in custody two months earlier. She had seen him once in the previous eleven years.

'When Dr Banda first came you could not imagine he would do those bad things,' she told me. 'He was actually dedicated – unless of course he was a very good actor. But there are some people who get drunk with power. Power corrupts and it corrupted him. It's a pity, a man who started quite well and he developed into an animal, a killer.'

By the late Eighties it was widely believed that Banda no longer had a hand in the day-to-day affairs of state. He was certainly relying heavily on John Tembo, his police minister and business associate, who was a co-accused in the murder trial and the uncle of the enigmatic 'Mama', the third member of the ruling triumvirate. When the murder trial opened, Banda was allowed to stay in Mudi House after the court was told he was too old to sit through the hearings. By the time of my interview his mind was clearly fading. It was almost as if he had reverted to being a schoolboy. He jumped to attention when asked if he would be photographed and grinned merrily when positioned in front of a giant portrait of himself. But every now and then the old wicked gleam would return.

As I rose to go I asked whether he had any regrets and whom he most admired. He seemed puzzled at the first part of the question. Penitent he was clearly not. He saw his detention as the ultimate endorsement of his low opinion of Africa. 'Bitter? Why? I am indifferent.' He needed no prompting however for the second part. 'Julius Caesar,' he said. 'He could be tough. He could be kind. But when he was tough he was tough . . . oh yes.'

The analogy was all too apt. Caesar's assassination ushered in a period of chaos before Octavian took over as *primus inter pares*. Banda's fall paved the way for the long-awaited democracy. Sadly for Malawians it was confused and confusing from its earliest days.

ﾊﾊﾊ

If there was one tale in the 1990s that illustrated the fragility of African democracy, it was the story of the president who was not himself. A fortnight after my interview with Banda I went to chronicle the last political gasp of another Big Man, his erstwhile neighbour and rival, the former Zambian president Kenneth Kaunda, who was plotting a comeback. I left the capital, Lusaka, after a few days with a far more ludicrous and yet ominous story about his successor than I could ever have imagined. Far from observing the last of a Big Man I wondered if I had been chronicling the birth of a new one.

'K.K.', who led Zambia from independence in 1964, always managed to avoid the opprobrium of his peers, but this was a sentimental not an empirical judgement, as his rule was a disaster. To be fair, his government was dealt a grievous blow when the price of copper, Zambia's main source of export earnings, plummeted in a harsh echo of the collapse of cacao prices which so devastated Nkrumah's Ghana. But his Utopian policies reduced one of Africa's most promising economies to a shambles from which it may never recover. He destroyed the country's rich agricultural base by introducing price subsidies which made it uneconomic to grow crops. An extravagant social welfare programme for the towns further encouraged peasants to abandon the land. By 1990 it was estimated that half Zambia's population lived in towns, an absurdly high figure for a country with such ideal farming land. Thousands of jobs were created in a bloated civil service and giant state monopolies. Money was printed to pay the salaries. Aid agencies then compounded the problem by saturating Lusaka with cut-price food, encouraging still more people to leave their plots and live off the state.

Frantic for funds for his ambitious plans, K.K. could not resist taking control of Zambia's 'golden egg', its copper industry. By nationalizing the mines he destroyed the threadbare remains of foreign investor confidence and entrenched a Western cynicism about African governments' grasp of economics which endures to this day. When Mandela's ministers introduced a textbook free-market economic programme which was designed to boost growth, officials angrily berated wary foreign businessmen for their 'racist' preconceptions about 'voodoo economics'. But caution was only to be expected, given that the ANC had still been talking of nationalization in 1990 when Mandela was released.

The Zambian leader was, however, one of the few genuinely likeable Big Men. Although corruption flourished under his chaotic rule, he was untainted. He would burst into tears and dab his eyes with a handkerchief at emotional points in his many public addresses. He had a lightness of touch remarkable for an African leader of his generation. He and his wife Betty once entertained President Nixon at the White House with guitar and song. When South Africa was several nervy months from its April 1994 election I watched him dance a jig on a Johannesburg television talk show while one of his oldest enemies, Roelof 'Pik' Botha, the veteran Afrikaner Nationalist foreign minister, hopped around a giant saucepan cooking his favourite stew. Kaunda's most valued political act, however, came at the very end of his long rule. After nearly three decades in office, he submitted to the voice of his people, a rare event in a continent where few leaders bow out of office.

The hero of that rare African good news story was an outspoken trade unionist, Frederick Chiluba, who rose to power in the mould of the Polish union leader, Lech Walesa, by daring to challenge the one-party state, and calling for reform. His election campaign was irresistible as it focused on one key demand – reform. The clamour for change had been growing steadily in the late Eighties as it became clear to Zambians that independence had been a disaster. With Western aid donors at last acknowledging there should be a reformist price tag to their largesse and threatening to cut off loans, Kaunda was under increasing pressure to change. Then came the fall of the Berlin Wall and a loosening of Africa's ideological strait-jacket. Like a gambler trying one last routine, K.K. agreed to multi-party elections and, much to his surprise, was voted from power.

On conceding defeat Kaunda regretfully said farewell to the sumptuous grounds of State House, where he had played many a needle golf tournament with visiting dignitaries on his private nine-hole course. One of his former golfing partners recalled to me wistfully that he had never been such a good loser on the course: 'You couldn't take your eye off him or he would be lying about his handicap, changing the lay of his ball in the rough and mismarking his card.'

His diminutive successor was a born-again Christian who clearly believed he was on a crusade. Chiluba saw himself as the first in a new breed of African leaders and was determined to prove to the world that Africans really were starting to take responsibility for their own affairs. He shattered the cosy support-system of the OAU, which had become little more than an autocrats' drinking club, when he stood up at a plenary session and denounced Africa's dictators. 'In Africa today the era of dictators, of hypocrisy and lies is over . . .' he told a startled audience in Washington a few months after taking power.

More than three years later he repeated the message in South Africa. 'To me democracy is not the preserve of the developed world,' he said. 'Democracy will succeed in Africa. Having broken the back of the one-party dictator and conscientized the people, we believe very sincerely that democracy is here to stay.' But this time his reception was distinctly muted. In a bitter blow to Africans' hopes of a rebirth, the parallel with Walesa, who turned out to be a disastrous president and was eventually voted out of office, proved all too apt.

Chiluba deserved praise in the early days of his presidency for his bravery in grasping the nettle of economic reform. He inherited an economy that had all but ceased to exist after two decades of inefficient statist policies. He promptly did what few African leaders have dared to do before or since: he slashed the old subsidies, curbed government spending and took a scythe to the bloated civil service.

The International Monetary Fund and the World Bank approved; it was textbook structural adjustment, the harsh reformist medicine which the West prescribed to Africa in the Eighties. But, as was proved time and again, the continent is too frail for such measures. On paper, structural adjustment has all the answers, but it failed to take into account Africa and the Africans and raised the ultimate dilemma of modern Africa – which comes first, economic or political reform? It is arguable that you cannot introduce the one without the other, but democratic leaders risked being overthrown at the ballot box if they imposed the austerity measures necessary for the reforms to work. Few, if any, Western electorates would be able to tolerate a fraction of the hardship required of Africans by structural adjustment. Two of the more successful free-market programmes were introduced by President Museveni of Uganda and Ghana's President Rawlings, authoritarian populists whose records raise a sensitive question: is autocracy the only way forward?

A year after Chiluba took office, consumer goods did at last start to appear on Lusaka's shop-shelves, but Zambians were too poor to buy them. Cafés opened but only the élite could afford their prices. For the peasants even seeds became too expensive. As K.K. lumbered out of unofficial retirement to capitalize on the dissatisfaction, Chiluba resorted to increasingly autocratic measures, arresting opposition journalists and critics. Cabinet members were linked to drug-dealing and corruption. As the cycle of repression looked set to start again, the old joke that democracy in Africa means 'one man, one vote, one time' was once again doing the rounds.

Unsurprisingly the furore delighted Rupiah Bandah, a leading figure in Kaunda's United National Independence Party (UNIP). We met in the courtyard of Lusaka's Holiday Inn, where the freshly painted white walls and nimble waiters symbolized the new free-market breeze blowing through a city that had been a byword for shortages and queues. Bandah was a jolly bear of a man with a booming laugh and fruity British accent. As we relished chilled South African beers, which had been unavailable in the old days of the UNIP government, Bandah happily acknowledged they had botched the past, before he proceeded to belittle Chiluba, in particular for a bizarre constitutional clause designed to stop Kaunda from standing against him.

The government had just proposed that only Zambians could stand for the presidency. This was patently aimed at Kaunda, whose parents had been born in Nyasaland, now Malawi. But instead it prompted an investigation of Chiluba's own past, which, to the delight of UNIP, backfired badly. In a front-page article which sent shockwaves through the government, the *Post*, Zambia's one truly independent newspaper, researched Chiluba's own background in a village on the Zairean border. He had, the newspaper claimed, been born in Zaire to Zairean parents. As for Chiluba's father, far from his having died, as the president said, the *Post* produced a Zairean called Luka Chabala, who claimed to be the president's father and who insisted that the president had changed his name.

Chiluba was outraged and flatly denied the allegations. Most Zambians were not so sure. It was not that any minded whether the president had been born on this or that side of a particular river. Borders in central Africa are famously fluid in a tribute to the absurdity of the lines colonial administrators had drawn on the map. The nub of the matter was that Chiluba's armour was less shining than had been thought. After years of taunting K.K. on the need to allow the people to choose, he now seemed reluctant to give the old stalwart another chance.

Elections did finally take place in November 1996 but without Kaunda, who had been barred. The muted and sullen atmosphere was a far cry from the rapturous joy which accompanied Zambians' previous foray to the polls. Chiluba's image was to sink still further the following year. On Christmas Day 1997 he arrested Kaunda on suspicion of involvement in an abortive coup attempt the previous month. When he was criticized in the West he started denouncing the colonial powers for meddling, just as K.K. had done at sensitive moments. Chiluba's aides later said they had decided to act on Christmas Day assuming the world would be on holiday and so would pay little attention. They could not have been more wrong. It was a quiet Christmas in the rest of the world. Day after day Zambia was on international television after an incident which might have escaped notice at any other time.

I had only a modicum of sympathy for Kaunda as he fulminated about the abuse of the very democratic rights he had denied his people so long. Grand old man of Africa that he is, on his release from prison in 1998 he probably did his people a service by announcing an end to his political career. But that did not excuse Chiluba, whose behaviour sounded all too familiar to the rest of the continent.

So after all these travails is Africa still not yet ready for democracy? Depressingly, Zambia's tale was hardly unique. The people of Blantyre were initially agog with the wonders of their new-found freedom under Banda's successor. When I met Bakili Muluzi at his Sanjika Palace I was impressed. His crisp answers and lack of protocol marked him out as utterly unlike the Big Men. Strikingly he announced he would forgo the chance of hobnobbing with other heads of state at the United Nations Development Conference in Copenhagen. The vast expense of taking his entourage there could, he argued, be better spent in Malawi.

But the 'new man' was less jaunty by the time of my interview with Banda, little more than a year after the election. Malawians' love affair with multi-party politics had long since died. The politicians, everyone muttered, spent more time arguing than governing. The cabinet was over-staffed. There were reports of officials driving convoys of food aid over the border into Mozambique for a quick profit. Newspapers and trade unions seemed to have mistaken freedom for licence. To the delight of the time-servers at the Malawi Congress Party there were even appreciative hankerings after the old days. 'At least you knew where you stood,' I was told time and again by frustrated Malawians. Diplomats mused that Muluzi's new broom was looking like more of the same. He had, it emerged, refused the Copenhagen invitation only after coming under massive pressure from the West to cut costs or risk forfeiting loans.

The refrain was familiar from Eastern Europe where, a few years after the fall of the Berlin Wall, electorates started hankering for the comfort and security of the old order. In times of hardship, memories are short. But in Eastern Europe democracy did at least have regional and historical foundations. Malawi, like much of Africa, has had to undergo in a matter of decades a political evolution that took centuries in the West. First, the colonists thrust much of the continent into the glare of the developed world. Then, in their haste to decolonize, they abandoned country after country with only the trappings of democratic institutions.

'It was a Catch-22,' a senior British government advisor from the period later mused to me. 'If we had sanctioned anything short of democracy we would have been pilloried. So we put in place the structures of Westminster-style oppositional politics and to no one's surprise it did not work.'

The blunderings and tribulations of Africa's new democrats were endlessly amusing to Banda's aides. He had long argued that multi-party politics was alien to Africa. The African continent, he once declared, needed a special style of democracy and it also needed time. 'Democracy did not come to Britain on the platter from the Angel Gabriel in heaven,' he told his party. 'There are varieties of cow, varieties of sheep and goat, varieties of chicken – so why should there not be varieties of democracy? We have to have our own kind of democracy based on African institutions.'[4]

This was, inevitably, a favoured line of crusty old autocrats, but it does contain a kernel of truth. The rights and wrongs of multi-party politics in Africa is one of the more sensitive debates in the continent. By suggesting that Africa is not mature enough for democracy you run the risk of being labelled racist or neo-colonialist. But it is unarguable that Western-style multi-party democracy has had a dismal record in Africa. All too often it has split states down tribal lines and led to chaos and war. As frequently it has provided a façade of respectability for the very tyrants outsiders hoped it would supplant. President Moi of Kenya and President Mugabe of Zimbabwe are classic examples. Both were elected in flawed multi-party elections enabling them to vaunt their 'democratic' credentials even though the opposition – which barely exists in Zimbabwe – knows all too well that it would be in trouble if it were to pose a serious challenge.

Africa's political difficulties, however, are more deeply rooted than just bad leadership. A range of factors has assisted the triumph of tyrants, not least poverty, as Mr Muluzi warned soon after taking office. It was, he said, the greatest barrier to democracy. 'People cannot eat democracy. They cannot eat human rights. All these problems we see in Africa are because people are poor.' Much of Africa has a harsh and unremitting climate which saps the strength of all but the most energetic.

The World Bank estimates that eighteen out of the world's twenty poorest nations are in Africa. With daily life little more than a battle for survival, politics is a luxury that only the wealthy have time for.

For the Big Men it was all too easy to dominate. For Africa watchers the acquiescence of many societies towards their élites is endlessly frustrating. But the abuses of Arab, European and African slavers, followed by colonial rule, have weighed heavily on the continent's psyche, spawning a culture of submission which impedes the growth of a vigorous opposition culture. The Big Men's greed and repression merely cemented a feeling that the little man was doomed to be trampled underfoot.

And yet it is a massive mistake to conclude that Africans do not want accountable government. You only have to witness the enthusiasm and patience of Africans lining up to vote at an election to understand people are aching to have a say in running their societies. It is just that they are seldom given the chance to cast a vote, and when they are, all too often the government machinery loads the dice against the opposition.

To understand the political currents that are swirling in late twentieth-century Africa you have to go beyond the utterances of its leaders, and one of the best places to start is the local news-stand. Publications with crisp new paper and shiny print are to be read with caution; their sheen suggests funding from a local bigwig. Instead, often the journals to head for are the ones with yellowy print-smudged paper. It is there that writers can be found criticizing the government, whatever its hue, as they fight to defend or attain a long-dreamed-of freedom.

I learned the lesson of the newspaper stand during my long vigil in Blantyre. It had been an especially frustrating day. I had trekked several times to the office of the government spokesman for pre-arranged appointments only to find an empty desk and the blank stares of civil servants with nothing to do. On a whim I bought a sheaf of newspapers, flagged down a taxi, thrust in the driver's face the *Independent*, which was at the top of the pile, and asked him to take me there. An hour later I was outside a launderette on the edge of town face to face with David Nthengwe, the newspaper's fresh-faced editor. In time I came to see him as the voice and face of the new Africa.

I arrived at a difficult time. The *Independent*'s last telephone line had been cut off that morning for non-payment. In a bitter twist their last incoming call had been from a chain of garages, the newspaper's main advertiser. The manager was transferring their business to another paper without a day's notice. No reason had been given, but the journalists did not need to be told. The firm had for months been warning that the newspaper was too critical of Mr Muluzi's government. The loss of the advertising meant there would be no salaries that month. It was enough to make the most dedicated newspaperman throw in the towel, but Nthengwe and his young team had not seen off Banda for nothing. There can have been no one older than thirty on the staff. They had already had to cut their weekly production from two editions to one. The *sine qua non* was their survival.

The *Independent* was one of dozens of newspapers that emerged in the dying days of Banda's regime. Journalistic training was in as short supply as funding and materials. But determination and energy made up the shortfall. When Banda lost the 1994 election many transferred their attentions to the new government. Tittle-tattle and conspiracy were often dressed up as news, undermining the newspapers' reputations. But it was the principle that mattered. The days of hagiography were over. Just because the 'good guys' had won the election, journalists were not going to stand back and watch another élite take charge – or at least, Nthengwe said with a devil-may-care smile, they would do their best not to.

'We are, I suppose, surviving only by the grace of God,' he explained. 'We take all sides on their merits and so we suffer. We want to be objective. The difficulty is that you have to fight between survival and objectivity. Companies warn unless we tone down our line they will leave us. What can we do? Governments in Africa are only interested in power and money. They are not concerned with freedom of speech. These new leaders are putting on their democracy jacket, but their shirts are cut from the same old dictatorial cloth.'

For journalists like Nthengwe it was difficult enough to get their hands on newsprint and notebooks, let alone a story. But somehow he managed. During his schooldays he had watched as Banda had frittered away his people's hopes, dreamed of wielding a critical pen, and waited for his chance. When the opportunity finally came, at the end of Banda's rule, he vowed not to waste it – and not to compromise his ideals.

He started at the *Independent* soon after it opened in the dying days of Banda's regime. Within a few months his writing was attracting unwelcome attention. His younger brother Donald was walking home one night when a man ran into his path, thrust a revolver in his face and threatened to blow his head off if he did not reveal where David was staying. Donald denied he had a brother and the vigilante, almost certainly a member of Banda's Pioneers, ran off into the bush.

Nthengwe became the talk of the town. He was one of Malawi's most prominent journalists in the countdown to the elections. But if Muluzi expected to be supported by him and Banda's other critics, he was sorely disappointed. Once the election was over, the *Independent* and other papers levelled their sights on the new team. The response was not long in coming. Nthengwe was walking with a friend from the office to his township home a few months after the election when police with automatic rifles ambushed them from behind a tree. Shortly before a gun butt crashed down on his head, he heard one of the policemen exclaim: 'I know this boy. He is the one writing rubbish things against Muluzi.'

Nthengwe lives and breathes the fire of educated Africans of his generation who are to be found all over the continent, men like Trevor Ncube, the editor of the *Zimbabwe Independent* who was a persistent thorn in the flesh of Mugabe, and Fred M'membe, the editor of the *Post* in Zambia who uncovered the allegations about Chiluba's origins, driven by a desire not to accept second-best.

In the old early days of independence it was the easiest thing in the world to gain popular acclaim. When Nkrumah came up with his mantra 'Seek ye first the political kingdom . . . the rest will follow', everyone cheered, seemingly blind to the implicit *carte blanche* it gave leaders to ignore the basic rules of economy and good government. A leader would call for the media to take a more patriotic line, would point the finger of blame at the white man and the West and his halo would grow. After the long years as second-class citizens in their own countries it was easy to see why so many African intellectuals and journalists fell into line.

By the late Nineties, however, the argument that Africans had to work together to throw off the burden of their submissive past had lost its allure. It was not often outside government offices that you heard the white man taking the rap for Africa's woes. Instead, governments were held to be accountable.

The most striking exception was South Africa. The African National Congress freely played the 'apartheid' card, not least because many whites disappeared into their laager and greeted the new order with resentment and fear. Black journalists were called in for a 'friendly chat' with Mandela and were urged to play a more constructive role. Critical white colleagues were accused of being racist and unpatriotic. It was a sensitive argument for black and white journalists alike. The former risked being branded as 'Uncle Toms', the latter as 'racist', and some did back down and take a less confrontational stance. But they found little sympathy among their peers north of the Limpopo who have no truck with such defeatist thought.

It is easy to be pessimistic about the chances of journalists like David Nthengwe. Like teachers, human rights activists, priests and imams who, all over the continent, bravely defy the Big Men, they are 'little people' who can be ignored or silenced. Even when they are allowed to publish, governments tend to ignore their findings. But they are, at least, a living proof of a more critical vein running through the continent. Two years after taking office in Malawi, Muluzi warned journalists that he would not tolerate 'inaccurate reporting'. Far from huddling nervously over their typewriters, as he had no doubt hoped, journalists celebrated, assuming that his outburst meant that he had been stung by newspaper allegations that he had taken bribes from a local garage. The Nthengwes' task is huge and their resources few. The detention and torture of a Zimbabwean editor and reporter in January 1999 for claiming that twenty-three army officers had been arrested for plotting a coup against Mugabe, was a sombre reminder of the contempt amongst African governments for free speech – Zimbabwe was, after all, still supposed to be one of the continent's less authoritarian states. But governments are at least finding it harder to fall back on the blather that helped sustain the Big Men so long.

ᛘᛘᛘᛘ

The Ngwazi maintained his disdainful distance from Africa to the very end. He also escaped the crocodiles: he was acquitted in December 1996. Banda was by then failing fast, but if he was aware of the verdict it almost certainly would have confirmed his belief that Malawi had gone soft. An acquittal in such a highly charged case would never have happened in his day. It was Banda after all who had authorized the traditional courts to try murder cases, as they allowed hearsay evidence, ensuring a conviction was a formality.

A year after his acquittal he was flown to a top hospital in one of Johannesburg's most exclusive suburbs, about as far from the gritty reality of Big Man land as you can get in Africa. He died a week later with 'Mama' at his side. For the first time in decades his great age was officially acknowledged. He was, it seemed, just short of his century. 'At ninety-nine the battle to recover from pneumonia is very difficult,' said a hospital spokesman. 'He went easy.'

In a tribute to Africa's spirit of forgiveness, but also to its short memory, his body was flown home for a state funeral. Large crowds met him at the airport. Many were genuinely sad to see the Ngwazi go. For Africa, however, there was nothing to mourn. Despots will continue to wield power. But the material for Evelyn Waugh parodies is waning. If they want the support of the outside world, African leaders are at last having to learn to behave in a less high-handed fashion – not that I would have guessed that as I sat in the waiting-room of Daniel arap Moi for the second day running with a crowd of importunate hangers-on.

3

Kenya – Where the Kalenjin are Kings

Daniel arap Moi – The Ties of Tribalism

The highway north from Nairobi through the Rift Valley has to be one of the more dangerous roads in the continent. It is the overland route to the interior, linking Uganda and the tortured twins, Rwanda and Burundi, to the Indian Ocean. Hundreds of lorries grind their way along it each day, bringing valuable transit currency to the Kenyan economy. And yet the potholes suggest an incipient Zaire. The markings have long since faded. In the rainy season the road is blanketed by thick fog. Any driver mad enough to take to the road before dawn will pass a jack-knifed or overturned lorry every few miles and end up as I did early one morning in a layby willing on the morning.

The road, however, suddenly changes on the far side of the central town of Nakuru. The tarmac is newly laid and the lines freshly painted. The fields mirror the transformation. Scrubland gives way to golden cornfields. Neat rows of sheaves gleam in the sun. A handsome school building fronted by a trim green lawn appears between black wrought-iron gates. The picture-postcard image falters as scarred fields and potholes testify to over-crowding and disrepair. But the landscape resumes its pristine state on the road to the hill-town of Kabarnet and in the rugged hills of the Baringo area. For mile after mile the road is deserted. The handful of villages have gleaming pylons and new telegraph poles. It is like being in a millionaire's private estate, and in a sense it is.

Back in 1924 when the hedonistic aristocrats of 'Happy

Valley' were in full swing, Daniel arap Moi was born twenty miles from Kabarnet, in a tiny village on the edge of a precipitous cliff. Sacho was then an impoverished and illiterate backwater among the last to be visited by missionaries, who were largely responsible for the spread of education through the region. Moi is a Tugen, a sub-branch of the Kalenjins, one of Kenya's smallest tribal groups, and although his 'herdboy-to-president' motif has been embroidered in state hagiography, his was an archetypal peasant upbringing. Contemporaries recall that the young Moi walked to school, milked the goats, and felt uneasy with city folk. In the eyes of the Luo and the Kikuyu, the two dominant tribes of the then British colony, the Kalenjin were country bumpkins to be tricked and teased.

By the time of my visit, however, a remarkable facelift was under way. Every second street in Kabarnet had a crane and a team of builders. Many of the sheerest slopes around Sacho had been expertly terraced. School-children were walking home from school as in Moi's time, but in bright blue uniforms with satchels. The average Kalenjin is as poor as any Kenyan, but no expense has been spared by the regional government on showpieces to give the impression that they are uplifting the president's backyard.

The contrasts reminded me of the difference between apartheid South Africa's impoverished tribal homelands and the white areas. As my guide, a Kenyan journalist, explained, the analogy was all too apt. The patch of pristine territory outside Nakuru was Moi's personal estate, Kabarak, a cornucopia of pineapple trees, oranges and sugar cane. The black wrought-iron gates belonged to the Moi High School.

The chief was, my friend said with a wry smile, 'merely seeing his people right'.

ᛈᛈᛈᛈ

The monopoly of a tribal élite is nothing new. It has blighted the history of post-colonial Africa like a terrible cancer. Hardly an African president has been able to resist the temptation of stocking his household, cabinet and often civil service and army with his own tribe. Mobutu's inner circle were all from his Gbande tribe. Banda promoted his fellow Chewe. Despite heady talk of reconciliation, soon after Zimbabwe's independence in 1980 Mugabe favoured his Shona over the Ndebele of his rival, Joshua Nkomo. After a bloody purge of Matabeleland, the Ndebele homeland, the two leaders effected a reconciliation, but Shonas maintained their most-favoured status. In 1989, after a scandal over government officials selling subsidized cars on the black market, Mugabe sacked senior government figures but pointedly excluded those from his own tribal group.

Namibia exemplifies how tribalism pervades African society and politics. To outsiders the sparsely populated barren country in south-west Africa is a role model for the continent, a rare and welcome case of a peaceful and prosperous state. From a Namibian point of view the perception is accurate as long as you are an Ovambo. When President Sam Nujoma's SWAPO (South West Africa People's Organization) took power in elections in 1989 after a long guerrilla war against South African forces Namibia became effectively the land of the Ovambos, the largest tribe. Driving through the parched interior I picked up a Herero hitch-hiker who spoke perfect English and had a string of qualifications but was struggling to find a job.

'The Ovambos have them all,' he said. 'They turn up in Windhoek [the capital], see the right person and the job is settled. The civil service is packed with them and even businesses give them preferential treatment so they are seen as doing the right thing.' I remembered his words that evening as I trudged up a hill in Damaraland, the rugged semi-desert region inland from the Skeleton Coast. Our guide, a Damara, told a grim story about the guerrilla war in the Eighties. Twenty-seven Ovambos were passing through the area, he said, looking for work. They stopped for the night in the same hills we were walking in, and made a fire from a poisonous shrub. The fumes impregnated their food and all but one 'who had not been hungry' died. Our guide pursed his lips without comment and walked on up the hill.

Tribal preferment almost always brings ruination in its wake, but the risks of a backlash are seldom heeded. The Gbande went on exploiting fellow Zaireans to the very end of Mobutu's rule. So intense was the resentment against them that many Gbande who had moved to Kinshasa fled across the river Congo to Brazzaville, the adjacent capital of the Republic of Congo, after his overthrow, fearing reprisals. An even more catastrophic example was in Liberia, where in the Eighties Samuel Doe, an uneducated Master Sergeant turned psychotic president, gave his fellow Krahns *carte blanche* to kill and plunder other tribes. Before he took power in a coup in 1980, Liberia's history was untainted by tribal bloodshed. By the time of his bloody over-throw ten years later – he was tortured to death – hundreds of thousands of Krahns were fleeing into exile to escape the tribes they had oppressed for so long.

The resentment against Kalenjins is not as intense, or at least not yet. My driver in Nairobi was a member of Moi's bodyguard until he was squeezed out because he did not belong to the right tribe – he was a Kikuyu, Kenya's largest tribe, which dominated politics at independence in 1960. Kalenjins dominate Moi's inner circle. Nicholas Biwott, Moi's *eminence grise*, is of course a Keiyo, another sub-branch of the Kalenjins. He has been linked to countless government scandals. He was named by Scotland Yard as a prime suspect in the February 1990 murder of Dr Robert Ouko, an outspoken former foreign min-ister who had called for an investigation into government cor-ruption. After an international outcry Biwott was suspended from the cabinet, but was later rehabilitated and brought back into the government.

Moi, however, was craftier in his tribal politics than many of his peers. As a shy Kalenjin with halting English he was consis-tently under-rated in his early career. His credentials as well as his bloodstock stood against him. He had served as one of five African members of the Legislative Council, the colonial con-sultative body set up by the British in the late Fifties while Jomo Kenyatta and other nationalists were in prison, thereby implicitly taking the British line. That should have been a death blow to Moi's ambitions as Kenya moved towards independence in 1963. Certainly he was seen as no threat by the Luo and Kikuyu powerbrokers when he was made Kenyatta's vice-president in 1967. Indeed, he was regarded as a useful compromise candidate. The Kikuyus even broadly welcomed his succession to the presidency in 1978 after Kenyatta died, assuming he would be a pliant leader who would do their bidding. How wrong they were.

The naive country boy routine was merely a brilliant act. Kikuyus were played off against Luos until the time was right to strike. The rise and fall of Charles Njonjo, his one-time attorney general and mentor turned 'non-person', was a classic case. As a Kikuyu powerbroker, Njonjo was a vital ally for Moi in the jostling for position in Kenyatta's last years. But Njonjo's lessons in the politics of power were clearly too good. As soon as Moi felt strong enough to cope without him, Njonjo was denounced, like an out-of-favour commissar from the Kremlin. Paul Muite, an ambitious lawyer and a leading light in the opposition party, Safina, which means Noah's Ark in Swahili, recalled acting for Njonjo in the mid-Seventies when it was clear Kenyatta did not have long to live.

'He [Moi] was just a hick. Njonjo used to joke to me that he had to take him shopping, that he did not know what to wear. He [Moi] also used to burst into tears in Njonjo's office, saying these Kikuyu will kill me when Mzee [Swahili for 'old man' an affectionate nickname for Kenyatta subsequently used of Moi] dies. And Njonjo literally took him by the hand and said, "Don't worry. Nothing will happen." Njonjo was vital to him and then when he felt strong he suddenly turned round and set the wolves on him.' The axe fell in 1983 when Njonjo was travelling abroad. Moi insinuated that a 'traitor' was hoping to replace him. Njonjo was disgraced and replaced.

Muite's cramped office in central Nairobi was packed with clients hoping for advice. It is harder and harder to find good lawyers as the judiciary, like so much else in Kenya, crumbles beneath the weight of political pressure and corruption. In a brief break between consultations Muite ridiculed Moi's official image as tribal harmonist. Tribal jealousy, he reckoned, has influenced every step of Moi's career.

Way back in 1980 he came to open a regional office of the attorney general. There were fifteen or so of us there and by coincidence we were all part of the educated élite. I became increasingly puzzled. He had this expression I could not quite work out. The penny dropped when the last person was introduced. Moi turned to Njonjo and said: 'You are very lucky. If only I had four people like these in Baringo [Moi's home district].' The rest laughed as if it was a great joke. But I did not laugh. I could see he meant it and there was an intense jealousy burning in his eyes.

He preaches to you as if he was a tape-recorder. 'I hate tribalism blah blah blah.' That is all the British government [traditionally one of Moi's staunchest allies] hears. But every now and then he lets down his guard. I had been brought to State House on one occasion after speaking out against the government. The 'tape-recorder' was whirring away and then suddenly the tortoise popped out of its shell. And he shouted in Swahili, 'Yes, it is you people, the Kikuyu, who will suffer. You are the ones with the wealth. What do my people have, the Kalenjins? One or two cows . . . isolated buildings.' There was the real man speaking from the heart.

By the early Nineties Moi was ringed by a coterie of Kalenjins, many of whom were, one old friend of his told me, 'country peasants trying to get in on every deal, the bigger the better, even when they had no idea of commerce.' Moi, however, is no fool. He appreciates the need to bolster his position outside the Kalenjin clique. In 1978, soon after taking office, he was given a copy of Machiavelli's *The Prince*. It was, one insider recalled with a note of derision, an abridged version, but the lessons were clear. Where tribal politics failed, Moi, like his predecessor and mentor, Kenyatta, flattered with money and land.

Koigi wa Wamwere, one of Kenya's most famous dissidents, knew Moi well in the Seventies when Kenya was a one-party state. Koigi was then an MP in the ruling party for Kabarak,

where Moi has his farm, but he later broke with the government, accusing Moi of betraying the independence ideals. For
his pains he has spent thirteen years in prison. His latest spell
ended in December 1996 when he was released on medical
grounds after serving the first of a four-year sentence on what
international legal observers said were blatantly trumped-up
charges.

We met on the verandah of a cavernous state-owned hotel in
Nakuru. Koigi was a distinctive figure with an extravagant whirl
of dreadlocks, which he once vowed not to cut off until Moi
left office, coiled up under a Rastafarian cap. He was accompanied by two young acolytes who sat on an adjacent table.
Two government goons – or at least I assume that is who they
were – sat a few tables back. With a wry smile, Koigi recalled
his early dealings with Moi.

> The funny thing is I felt sorry for him in his early days. He
> was an underdog. When he was vice-president we had some
> empathy for each other as the ruling class did not want to
> see him inherit. He wasn't one of us [a Kikuyu]. He sum-
> moned me and my wife one morning to Kabarak when I was
> in trouble for criticizing the government.
>
> It was early one morning and we had breakfast and then
> he asked me into a very small room next to the kitchen. He
> got straight to the point and said, 'Don't allow yourself to be
> used.' The threat was clear but then he softened and he
> asked me, 'So where do you stay?' And when I said I lived in
> town he said, 'But that's terrible. Why don't you stay in your
> constituency? You mean you don't have any land?' And he
> picked up the phone and said, 'Is there any land free in
> Koigi's constituency?' He then took out some money from
> his pocket, the equivalent of about 100 dollars, and gave it
> to my wife.

By admitting he took the money, Koigi somewhat undercut
his dissident credentials. But he did later spent several stints in
prison for dissent. The next and last time he was at Kabarak, he
was given an even more straightforward choice. 'Moi told me,

"You are a young man. Listen to an older man. Do not waken those who are sleeping because when they wake you may be the one to sleep." Then he opened three suitcases lined up in the hall and they were full of money. And I realized I was being tempted by the devil . . .'

***

Sixty undulating miles west in the tea-station of Kericho, the view from the Kalenjin side of the fence was of course very different. If anyone is qualified to put Moi's defence it is Mark Too, the head of Lonrho East Africa, who is widely believed to be Moi's illegitimate son. He is a Kenyan multi-millionaire wide-boy who refreshingly has no time for the stuffy protocol favoured by many of Africa's new élites. He is also, like Moi, a Kalenjin, and bears more than a passing resemblance to the president, but he deftly denies the story that they are related. They met, he says, when he was a young boy in the mid-Seventies. He was herding cattle by the side of the road when Moi's Land Rover got stuck in a mudslide as the then vice-president made his way to open a cattle dip.

'He said "Who are you?" And I said: "I'm Mark Too." And he said: "I'm Moi." So I said: "Hello, Mr Moi." And he lightened and we were soon chatting away.' The story has a strong whiff of mythology, but the idea of Moi bonding with a bouncy young Kalenjin is plausible. The aspirant politician would have been on the hunt for men he could trust, and who better than a fellow tribesman who needed a leg-up in the world?

Too likes to think he has maintained his credibility by his forthright ways. He claims he infuriated Moi when he called for action against officials accused of swindling the Central Bank of more than £300 million for non-existent mineral exports in what became known as the Goldenberg scandal. He also insists he was an outspoken supporter of multi-party democracy in the late Eighties when Moi was dragging his feet. But it is hard to imagine there has ever been a rift. Too has been Moi's special envoy on secret missions all over the continent, as, with obvious pride, he kept reminding me.

Too argued long and hard that Moi was misunderstood. He started in the late morning when the sun was high in the sky, continued over lunch in his old white-washed colonial tea-planter's house, and was still going strong as a late-afternoon thunderstorm forced us to abandon our coffee on the lawn and run inside, pursued by a butler carrying our chairs, as must have happened in the old days. Too's main thesis was that Moi was happier tending his cattle than running the affairs of state.

> When you are president a lot of things happen in your name. Maybe his one fault is he has been too tolerant. People say 'I don't know how he will react' and so they say what they think he wants to hear. They give answers before they have heard his question. They should treat him like a human, like everyone else . . .
>
> Only last Saturday he was out early in his farm checking the seeds had been planted in the right way. He knows every corner of his farm. I promise you he is a different man when he gets behind his gates. He doesn't have a special table setting for himself. Whatever there is to eat, he will share. He is determined to set an example to Kenyans.

Moi is in many ways a very British Big Man. He goes to church every Sunday where he delivers impromptu homilies. He wears sombre suits, rises at dawn and neither drinks nor smokes. Bar the odd indulgence such as a private jet with white leather seats he eschews flamboyance, which he leaves to his playboy sons. He more than compensates for his lack of charisma by his prodigious energy touring the country and meeting Kenyans. He is estimated most years to have spent more than 200 days on the road.

The picture of a benevolent pastoralist is no doubt how Moi likes to see himself. He maintains he runs Kenya as he does his household, like a philanthropic seigneur – an argument familiar to defenders of Banda and Mobutu, or even Romania's late dictator Nicolae Ceausescu, who liked to play up his peasant background and his love of rural life. Too was still doggedly defending his man at midnight over a late supper in his house in Nakuru when the telephone rang. He picked up the receiver, stiffened and mouthed to me, 'It is the chief.'

Moi's gravelly voice came down the line. He had been going to see me the next morning following Too's intervention on my behalf. But he had changed his plans. He was flying to the coast to visit a village badly hit by floods. 'Tell him to see me in Nairobi.' The line went dead.

I flew home for a week imagining I had seen from the inside the workings of a Big Man, and concluding from the telephone call that Moi made every decision himself and did not trust anyone to do the right thing in his place. Such was certainly the way of Mobutu and Banda. But, as I later learned, Moi was not as decisive as he made out – all too often he listened to the twisted information of bad advisors and let them act on it.

⁂

For the home of a Big Man, State House, Nairobi, was remarkably low-key. In contrast to Mobutu's palaces, where goons with sunglasses manhandled you if you so much as looked at them, sentries in pressed khaki drill with crisp blue berets jumped to attention and guided me to the waiting room where attendants were waiting with pots of milky tea. It was more county squire than Third World autocrat. There were even prints of stag hunts and partridge shooting in the entrance hall and a set of ever so slightly dilapidated comfy chairs.

But to sit in Moi's waiting room, as I did in October 1997 a week after his late-night phone call, was to take on the role of sycophant at the court of Louis XVI. Perched on the chaise longue opposite me was a senior executive from Kenya's Tourism Board splendidly attired in a bright blue suit with gold buttons. Beside him sat an archbishop, a mayor and – I assumed from his chatter about constituencies – a would-be MP, a popinjay of a man in shiny designer clothes. Our elaborate courtesies had the thinnest veneer for we were bitter rivals for the ear of the chief.

Halfway through the first afternoon, out of boredom I rose from my chair, wandered over to a set of shelves and leafed

through the leather-bound family photo albums with their blurred and amateurish pictures of Moi's foreign tours. Behind me I
sensed a prickle of unease. My neighbours clearly feared that
my insouciance indicated I was at the head of the queue. Their
concern, however, was unfounded; the following morning found
me once more in their midst. Nine o'clock, ten o'clock, eleven
o'clock passed. Then a thick-set official in a dark suit poked his
head around the door. 'The reporter?' he barked. Pathetically
grateful, I jumped to my feet, and followed him out.

Moi was in cracking form: his arms swung at his side as if he
was half his seventy-four years; he was whistling a jolly tune;
he was clearly still revelling in the events of the night before
when parliament had passed a package of political reforms, out-
manoeuvring his critics for the umpteenth time in his career. But
quite what he had to be so jaunty about was hard to imagine.

Moi is a second-generation 'Big Man' but he has been in
politics since before independence and he learned all too well
from Kenyatta's heavy-handed and venal ways. Dissent has been
ruthlessly crushed for most of his rule. Persistent opponents
have been assassinated. By the late Eighties Kenya had scores
of political prisoners, many of whom were held and tortured
in the Central Police Station, just 200 yards away from the
verandah of the Norfolk, Nairobi's premier hotel, favoured by
the wealthier tourists in search of the *Out of Africa* dream.

The repression eased a little in the early Nineties when Moi
succumbed to international pressure and allowed multi-party
elections in 1992. But when pressed he instinctively resorted to
force. Dozens died in the countdown to Kenya's second election
in 1997 in fighting between opposition demonstrators and the
police and in so-called tribal clashes which looked suspiciously
like the work of government *agents provocateurs*. The worst
violence occurred near Kenya's Indian Ocean beach resorts.
Tour operators bemoaned the damage to tourism, but Moi's
opponents pointed out that at least tourists might start to
appreciate the discrepancy between the pictures in Western
holiday brochures of gambolling giraffes and smiling black game

guards in trim khaki shorts and the truth, namely that Kenya is spiralling relentlessly downhill.

As the millennium approached, Kenya's image as an island of prosperity in a sea of chaos was seeping away in a flood of corruption scandals. Even as most Kenyans struggled to feed let alone educate their families, grasping officials creamed off state resources. Month by month the roads became more potholed and the hospitals and schools more down-at-heel. An opposition leader claimed in parliament that nearly $2.5 billion had been stolen from the state since 1990. Moi's sons were frequently linked to financial scandals. Even Britain, traditionally Moi's most loyal Western ally, was starting to reassess its position amid fears that Kenya was going the way of Nigeria and becoming another conduit of fraud and drugs. All the while, whether attending a church service or a cattle market, Moi was, of course, the lead item on the nightly television news, dispensing largesse as if it was his own.

'I am very busy,' Moi growled as I sat down. 'You have two minutes.' But he was under pressure from a British public relations team to launch a charm offensive and belatedly he remembered the script. He was also mortified by claims he is no better than Mobutu, and determined to change his image. One government insider later told me that when in 1982 Moi heard that air force officers had launched a coup he burst into tears – not out of fear but at the thought that there were Kenyans who did not like him. Our conversation lasted half an hour, but it was more of a lecture than an interview. He returned time and again to the 'treachery' of the West, in particular Britain. He had backed them in the Cold War and yet all he got was abuse.

The Western world have in recent years applied double standards. I have known British leaders from Churchill onwards, the whole lot, Callaghan, Wilson, Heath. I knew their colonial secretaries and their attitudes. Here in Africa Kenya has always been called a stooge, an American stooge, a British stooge. And all of a sudden they abandon Kenya with all this talk of democracy and human rights . . . All around us we have military regimes and yet no one seems to protest about them . . .

I recognized the injured tones from government offices all over the continent. The collapse of the Soviet Union transformed Africa almost as much as Europe. Overnight the rules changed. The West no longer needed to turn a blind eye to the excesses of its ideological soulmates. A victim of the changing times, Moi was bewildered and annoyed by his rejection. For years for the West he was the Slobodan Milošević of east Africa. Just as the Serbian leader was seen as indispensable to security in the Balkans in the mid-Nineties before the conflict in Kosovo led to the vilification that he deserved, so Britain identified Moi as a regional bulwark, discreetly overlooking his excesses, in return for his support. He was the first African leader to volunteer troops for the Commonwealth monitoring mission for Rhodesia's transition to Zimbabwe. He boycotted the 1980 Moscow Olympics, and yet the West had abandoned him. Trying to sound a note of self-pity, Moi closed by pleading he had also kept Kenya intact while most of the region had fallen apart. With tribalism so deep-rooted, what could he do? How could he be expected to crack the whip?

'At independence our forty-two tribes all became united under one flag. I am accused of not acting against corrupt civil servants. We'll do the best we can, but it takes time . . .'

Ever since taking office Moi had preyed on the West's fear of tribal bloodshed – something of an irony, given that the British colonialists refined the concept of 'divide and rule'. The assassination of Tom Mboya in 1969, a Luo tipped as Kenyatta's successor, had shown how deep-rooted tribal antipathy was. When a Kikuyu was convicted of the killing, there were ugly clashes between the police and Luo mourners who were convinced there had been a plot to deny Luos power.

By the time of my interview Moi's argument was looking increasingly weak. Although Kenya avoided the fate of many of its neighbours and did not fissure down ethnic lines, that was no justification for overseeing the demise of Kenya's bright independence hopes. He himself had frequently exploited tribal rifts to bolster his position.

And yet Africa is a continent of degrees. Kenya is ringed by some of the most bloodstained states of the late twentieth century. A foray across the frontier in any direction leaves you acutely aware of the hideous shadow that tribalism, or rather the manipulation of tribalism, has cast over Africa.

𝕏𝕏𝕏

The skeletons lay where they had fallen between the pews. Heaps of bloodied clothing filled the aisle. Jagged holes in the walls showed where the killers threw in grenades. Splintered skulls testified to the machetes used for the *coups de grâce*. Several thousand people were slaughtered in the simple red-brick Catholic church at Ntarama, a village twenty miles from the Rwandan capital Kigali, on 15 April 1994, in just one of the massacres of the genocide. The killers were from the majority Hutu tribe fired up with bloodlust by extremists in the Hutu ruling party to eliminate the minority Tutsis. When I visited the scene two years later the flesh had long since rotted away but the ghosts were everywhere. You could sense them behind the sweet-smelling tropical bushes. They hung over the church like the damp equatorial heat.

After overthrowing the Hutu extremists the Tutsi-dominated Rwandan Patriotic Front had left the church untouched as a memorial. There was something distasteful about the caretaker as he rummaged through the debris to illustrate the horrors of that awful day. I almost remonstrated when he asked for a tip. But as I sat on the track leading away from the church listening to a survivor describe how his family were butchered, I appreciated the caretaker's woeful task, and understood the outburst of anger that had followed my suggestion that maybe the time had come to bury the dead. Without such grisly monuments revisionism could set in and allow the world to sit by and watch again.

Georges Ngalinde remembers the night of 6 April 1994 with nightmarish clarity. He was tilling his plot when a neighbour rushed over with a crackly radio to announce that their president, Juvenal Habyarimana, and the president of neighbouring Burundi had been killed when their plane was shot down over the capital, Kigali. Ngalinde hurried home to discuss the implications with his family and they sat up all night fearing trouble. But not even Rwanda's bloody independence history of pogroms could prepare them for what was to come.

Habyarimana was a Hutu who had reluctantly signed a ceasefire and power-sharing settlement the previous year with the Rwandan Patriotic Front, then a rebel movement controlling a third of the country. It is widely assumed that his plane was shot down by extremist Hutus opposed to the deal. It later emerged that local authorities had been drawing up lists detailing the ethnic breakdown of each community to facilitate the slaughter. In a well-planned operation, on the night of the plane crash mobs set up roadblocks and started to butcher Tutsis and moderate Hutu politicians.

On the advice of the local Hutu authorities Ngalinde and other Tutsis from his commune took refuge in their church. For all but a handful it was to be their tomb. Ngalinde was scouting for food outside when trucks of militia drew up alongside the church accompanied by a crowd of local Hutu peasants, including many of his neighbours. First they fired through the holes in the walls, then they finished off survivors with garden tools. His two children were among the victims. All the while Ngalinde was watching from a plantation on a nearby hill. He had been haunted by the screams ever since. He stared at the ground; his face was the proverbial African mask in the face of tragedy.

Up to a million Tutsis and moderate Hutus were killed in the Rwandan genocide in about a hundred days, a rate which makes even Pol Pot's genocide of Cambodians seem slow. Manning checkpoints with bloodstained machetes, the killers boasted to foreign correspondents about what they were doing. Women and children gleefully took part. In village after village butchering Tutsis became part of the daily grind. There were

Right: Mobutu Sese Seko, President of Zaire, one of Africa's longest serving and most corrupt despots, in his traditional leopard skin hat.

Below: Mobutu at the controls of his private jet. In his heyday he would fly foreign visitors around his vast country buzzing low over the Congo and waving at his subjects.

Above: Dr Hastings Banda, life president of Malawi, with his ever-present fly-whisk with which he would belabour importunate petitioners, on one of his regular rural tours.

Left: Dr Banda under house arrest for murder in his official residence, at his interview with the author 1995. Banda was then in his late nineties and this was one of his last public audiences.

Kenneth Kaunda, the former President of Zambia, is one of the most likeable of Africa's Big Men. His policies bankrupted his people but following his defeat in elections he has become a regional sage.

Above: President Daniel arap Moi of Kenya makes a political speech. He is a ponderous speaker in English but witty and sharp in Swahili.

Above right: Jonas Savimibi, leader of Angola's rebel UNITA movement and one of Africa's longest-serving guerrilla leaders, harangues his troops in the bush.

Right: Savimbi in Western politician mode. He for many years played on the West's fears of Soviet domination in Africa and is an expert at tailoring his message to suit his audience.

Left: A train pulls into Benguela station. Angola's Benguela Railway was once one of Africa's main trade arteries, snaking 1200 miles from the Atlantic to the heart of the continent. Jonas Savimbi's father was one of the first black railway officials.

Below left: Conductors of Angola's Benguela Railway. More than 30 years of civil war have reduced it to a small stretch along the coast, but its tarnished silver fittings and teak compartments hint at its colonial past.

Below: F. W. De Klerk, South Africa's last apartheid leader, dons traditional Sotho dress on the 1994 election campaign. His attempts to woo black voters proved fruitless.

Charl van der Merwe, the former mayor of the small town of Koppies, in his grocery store. Over the transition he proved himself the 'F. W. De Klerk' of Koppies, a pragmatist wanting to move forward but unable to shed his past.

even cases of death squads taking a breather from the slaughter and leaving potential victims overnight in mounds of bodies, before resuming their work the following day.

Correspondents covering the genocide were appalled by the sluggish reaction in the West. For weeks Rwanda barely made newspaper front pages and elicited the most grudging responses from governments. Rwanda was the stereotypical faraway place about which people knew nothing. Editors were fixated by the dramatic events in South Africa where apartheid was finally laid to rest. As for the Western powers, unless pressed they were never going to put Rwanda on their agenda. It had no strategic nor economic interest, the factors that have encouraged intervention elsewhere. Moreover, Bosnia was causing enough heartache and the botched American operation in Somalia the previous year had inspired a terror in Washington about involvement in Africa. Before the genocide started, a UN force that had been despatched to monitor the peace settlement had warned its headquarters that extremists were stockpiling weapons. Major-General Romeo Dallaire, the Canadian commander of the force, sent a memo to New York detailing plans for a genocide, but, inexplicably, it went missing. In Washington in mid-May the State Department indulged in linguistic contortions to avoid using the word 'genocide', favouring instead the 'breakdown of a ceasefire', in a bid to play down pressure to intervene. The contrast was striking five years later when Nato accused Milošević of 'genocide' in Kosovo at every opportunity.

The overwhelming factor was the *ennui* that African carnage inspires in the outside world. Since the early Sixties when up to a million people were killed in Nigeria in the Biafran war, the continent has given the impression of being permanently convulsed by tribal conflict. Biafra was merely the beginning. From Chad to Uganda it often seemed that barely was the colonial flag furled before one tribe was at the throats of another.

Nowhere in Africa has tribal identity had such a disastrous legacy as Rwanda and Burundi in the last forty years. Both have – or in the case of Rwanda had – a 15 per cent minority of Tutsis, a Nilotic race who moved into central Africa and lived alongside the resident Bantu tribesmen several centuries ago. Contrary to received wisdom they were not always at each other's throats. Many intermarried. While there is some truth to the legend that in the pre-colonial era Tutsis were cattle-herding aristocrats and the Hutus were serfs, the division was entrenched only in the 1930s when Belgian colonists issued tribal identity cards and set up an apartheid system. Ever since the Belgians bequeathed power to the Hutus in Rwanda, the tiny state has been beset by anti-Tutsi pogroms. Across the border in Burundi the boot was on the other foot. There the Tutsis had kept power and they did all they could to avoid sharing it. When about 100,000 people were killed in Burundi in late 1993 the news was judged in most Western newspapers to merit only an occasional mention.

Such is the tension in Burundi that aid-workers in the capital, Bujumbura, developed a code and referred to Tutsis and Hutus as 'tacos' and 'hamburgers', or 'trees' and 'hedges'. I accompanied Sylvestre Ntibantunganya, who became president after the April 1994 plane crash, into the interior on a mission to urge his people to lay down their machetes and save themselves from the horrors of their Rwandan neighbours. He was a Hutu whose presence was tolerated by the dominant Tutsi power-brokers to reassure the Hutu majority. In a tiny village surrounded by lush plantations he delivered a thunderous speech.

'How long is blood going to have to flow in this country? What do you gain when you start killing and shedding blood? Can you drink it? Can you make bricks from it? Who has ever benefited from blood running in the streets? You must live together. It is time for the people to work for peace. I come with a present: justice, unity and peace.'

Backed up by a vigorous drum roll his appeal for reconciliation was worthy of Mandela. The colourful rhetoric clearly moved his retinue, but it meant little to the thousands of villagers squatting on the deep red earth in front of him. They did not want fine words, they wanted a guarantee of protection from the random vicious attacks of both the Hutu guerrillas and the Tutsi security forces. Two hours later we bounced back in our heavily guarded convoy of four-wheel-drive vehicles to the capital. Within a few days the village was once more the scene of vicious fighting.

Ntibantunganya was Burundi's third president in seven months. He escaped the violent end of his two predecessors but his tenure, too, was abruptly cut short. In 1996, after eighteen months in power, he took refuge in the American Embassy following a coup by hardline Tutsi army officers, much to the irritation of the Americans, who were believed to have tacitly encouraged the change. For more than a year he was stranded in the embassy and was spotted at receptions, a lonely haggard figure slipping sandwiches into his pockets before being shooed back out of sight by embarrassed American officials.

After the Rwandan genocide it is easy to understand the West's despair about Africa. It is impossible not to feel heavy-hearted when you visit Kigali. Months after the massacres the whiff of rotting flesh lingered in the streets. I found myself longing for a breeze not just to freshen the air but also to cleanse the moral taint. Nowhere was free from the past. Shortly after the genocide I stayed in a Jesuit centre. It was only in the candle-light on my first evening that I saw bloody handprints still marking the walls. Our guide advised us to stay away from Room 28. The next morning I heard how the seventeen priests and novices were first hacked with machetes and then dragged to Room 28 and shot. A mound of bloodstained blankets still lay in the corner. On a back wall was an icon with an inscription: 'God please don't let us waste the world's beauty and joy.'

The genocide fuelled the weary conviction in the West that the word tribalism in Africa equals 'barbaric' and 'bad'. It was not accidental that, when the Soviet Union and Yugoslavia splintered after the collapse of Communism, the hatreds were described as ethnic, not tribal. The distinction lies at the heart of a perceived divide between the civilized and primitive worlds.

African commentators rightly decry the hypocrisy. The litany

of atrocities in the Yugoslav and post-Soviet wars of the early
Nineties shows that Africans are far from having a monopoly on
tribalism. Arriving in Africa after reporting in Bosnia, I needed
no reminding of the similarities between Europe's and Africa's
rifts. Both are linked to the feverish attempt to fashion nation
states on the lines of Western Europe. Africa's added burden is
that the faultlines are more profound than in Eastern Europe;
borders are not only a recent creation, but also in most cases
lack the slightest historical or even geographical justification,
although this does not apply to Burundi and Rwanda as their
boundaries are based on the frontiers of centuries' old kingdoms.
With its straight lines and the occasional river frontier, the map
of Africa at the Berlin Congress of 1878 no doubt looked very
fine to the civil servants in Whitehall or the Quai d'Orsay. But
the colonial map-makers were influenced more by the politics
of Western Europe than by the reality on the ground. Most of
the colonies were a mish-mash of tribes which traditionally had
had little in common, like Nigeria with its divisions between the
Hausa and Fulani of the north, the heirs of old Muslim kingdoms, and the mainly Christian peoples, the Ibos in the east and
the Yoruba in the south, or the Sudan with a similar religious
divide, rifts which dictate politics to this day.

The colonial administrators provided a common enemy for
their varied subjects. But once the colonies had been swept into
independence the consensus in most cases ended. Consisting of
some of the world's most unwieldy and artificial nation states,
the new Africa was dangerously vulnerable to tribal infighting.
But the real villains of the piece are not the map-makers but
the politicians for whom stoking tribal resentments is often a
first resort.

The tribal carnage which blights Africa is not inevitable as
many in the West suppose. When war erupted in the former
Yugoslavia in 1991, Western politicians blamed 'ancient ethnic
hatreds' as if somehow amorphous primordial forces were
responsible for the bloodshed. The 'inevitability' argument provided a convenient pretext to rule out the need for serious
analysis and policy decisions. It also created a smokescreen for

the guilty politicians. If the Flemish started to massacre the Walloons no doubt there would be voices in London urging caution on the grounds that the two peoples had always been at each other's throats. In just the same way there is a perception in the developed world that tribal massacres are an ineluctable part of modern Africa, whereas in reality tribal identity only leads to bloodshed because of callous politics.

Just as the Serbs and Croats were primed by their leaders' propaganda into a crude form of ethno-nationalism, so when put to the test many African politicians rely on whipping up tribal passions to stay in power. The brutality of the Rwandan genocide reinforced Western stereotypes about the African savage. There was something about hoes and machetes that made the killing seem still more primal than the idea of neighbours shelling neighbours in Bosnia, and pandered to the old stereotype of Africans as tribal barbarians. But there was nothing random about the massacres. They had been carefully planned. Hutu peasants were whipped into a murderous frenzy by state radio, in an extreme version of the role played by the media in Croatia and Serbia in the countdown to conflict in 1991. It was the old 'them' or 'us' message: Hutus should kill Tutsis before the Tutsis turned on them.

In a poorly educated society such as Rwanda, where radio was for most people the sole source of news, the broadcasts were especially potent. In Rwanda's patriarchal society it was always unlikely that illiterate peasants would question their orders, particularly because land, or rather greed, provided a tempting personal incentive to take part.

Known as the country of a thousand hills, Rwanda is not for claustrophobes. It is Africa's most densely populated state – or at least it was said to be in 1994. Every ridge is neatly terraced. Every speck of land is tilled. Once you step off the roads you feel choked by humanity. Before the genocide, about eight million people were eking out a living in a territory smaller than Wales. If it were not for the tropical climate, which assures at least two harvests a year, the nation would starve.

The calls to kill Tutsis offered an answer to the age-old

problem – no more competition for land. And as the radio presenters helpfully pointed out, as long as they killed Tutsi babies and children there would be no chance of another generation returning to haunt them.

ɩɩɩɩ

So can Africa's tribes learn to live at peace? African politicians keen to develop an allegiance that stretched beyond the interests of their tribe could do worse than look to South Africa, one of a handful of states to move into independence without a tribal élite. It is blessed by three advantages. First, it has no obvious dominant tribe: eight million Zulu-speakers are balanced by almost as many Xhosas; Sothos come a close third. Second, its industrial economy has given rise to scores of vibrant urban black communities where tribe and tradition have waned, and where savvy, not bloodstock, is what counts. Third, the ANC had the benefit of long years in exile to muse on the reality of power and to watch its peers' mistakes.

The issue of tribe has not been eradicated, particularly in rural areas. With the exception of Chief Albert Luthuli, a Zulu, who won the Nobel Peace Prize in 1961, the ANC leadership has in the last fifty years been dominated by Xhosa-speakers from the Eastern Cape. Mandela and his contemporaries Oliver Tambo, Walter Sisulu and Govan Mbeki, the father of Mandela's successor, were all Xhosas. But this was as much a reflection of geography as ethnicity. The Eastern Cape had been at the forefront of black politics in South Africa since the early nineteenth century when the Xhosas defied the first white settlers in a succession of 'frontier' wars.

Party insiders whispered that the 'Xhosa connection' played a part in the eclipse of Cyril Ramaphosa, who before the April 1994 election was Thabo Mbeki's only contender as Mandela's successor. Ramaphosa is a Venda, one of South Africa's tiniest tribes. Traditionally in townships they are yokels to be teased and tricked. They are as far in geography and status as you can get from the Xhosas of the Eastern Cape – hardly good presidential stock. But among cosmopolitan types such stereotyping was more of a joke than reality, akin to the British making fun of the Irish. Such is the party's political correctness that it has moved to the opposite extreme and it is seen as anathema for members to raise the issue of tribe.

Unfortunately, however, the rest of the continent has a long way to go. The quest to accommodate the tribe within the nation state is fundamental if the continent is to emerge from its cycle of despair. Samora Machel, the late independence president of Mozambique, famously declared that, 'For the nation to live, the tribe must die.' But Africa has stubbornly resisted his vision. For most Africans the tie of the tribe comes far before the call of country. It is a prop at times of trouble and an identity, and in some countries its importance has increased as the nation state has failed. Indeed as central government continues to wither all over Africa the twenty-first century may well see the heretical view take hold that Africa's problem is the nation state and not the tribe.

The only seeds of hope in such bleak environments are to be drawn from the spirit of individual Africans, not the politicians but people like Georges Ngalinde, the Tutsi smallholder who watched as his children were killed at Ntarama. Just two days before my visit he was sitting outside his hut when he saw three of his children's murderers walk past. They had joined the Hutu exodus into Zaire when the RPF stepped up their assault. Now, more than two years later, they were back, following the RPF's decision to close down, by force, the UN's Hutu refugee camps – and he was planning to welcome them home.

'How could I mistake them?' said Ngalinde. 'Remember I saw them, machetes in hand, as they went to work [killing his family]. Truly at first I was afraid to see them come back, because it made me think of those days. I am frightened. What happens if they start killing again? But we cannot take up a machete. We cannot behave like those killers. If Hutus arrive and they submit to the process of law they can live in peace.'

His words were an inspiring testimony to Africans' resilience and dignity in the face of terrible suffering. I was reminded of Ngalinde several thousand miles to the north-west in Sierra

Leone during one of the lulls from its intermittent chaos. I had spent two days travelling with a local representative of the aid agency CARE, first down the coast in a fishing boat and then walking and hitching rides inland, to reach a community that had been cut off for several months by fighting. We were talking to some of the villagers about how they managed to survive when a man came into view carrying a blow-up Father Christmas. The Rev. Jacob Johnson had arrived with his supplies. He came every week, he said, on the road from Freetown which had been officially closed for three months. He was usually fired on by one side or another. But only once had he had to turn back. Would we like a lift home?

It is often said that countries get the rulers they deserve. If only that were the case in Africa.

♟♟♟♟

Moi stood ramrod-straight before 20,000 *wananchi* (people) as the military band in their bright red tunics and black pillar-box hats oompah-pahed back and forth. Paratroopers, forest guards, city council workers, even the national youth service filed past. Not a step was missed, not a toecap was unshined. By the standards of African parades the annual Kenyatta Day commemoration, marking the anniversary of the arrest of the then freedom fighter by the British, was an impressive performance. The crowd, which initially gave the distinct impression of having gone there against their wishes, warmed to Moi's remarks, particularly when he switched from English to Swahili and poked fun at the ranks of foreign diplomats on the podium behind him. There was a ripple of approval as he decried the 'tribalism' of his opponents.

And yet even as Moi spoke, the bully boys of his ruling KANU party were on the rampage intimidating opposition strongholds. In the countdown to the 1992 elections he played on the ethnic rivalry in the opposition and served warning that political pluralism would lead to tribal conflict. Then as soon as he had won, party bosses set about making his predictions come true, letting loose thugs from his Kalenjin tribe and from their

90

allies, the Masai, on Luos and Luyha and Kikuyu peasant farmers in the Rift Valley, accelerating an ethnic cleansing that began before the elections. More than 300,000 people were forced to leave their smallholdings and were driven into refugee camps. Such is the reality of Moi's non-tribalism.

Old-school white Kenyans argue that Moi is misunderstood. As legend has it, white Kenyans were 'officers' mess' as opposed to the 'NCOs' who flocked to Rhodesia after the Second World War. The older generations speak the language of the British establishment and their attitudes reinforce the British line, namely that, while a rogue, Moi was at least 'a steady hand'. He was the man to prevent the 'nightmare' scenario of Kenya's British passport-holding Asians fleeing in their thousands to Heathrow. Over toast and Earl Grey Tea early one morning in Karen, the old colonial suburb named after Karen Blixen, the author of *Out of Africa*, overlooking Nairobi, I heard how Moi is surrounded by a 'rotten lot', but is not all bad. My host was an enlightened man who had had extensive dealings with Moi, but he did not come from a rival tribe.

Richard Leakey, the celebrated conservationist, is one of a handful of whites to have 'broken the compact' and taken a role in opposition politics. He has known Moi well since the early Seventies and had regular contact with him between 1989 and 1994 when he was head of Kenya's Wildlife Service before he resigned in frustration at government attempts to undermine him. He readily admits that in his one-to-one encounters their relationship was quite cordial. He remembers countless meetings when he would walk out of Moi's office convinced that he had won his point, only to hear the next day that Moi had changed his mind. With hindsight he appreciates that Moi is a master at saying what people want to hear.

'When you sit down and talk to him he doesn't come across as venal, scheming or dangerous,' Leakey said in his office in a run-down side-street in Nairobi. 'He comes across as congenial, compassionate, a benevolent leader . . . You can tell him your frustrations and you leave feeling, "Boy, that man is really concerned." But it doesn't stick. He is the sort of man who will agree with you that red is his favourite colour. But then the next day when someone else says: "Don't you think red is ghastly?" He will say: "Absolutely, I couldn't agree more."'

Their relationship changed dramatically, however, the year after his resignation when Leakey formed Safina, the opposition party. Masai warriors paraded outside his home. His rallies were attacked. In the worst incident he was whipped and beaten by police and prison officials. The clubbing continued even as Leakey, who had lost both legs in a plane crash two years earlier, fled on his artificial limbs to his car. He was a racist. He was a colonialist. He was fair game. Leakey laughed hollowly as he recalled all the anti-colonial slurs he had endured. 'When I was thirteen Moi actually applauded the British suppression of the Mau Mau [the anti-white Kikuyu guerrilla movement] and the "cancer" of the freedom fighter. How he slipped past that I don't know and yet now he is branding me a colonialist . . .'

Significantly, Moi's attacks on Leakey caused more of a stir among conservative white Kenyans than among blacks: he stood accused of 'rocking the boat'. A delegation, including Leakey's brother, Philip, with whom he is not on speaking terms, made a highly publicized visit to Moi to take tea with the president to pledge their support. Against the lurid backdrop of East Africa's tribal divisions it is easy to understand their logic. It is true he is neither a Mobutu nor an Amin and he has kept Kenya together. Nairobi has an active parliament and vibrant opposition press. It is easy to see how Moi's apologists argue that things could be a lot worse. He should not be judged by Western standards, they cry. This is not Europe. This is Africa. You need to be ruthless to survive.

It is one of the tragedies of Africa, or rather it is a reflection of the tragedy of Africa, that a man like Moi can with some justification be seen as a compromise. Moi is not in the first rank of Big Men: he is too astute to have sown the seeds of his own downfall and he looks set to follow the path of Banda and Kaunda and accept retirement rather than wait to be forced from power. He duly won a convincing victory in his second multi-party election in December 1997, reflecting the durability of his ties of patronage and powers of intimidation as well as the success of his attempts to present himself as the father of the nation, and the chronic divisions of the opposition. Required by the constitution to stand down in 2002, he set about rehabilitating his image for posterity. Andrew Morton, the biographer of the Princess of Wales, wrote a biography, *Moi: The Making of an African Statesman*, which Moi's critics labelled a one-sided pro-Moi account. Parliament proposed a comfortable presidential retirement package of about $400,000 a year including, according to media reports, a staff of twenty-seven and three limousines. His old friend Biwott applauded the proposal, saying it was important that a president 'who has sacrificed so much for his country must be accorded good living in his retirement'. More pointedly, Anyang' Nyong'o, the opposition MP who introduced the measure, said it aimed to encourage presidents to retire rather than cling to power.

Moi closed my interview with what he no doubt thought was a Cassandra-esque prediction. 'I am not a dictator. Although people blame Moi now, one day they will understand what Moi was.'

The perennial difficulty of assessing Africa as an outsider is knowing whose standards to apply. For an increasing number of Kenyans, however, the question requires no reflection. Moi's opponents throw up their hands at the thought that the world should apply second-rate standards to their country. They could not care a jot that Leakey is white. All they want is to see an end to the corruption that has flourished under Moi and to have the chance to start again.

As I boarded my plane home, an Indian fridge salesman collapsed into the seat beside me. He had never encountered such a corrupt country in ten years travelling the world. As he recounted his tales of grasping government officials I heard the contemptuous laugh of Koigi, the dreadlocked dissident, ringing in my ears.

'Moi believes whites are fools because we [blacks] don't

blush. Whites do not understand when they are being lied to. And you must remember: you have to be a rabbit to know how cruel the jungle is.'

It is all too easy for whites travelling in Africa to take away an idealized view of the continent. But, as I was to find, there is no such danger if you take a train in Angola, the ultimate victim of the superpowers' meddling in Africa.

4

The Cold War Crooner

Jonas Savimbi – Western Disengagement or Disarray?

The conductor brushed down his faded grey uniform and straightened his peaked cap. His fingers faltered over his fading gold brocade. Then he glanced at his watch. It was time. As his whistle resounded over the platform, stragglers rushed to take their seats. School-children in black and white uniforms shouted and waved from the windows. With a final root toot toot from the engine driver, the pastel station buildings of Lobito, once one of the premier ports on Africa's Atlantic coastline, receded in the early morning haze. Against the odds, or at least against my expectations, the dawn train to Benguela was leaving bang on time.

A faded photograph of Portuguese colonial architecture was inlaid in the compartment wall opposite me, a reminder of the days when Europeans took a liner to Lobito and then headed inland by train, bolstered by silver service in the restaurant cars and hot showers in the berths. The photograph was unharmed in the twenty years since the Portuguese had abruptly abandoned Angola and returned whence they had come, by sea, five centuries earlier.

The carriage's teak fittings and brass and silver work, while in need of a polish, were also in fine nick. But then again I should not have been surprised. For railway buffs and indeed Africa-watchers Benguela has been a name to conjure with for almost a century. In the best traditions of the railway's indomitable founding engineers, it was clearly going to take more than a war to make the last of its employees lower their standards.

In 1902 Robert Williams, a canny Scots business associate of Cecil Rhodes, won a concession from the Portuguese to build a railway through their territory to link the minerals of northern Rhodesia and King Leopold's Congo to the coast. Within thirty years his task was complete. It was a triumph of engineering, opening up southern and central Africa. Starting at Benguela it snaked more than 1,000 miles up and across the central 6,000-ft plateau through the forests of the hinterland which powered the locomotives' wood-fired boilers into the heart of the continent, where they linked with a railway from Beira, on the Indian Ocean. For the Portuguese it was also extremely lucrative. By the early Seventies, rail traffic was generating an estimated $43 million a year.

The railway timetable still dutifully records the destinations of those glory years. Several of my fellow passengers were from Huambo, the first significant town to the east, and they gazed out the window imagining they were bound for home. Johnny Alcides, a twenty-year-old student, had not seen his four brothers and two sisters in Huambo since he fled into the bush eighteen months earlier when his father was killed in the latest eruption of Angola's thirty-year-old war. He had walked to Lobito in March 1993. He longed, he said, to be able to queue up at Lobito ticket office and order a single to Huambo. But to return home by train, such a potent symbol of normality, was, he knew, only a dream.

The Benguela Railway has been blocked for all but a few stretches since the Portuguese pulled down the flag and left in 1975. The three liberation movements had forged a power-sharing agreement for the post-colonial era in an attempt to overcome the differences which had riven their fight against white rule. But the settlement collapsed even before the Portuguese left, reigniting what would become Africa's longest-running civil war.

In the words of Ryszard Kapuściński, the Polish writer who reported the chaotic countdown to independence, the fighting was 'sloppy, dogged and cruel. Everyone was everyone's enemy, and no one was sure who would meet death.'[1] His words apply to each and every African bush war. In Angola, in the absence of front lines, the Benguela Railway was an obvious and easy target.

My train-ride, in July 1995, coincided with a lull in the fighting as the United Nations tried to implement a peace agreement between the two protagonists, the ruling MPLA (Popular Movement for the Liberation of Angola) and the rebel movement, UNITA (National Union for the Total Independence of Angola). The third liberation movement, the FNLA (National Front for the Liberation of Angola), had long since disintegrated. The railway, however, was still firmly closed after a series of fruitless attempts to reopen it, most notably by Tiny Rowland, the late chief executive of Lonrho.

With Lonrho's vast mining and agriculture interests in the region Rowland was interested in an offer by the MPLA to relaunch the railway in the mid-Eighties. He was the arch Africa-hand among Western businessmen. When he died in 1998 tributes flowed in from all corners of the continent, including from politicians whose careers had supposedly been founded on opposing the very capitalist principles Rowland so ruthlessly espoused. But not even his web of contacts, which extended to every regional seat of power, rebel and official, could make UNITA's primary African backer, South Africa, agree to leave the railway alone. For Pretoria it was too important a target. If the Benguela Railway reopened, the 'front-line' states of Zambia and Zimbabwe would be able, if they so wanted, to impose their much-vaunted but hitherto anodyne economic blockade. The closure of the railway meant that the black governments of southern Africa had to swallow their pride and rely on apartheid ports, a useful source of income for Pretoria and an even more vital piece of political leverage on their enemies.

Thirty-one miles from Lobito the train chugged into Benguela. My trip was at an end. The journey had provided a poignant taste of Angola's might-have-been. On paper Angola is doubly blessed, with the mineral riches of its northern neighbour, the Democratic Republic of Congo, or Zaire as it still was at the time of my ride, and the agricultural potential of its eastern neighbour, Zambia. The railway could have been the communications hub of the sub-continent. Instead it is little more than a museum piece.

In an irony that I only learned later, the man most responsible for the destruction of Williams' and Rhodes' dream was raised on stories of the Benguela Railway. On 3 August 1934 one of Angola's first black railway officials, a Protestant pastor who had been forced by debt to seek work where he could, had a son. The baby's name was Jonas Malheiro Savimbi.

ᛉᛉᛉ

Even allowing for the distortions of African leaders' biographies it seems fair to say that the history of Angola runs in Savimbi's veins. His grandfather, Sakaita, was a chief of the Ovimbundu, the country's largest ethnic group, which makes up more than a third of the population. Outraged by a second wave of colonization by Afrikaner and Portuguese farmers, and devastated by falling rubber prices, Sakaita led an ill-fated rebellion against the Portuguese in 1902 in the central town of Bailundo, which ninety years later was to be Savimbi's base. The uprising was brutally suppressed after four months, and Sakaita lost his chieftainship as punishment, but he never lost hope that another Savimbi would take up the revolutionary baton.

By deciding to work with rather than against the system, Sakaita's son Loth, Savimbi's father, had a very different but in its own way equally frustrating experience of colonial rule. He defied Sakaita's prohibition on having contact with whites and went to the local missionary school. Stricken by debt over an unpaid bill for a traditional healer, he looked to the Benguela Railway for employment and rose in due course to become Angola's first black station-master.

His post was a dazzling achievement for Africans of the time, especially in one of the Portuguese colonies where the slave trade had died out only in the late nineteenth century and where blacks were still assumed to have a duty to do menial work. In Portuguese eyes Loth had attained the greatest of good fortunes for an African, having qualified as an *assimilado*. Like the *évolués* of the Belgian colonies, the *assimilados* had a special status which, on paper at least, accorded them the rights of the Portuguese. But in practice these privileges were all but impossible to attain, as to qualify you had to be able to speak and write fluent Portuguese, and the authorities provided no primary schools for Africans. By 1960 it is reckoned that fewer than one in a hundred Angolans were *assimilados*. The 'promotion' also came at a humiliating price, as their compromise laid them open to charges of being 'Uncle Toms'.

These twin strands of family experience fuelled Savimbi in his early crusade to defy the Portuguese. Sakaita is said to have taught him the old tribal languages which would prove vital in his bid for rural support, and also the importance of stockpiling ammunition, another useful lesson for the years ahead. Embittered by his very different experiences, Loth reared the young Savimbi to believe he had to play a role in changing Angola, and in pursuit of this goal he ensured his son was educated by Protestant missionaries.

It was these same missionaries who are said to have organized a legendary football match between their black pupils and white children from the local town, Andulo, which, if true, provides a telling insight into Savimbi's mindset. The story, which was first told by Savimbi to his biographer, Fred Bridgland, does have the ring of truth. The arrangement was that Savimbi provided the ball and the whites provided the referee. All went according to plan until the game started and the Portuguese referee disallowed every goal the black pupils scored. So enraged was the young Savimbi that he walked off the pitch with his ball in his hands. 'My own team shouted that I could not do it because the administrator's son was playing,' he told Bridgland. 'I carried on walking and the game had to be abandoned.'[2]

The stubborn streak is one of the few consistent strands in Savimbi's subsequent career. Having transferred to a better school, run by another set of missionaries, he promptly incurred their wrath by defying their ban on ballroom dancing, which was all the rage among educated Africans of the time – and indeed still is in South African townships at the end of the twentieth century. Loth is said to have suggested that he should tango in secret with his sisters. But the fiery young Savimbi refused to back down, arguing that it was practically the only pastime available to him, as the Portuguese had banned would-be *assimilados* from traditional African dancing. Savimbi was suspended for a year. Defying his father once again, he walked for several days to the bustling town of Silva Porto, where, through brilliance and determination, he won a coveted scholarship and a ticket to Lisbon.

He soon, however, transferred his passion to a national stage as politics began to predominate over the desire for a profession. While in Europe in his early twenties he met many of the icons of black nationalism, including Kenyatta and Nkrumah, who kindled his revolutionary spirit. He briefly worked with the exiled leaders of Angola's liberation movements. But he later said they had despised his village upbringing. He also claimed they did not represent the aspirations of the Ovimbundu. With the backing of the Chinese, his first political friends, who trained him in guerrilla warfare, he slipped into Angola in 1966 with ten other Angolans and later the same year officially founded UNITA. He has been in the bush since then with barely a break.

↟↟↟↟

Savimbi's career over the next twenty years was a host of contradictions – at least it was in Western eyes. An admirer of Mao's 'long march', he promoted peasant socialism over the Soviet-style Marxist-Leninism of the MPLA. But in the Eighties he became the darling of Western conservatives because of his stand against Communism. UNITA trumpeted that it was the party of '*négritude*', a potent cause among the Ovimbundu, who felt they had been marginalized by the *mesticos*, people of mixed race, in the coastal cities. And yet for many years Savimbi's principal supporter was South Africa's apartheid government;

he even appeared at the inauguration of South Africa's authoritarian president P.W. Botha in 1984.

His foreign backers hailed him as a hero of capitalism and the free market. But these labels reflected more the wishful thinking of the West – and a brilliant public relations campaign by his aides in Washington – than reality. He was dubbed pro-Western because he was against the Marxist MPLA, but his real skill was that he knew how to impress the West. On infrequent tours of Europe he held court in smart London hotels. Little did his admirers know it but, if called upon, he could have quoted at length from Marx, a legacy from the dabblings of his youth. Instead, however, he would pander to his audience and quote Machiavelli, Churchill and Clausewitz. His command of French, English, German and Portuguese inevitably entrenched his standing as an 'intellectual' who understood the sophisticated subtleties of the West. But back home in true Maoist style he condemned intellectuals and praised peasant thought.

President Reagan was intrigued by him. The two had a fireside chat at the White House, an honour usually reserved for heads of state. But his vision and his personality were far more complex than American officials – in public at least – understood. He is at heart a tribal leader and his style and instincts reflect some of the complexities of Africa which so baffle the West. He despises Christianity, banning Bibles in areas under his control, in spite of – or maybe because of – his missionary upbringing. He led UNITA like a tribal chief in a pre-literate society bolstering his appeal with recourse to poetry, tradition and myth. His praise-singers spread fantastic tales of his voracious sexual appetite and his heroic powers of endurance in the bush, attributes which won him a fanatical following and entrenched his absolute authority.

Because of his free-market rhetoric, Savimbi was assumed also to espouse Western liberal democratic values – or at least it was hoped that he did. But it was a mistake to assume that just because Savimbi spoke the West's language he had forgiven the role of the white man in Africa. He has a strong Africanist streak. His grandfather had, after all, been defeated by the Portuguese, and his father had had the humiliation of being dubbed 'almost white'. Like Mobutu, Banda, Moi and many other Big Men, Savimbi used the West for what he could get from them, but he was never a liberal *manqué* as some of his Western supporters naively hoped.

By the late Eighties Savimbi's rationale was clear. All his ideals, if indeed he had ever had any, had become subordinate to a hunger for power. He talked of the need for accountable government and berated the MPLA's totalitarian record. He was an inspirational guerrilla leader. In the Seventies he emulated his hero Mao and disappeared on a 'long march' through the hinterland, leading the world to believe he was dead. But he led UNITA with a ruthless intolerance of dissent. Critics were tortured and killed in his presence. Joseph Conrad would have recognized and understood the apparent contradiction between the smooth-talking sophisticated Savimbi of the White House encounter and the cruel chieftain of the bush.

In the Seventies and early Eighties, claims that UNITA operated in a climate of fear were widely played down as the propaganda of the MPLA, which itself had an appalling record. But in 1989 the stories became irrefutable when dissenters disclosed how over the years Savimbi had systematically purged high-ranking UNITA supporters and their families. Women and children were thrown on bonfires on trumped-up charges, including witchcraft. Among them were wives of dissenters who had already been executed and women who had refused his advances. Amnesty International reported that crowds were made to watch as whole families were burned alive in Jamba, his headquarters in the far south, a scattering of bases in a wilderness of forest, savannah and bush.

The disclosures came ironically just as Savimbi's chances of inheriting power in Luanda, the capital, seemed stronger than ever. *Perestroika* had enabled the impoverished and crumbling Soviet Union to retract its tentacles from far-flung corners of the globe. After months of tortuous negotiations a peace accord was signed in Lisbon in May 1991, paving the way for Angola's first multi-party elections scheduled for September the following year. Savimbi was expected to do well even in the MPLA's urban heartlands as the party's record of inefficiency and corruption had disillusioned many of its traditional supporters. President José Eduardo Dos Santos, the party leader, was a colourless *apparatchik* with a fraction of Savimbi's charisma. In a clear sign that government officials were not confident of victory, the embezzlement of oil revenues from the rich off-shore fields reached new heights between the peace accord and the election. If Savimbi had presented himself as the man to unify the nation, he might have coasted home to a comfortable victory. Consensus and unity have a powerful resonance across Africa. But so, too, at least in the eyes of politicians, do authority and power. Far from promoting himself as the man to heal Angola's wounds, Savimbi talked of how he would crush the élite 'Ninja' security forces of the MPLA, not the most astute campaign in a country that was full of people like Johnny Alcides, my railway carriage companion, aching for peace. The chilling account of the fall from grace and murder of one of his most brilliant aides, Tito Chingunji, further damaged Savimbi's image in the countdown to polling day and destroyed his credentials in the West once and for all.

Whether it was because wavering MPLA supporters at the last minute turned back to the 'devil they knew' or that Savimbi's support had been over-estimated, provisional results for the election indicated that Dos Santos had about 50 per cent while Savimbi was trailing with 39 per cent. Tragically for Angola this was the cue for the spirit of the teenage Savimbi on the football pitch to reassert itself. Claiming the results were rigged, he returned to the bush and led his long-suffering countrymen into some of the bloodiest fighting in their long war.

Before the peace process, Angola's war was fought mostly in the bush. Savimbi's success as a guerrilla leader had hinged on avoiding pitched battles and leaving the towns in government hands. But his strategy changed in 1992. This time he aimed to take over the cities, starting with those in the Central Highlands, his Ovimbundu heartland. By November 1994, when a new peace settlement was signed, a series of towns whose names meant nothing in the West were in ruins and up to 100,000 people had been killed – all in the name of one man's pride.

Among the most hotly contested targets was Huambo, the second city, which Savimbi had coveted during his long years in the bush in the Seventies and Eighties. When I visited it, months after the ceasefire and a few days after Johnny Alcides had confided his dream of returning, the bougainvillaea were in flower. If I blurred my vision on their vivid pinks and crimsons I could have been in New Lisbon, as Huambo was known under the Portuguese, when it held Formula One races through its streets. But there was little left of the old town. The streets of stuccoed colonial villas had been flayed by small-arms fire, mortars and artillery shells, first by one side, then by the other. Every now and then the sharp crack of a landmine could be heard testifying to the destructive seeds both sides had laid.

The villain of the piece was Savimbi. Bitterness and pride consume O *Mais Velho* (the eldest one), as he is known to his supporters. As so many times before, once the war restarted after the election he dropped out of sight, fuelling rumours that he was wounded or dead. As a UN mission tried to breathe life into a new peace process in 1995, Savimbi became as elusive as Angola's long dreamed-of peace.

♦♦♦♦

Tucked away in the Angolan bush, Bailundo airstrip is a sight familiar to a dozen African countries: a bumpy clearing with a thatched hut as control tower, a khaki tent as passenger lounge, and the debris of war for decoration. I was squatting by the side of the airstrip, watching a United Nations airliner circle over-head, when there was a low rumble behind me. Twenty yards away the bush parted to reveal a black Mercedes. It was in perfect condition. The sun glinted off its silverwork. Its wheels were unflecked by the airstrip's ever swirling clouds of dust. It purred past me at a walking pace and drew to a halt on the edge of the 'runway'.

With immaculate timing, even as the aircraft drew to a halt to reveal its distinguished passenger, the then UN Secretary General Boutros Boutros-Ghali, the side-door of the Mercedes opened and out stepped a figure whose appearance seemed more appropriate for a concert hall than an African battlefield. A crisply ironed black shirt in the Mao collarless style was just visible under an immaculate cream jacket. Clutching his familiar silver-topped walking stick, Savimbi strode forward to greet his visitor like a lion emerging from the bush to consume his prey.

In the Eighties, at the height of his international prestige, the UNITA leader was known as Africa's 'Gucci guerrilla', both for his snazziness and for his ability to tailor his style to suit his audience. In the bush he favoured hip-hugging fatigues with a pearl-handled revolver at his belt. When touring the West he opted for well-cut suits. But his sartorial instincts deserted him after the collapse of the peace process in 1992. With his white jacket, which he wore throughout the tortuous negotiations of the Nineties, he clearly intended to cut a dash as a serious world leader, but the outfit was instead likened to the garb of an ageing crooner. The analogy became increasingly appropriate as time passed: like a has-been artiste, Savimbi only had one tune.

The two leaders embraced in a mêlée of suited UN aides and khaki-clad UNITA guards. The encounter had been billed by optimistic UN officials as one of the most significant for southern Africa in several years. Since the election, Savimbi's public appearances in his own country could have been counted on the fingers of one hand. The UN saw the Secretary General's visit as a chance to secure a much-needed success following the disastrous operation in Somalia of 1992–3 and amid the continuing chaos of their mission in Bosnia, which was then in the throes of one of its many crises.

The two delegations bumped a few miles through the bush to a stifling and gloomy old colonial villa with crumbling pink plaster walls. Many years before Bailundo had been a bustling community. Like the other towns on Angola's Central Highlands plateau it was favoured by the Portuguese in the colonial era because of its dry climate, which offered relief from the relentless humidity of the coastal strip. It was here that Savimbi's grandfather had taken part in the abortive revolt against colonial rule. Now it had become a UNITA garrison town and the accompanying journalists were policed with a manic intensity.

Every step we took was monitored. Every building we visited had been carefully pre-selected and approved. No soldier was prepared to go beyond formulaic answers. Someone had prepared a meal of charred chicken wings and warm beer which were served in a shell-scarred building on the edge of the town. We were herded there by UNITA aides, who hovered at our elbows monitoring our conversation as we nibbled the fare. All the while we willed a quick conclusion to the summit. No one was expecting anything significant to emerge.

Perched on a sofa under a large UNITA banner, Boutros-Ghali talked of his delight at seeing his 'very old friend', a reference to the early Sixties when Savimbi was in self-imposed exile and they had met in Cairo. The UN head spoke fulsomely of Angola's will for reconciliation and the 'irrevocable' peace process. But he must have known the encounter was little more than an exotic photo-opportunity.

Elegant and aloof, in marked contrast to the apologetic figure cut by the UN Secretary General, Savimbi said barely a word. His body language would have made him an ideal James Bond villain. Like all Big Men he clearly demanded the adulation of his aides. Boutros-Ghali was on paper one of the world's most influential men and yet he seemed like an apprentice before a grand-master.

By the late Nineties Savimbi was possibly the most dangerous politician on the continent. He had one of Africa's most experienced and well-equipped armies, access to an endless supply of minerals, and like Frankenstein's monster he had long since outgrown his handlers.

♦♦♦♦

It is received wisdom that the Cold War arms race, while a drain on finances, at least served as a deterrent which staved off a Third World War. Seen from Washington or Moscow it is a glib argument, but the view from Luanda, Bailundo or indeed any other part of Angola is not so simple. At its height, Africa was a patchwork quilt of spheres of influence. Just as the pre-independence map was coloured according to colonial power, so the post-independence map was shaded according to political orientation. African leaders were either on one side or the other. Their officers were trained either in Moscow and Berlin or Sandhurst and West Point.

Many of the bloodiest battles of the Cold War were fought thousands of miles from the superpowers in African countries which most Soviet and American citizens would not, if asked, have been able to place on a map. No one knows how many people died in Angola as sacrificial victims on the altar of superpower politics – nor how many were mutilated by the landmines which both sides sprinkled over the interior. But the answer to the first question lies somewhere in the hundreds of thousands, and the answer to the second is yet to be calculated – Angola is thought to have more landmines than its 11 million people.

Mother Superior Sao Paolo, the head of a Portuguese order of nuns, watched the appalling saga unfold. She arrived from Lisbon in 1962 shortly before the start of the anti-colonial war as a young idealist committed to living God's word. Since then her faith has had to struggle to survive as she watched Angola sink back into the pre-industrial age. Her order expanded and shrank as the fighting ebbed and flowed. For several years she was forced to live in the bush. Each time she reopened her community, a different band of soldiers would commandeer her set-up and force her to close down. Now she is a wrinkled chestnut of a figure.

'We're starting from nothing,' she told me. 'It's like when the Portuguese came here all those years ago. We are starting afresh.'

Her wistful invocation of the arrival of the first Portuguese in the late fifteenth century would until recently have outraged most Angolans. The Portuguese were by common consent the most tenacious colonists. They saw their three African colonies, Angola, Mozambique and Guinea-Bissau, as reminders of their glorious sea-faring days and, disdaining what they saw as the defeatism of the British, Belgians and French, had no intention of sailing home without a fight. Even as black nationalism was sweeping through the continent in the Fifties and Sixties, they invested in a massive construction and public works programme, although the Angolans, of course, saw little of the wealth. The departure of the Portuguese in 1975, following a coup by left-wing army officers in Lisbon the previous year, was as selfish and spiteful as anywhere else in the continent. More than a quarter of a million colonials fled Angola in the eighteen months between the coup and independence. Most stripped their homes and offices down to the electric fittings. The Polish correspondent Kapuściński described how Portuguese traders packed all their stocks into wooden crates and waited at Luanda docks for ships to take them anywhere. 'I don't know if there had ever been an instance of a whole city sailing across the ocean,' he wrote in his memoirs. 'But that is exactly what happened.'[3] There were even reports of people filling wells with cement and parking their cars and throwing away the keys.

After a few days in Luanda, however, it is easy to understand the sad logic of the Mother Superior's sentiments. At independence it was one of Africa's most charming and lively capitals. But by the time of Boutros-Ghali's visit it had been reduced to a foul-smelling shambles. On the outskirts the Roque Santeiro market, a teeming mass of hundreds of stalls stretching over several miles, had become the commercial hub of the nation. Traders came from all over Africa to take advantage of the captive audience. A Malian sold me a CD of one of Angola's favourite musicians. He had just closed the bargain with the tale of how each month he made his way from Timbuctoo across some of the most anarchic countries in Africa when, with a weary inevitability, a squad of jumpy and ill-kempt policemen waylaid my car and held me and my companions from the BBC hostage until the right 'fee' was agreed.

One of the enduring mysteries and marvels of Africa is the ability of its peoples to pick themselves up from the most appalling disasters. It is a tribute to the extraordinary spirit of the Angolans that the capital maintained a spark even in the gloomiest days of the war. It boasted some of the finest seafood and liveliest nightlife in the continent. But the glitter of the beach-front bars was merely a façade: they were of course available only to the élite of businessmen, diamond dealers and mercenaries who thrived in such conditions. Luanda is a monument to the disasters of the post-colonial years. It is also a mausoleum for the Cold War.

America and the Soviet Union were equally culpable – although intriguingly both were relatively slow starters in what was to become the second 'scramble' for Africa. Having not shared in the colonial dismemberment, Moscow lacked the commercial, missionary and expatriate sources which kept the European powers abreast of the latest African developments. With its vast natural resources, the Soviet Union also did not need to compete in the scrimmage for Africa's mineral wealth, the continent's primary magnet. Thus, as the era of independence dawned, Moscow had a relatively sketchy knowledge of the continent. But amid the fiery denunciations of colonial rule by black nationalists the Kremlin swiftly grew to appreciate that Africa could be a useful piece on the global chessboard. The Marxist governments in Angola, Mozambique and Ethiopia received massive shipments of arms and equipment. In the Seventies the MPLA had an estimated 1,500 Soviet military advisors as well as 30,000 Cuban troops who were funded by Moscow. In the Eighties American diplomats estimated that Angola received $800 million of Soviet military aid a year.

America was caught off-guard by Moscow's involvement. In the Sixties and early Seventies Washington was not over-exercised by events in Africa. The success of the CIA's contact, Mobutu, in Zaire and the overthrow of the leftist icon Nkrumah in Ghana in 1966, just nine years after he took power, were deemed to have crushed Soviet hopes in Africa. But the 1974 coup in Portugal changed everything, raising in the West and South Africa the spectre of a large swath of Africa falling under Soviet control.

The CIA launched an emergency operation to check the MPLA, first by backing the FNLA, Angola's third and northern-based liberation movement, and then by helping South Africa's white minority government to assist UNITA. Initially the support was covert. America had only just disengaged from Vietnam. Washington knew that public opinion would never accept a fully fledged foreign adventure. But the support became official in 1985 when Congress lifted a law that prohibited aid going to the rebels. It was estimated to have peaked at about $60 million a year in the mid-Eighties under President Reagan. The British secret service, MI6, and the French and German intelligence agencies also poured in support. Intelligence officers used to boast that Savimbi had enough weapons to fight a Third World War – not bad for a man who first invaded Angola in 1966 with a single pistol given to him by a sympathetic friend, Sam Nujoma, who was to become the first president of Namibia.

†††††

Over the years the communications industry in Africa has shown a remarkable versatility in overcoming chaos. In the late Nineties there was a cellular telephone revolution as businessmen realized that cordless phones were the answer for a continent where thousands of miles of cable had been destroyed in war and dug up and used for fencing and homes. Then there is always the 'bush telegraph'. If we are to believe folk legend, news travels more quickly in Africa along informal channels than anywhere else. It is a delightful, if slightly patronizing, notion that by reverting to an older system, Africa has managed somehow to surmount the collapse of its infrastructure. But it is, of course, not always the case. I had barely brushed off the dust of the Benguela Railway following my dawn ride from Lobito before I became aware that more than five years after the fall of the Berlin Wall there were parts of Angola which had yet to appreciate the Cold War is over – although, to be fair, in Benguela the problem was more a case of short-sightedness than of missing the news.

A mile from Benguela's handsome pastel-coloured railway station was the squat, heavily guarded mansion of the provincial governor, Paolo Jorge. He was a veteran MPLA leader who had been one of Angola's first foreign ministers and who was renowned in Washington for stymying talks with the Americans with his incomprehensible dialectic. In an impromptu interview it soon became clear that little had changed. The ageing *apparatchik* was still convinced the Marxist dream was nigh.

Loyal party man, he was cautious and stilted. The only time he broke off from his dogma was as I rose to leave, when he delivered an encomium to a prominent British journalist whose enthusiasm kept him going, he said with a flourish, even in moments of doubt. Indeed they had spoken on the telephone just the other morning and he had been assured he was still on the right track in pursuing a Marxist-Leninist course.

I walked away down the long central corridor past rows of empty offices with their mounds of meaningless bureaucracy, shaking my head at the absurdity of a Briton in the comfort of London still having the nerve to preach to Africa. Over the years, ideologues from both Left and Right have done much harm to Africa in trying to promote their views, and still, it seems, they have not learned to leave the continent alone.

Jorge was far more expansive that night after a few glasses of wine. He was, of all incongruous settings for a diehard Communist, dining on board a Royal Navy warship which was docked at Lobito to support a British UN contingent. His hosts were one of Britain's highest-ranking generals and a senior diplomat from Whitehall. 'You mark my words,' Jorge confided to a BBC colleague over coffee. 'One day you will remember what an old African had to tell you. Communism is on its way back.'

In Jorge's defence, the end of the Berlin Wall came to many politicians in Africa as a terrible shock. Moi and Banda both spoke to me of their 'disappointment' with the West. Mobutu vowed there would be no change in Zaire and fiddled for eight more years until he paid the price for his long years of misrule. He fled his capital baffled that the West, which had bailed him out so often, had deserted him. Africa's Left was equally strained. The *Ghanaian Times*, the then mouthpiece of President Jerry Rawlings, condemned the upheaval in Eastern Europe as the 'work of imperialism'.[4] But mercifully for Africa, by the early Nineties most African governments accepted that Soviet-style planned economies had failed. It pained them to admit it, but Savimbi had been right when he told the revolutionary Che Guevara in the Sixties that Soviet-style Marxism would not work in Africa.[5] It failed miserably, leading merely to bloated and corrupt bureaucracies, the destruction of indigenous agriculture and the impoverishment of peasants.

Four years after my encounter with Jorge I met his successor in the pink-plastered governor's mansion. He too was an old-school *apparatchik*, but he could see the way the world had changed and gave me a lecture about the wonders of the free market. For most Angolans, however, ideology was less important than peace which in 1989 at last seemed near.

By 1989 the Angolan war had reached a hideous stalemate with neither side able to deliver a knock-out blow. Even with the help of South Africa's armed forces, the most powerful in sub-Saharan Africa, UNITA could not defeat the MPLA. South Africa and Cuba withdrew their troops in accordance with the terms of a peace agreement in 1988. Although the fighting continued into 1991, this was widely seen as the final skirmishing as UNITA and the MPLA sought to gain the best bargaining position before negotiating peace. With talks under way for the end of white rule, South Africa's old guard had more pressing matters to confront. Washington and Moscow continued to provide funds and munitions until 1991 but agreed to stop as part of the peace settlement that was to end in the election. The irony was that the intensive Western involvement of the Cold War era was succeeded by a withdrawal that threatened to be almost as damaging. Africa badly needs all the help it can get.

The departure of the Russians was no great loss. The Soviet President Gorbachev was desperate to cut his puppets' strings – he could barely afford to pay his own army, let alone fund adventures in southern Africa. The only Russians in the continent these days are blue-eyed blond Slav 'men of action' piloting the 'seat-of-your-pants' flights that go where commercial airlines have long since feared to fly. They are key players in the network of organized crime, private armies and shady businesses that criss-crosses the continent and deprives Africans of the mineral revenues which could fund much-needed development. But at least they are no longer directing bombing raids on densely packed villages as was frequently the case in the Cold War in Angola and Mozambique.

America's withdrawal, while less thorough, was even more momentous. As the sole superpower, it has maintained a profile and interest in Africa: Washington sees East Africa as an important base to keep track of the world's radical Islamic movements traditionally backed by Sudan; the upheavals in the Great Lakes region which led to the overthrow of Mobutu were treated by the CIA with the same short-sighted intensity that marked their record there in the early Sixties. But nonetheless, when President Clinton visited Africa in March 1998, he was able to claim with some justification that it marked the start of a new partnership between America and Africa.

The Clintons' ten-day tour, which was billed by his aides as an end to 'paternalism, dependency and indifference', drew a line under the more brazenly interventionist policies of the past. Halfway through the visit, Mr Clinton came the closest that Washington has ever done to apologizing for its Cold War role when he conceded that America had not always 'done the right thing by the continent'. He also promised a new relationship via America's new 'Africa Growth and Opportunity Act' which he vowed would help revitalize the continent's economy.

'It used to be that when US policy makers thought of Africa

– if they thought of Africa – they said: "What can we do for Africa or about Africa?"' he told South Africa's parliament. 'They were the wrong questions. The right question today is what can we do *with* Africa? Yes, Africa still needs the world, but more than ever the world needs Africa.'

But Africans were probably right to be sceptical. Many politicians were concerned that the Americans' talk of trade and not aid was tantamount to neo-colonialism. Thabo Mbeki, then South Africa's deputy president, pointed out that most of the continent still badly needed development, and could not hope to compete with American markets. As the American entourage swept through Africa, I asked a Ghanaian guide at St George's Fort, one of the old Atlantic slave centres on the Ghanaian coast, for his thoughts on the American promises. 'Apologies are free,' he said, gesturing to the mouldy dungeons behind him where hundreds of thousands of slaves were kept before being shipped to America. 'What about some money?'

Not only is the flow of money drying up, so is the attention. Events on the ground in central Africa suggested that Washington was often struggling to keep pace with events. The disappointment of Kabila's government in Congo fuelled a disillusionment in Washington about Africa and a belief that there was little point in getting involved. Nowhere was this *ennui* more apparent than in Angola, where the UN ran a series of operations whose shortcomings and lack of funding and support reflected how the West was losing patience with Africa.

⋀⋀⋀⋀

With its shiny white paint glistening in the sun the washing machine shimmered in solitary splendour. It had arrived a week or so after Major Kundalkar had taken up his post at Quibala, a collection of huts deep in the Angolan bush. Amid the dust and flies it was understandably his pride and joy.

The major had been posted there in early 1995 on reconnaissance for the UN's third Angolan mission in the previous decade. Even as he started work, the UN's bureaucracy was whirring remorselessly in his wake. According to the rule book, new UN posts were to be equipped with a washing machine. Quibala, some bureaucrat looking at a map in New York had decreed, was to be no exception, even though, as every Angolan knew, it was in the middle of the war zone and had had neither electricity nor running water in years. Loyal soldier that he was, Kundalkar would not consider ridiculing his superiors. Instead he proudly related the tale of his washing machine's delivery.

'It came by air, of course, as the roads from Luanda are impassable. One day we were told on the radio to expect a shipment and suddenly there it was sitting on the airstrip. It was a terrible to-do getting it from there to here. We could hardly fit it in a vehicle. Now we use it as a table when we are entertaining visitors.'

As we bumped down the track away from Quibala I caught a final glimpse of the washing machine. It was, I reflected, a striking symbol of the UN's mission. There was a remote chance that one day it could work, but like the UN it would need considerable ingenuity, effort and good fortune.

A vast administrative machine like the UN lends itself to satire. As the UN's peace-keeping mission ground into action in 1995 there was no shortage of 'washing machine' material. The supply depot housed 250 ten-tonne containers shipped from the UN mission which had just ended in Mozambique. The British UN officers in charge of the warehouse were more forthright than my Indian host at Quibala; their guided tour was deliberately brimming with farce.

First, we inspected the rows of shiny Chinese 'Pheasant' bicycles which had been sent from the UN mission to Cambodia. Quite who would dare to ride a bicycle in the most densely mined country in the world my guides failed to understand. Po-faced they passed on to boxes full of 'Bright and Breezy' washing powder, presumably soon to be shipped at considerable peril (not to mention expense) to my Indian major friend. Like conjurors they saved the best for the end – a ten-tonne container of rubbish which had come via Mozambique from Phnom Penh.

The UN embarked on the Angolan mission inspired by the successful conclusion of their operation in Mozambique, which, as a former Portuguese colony embroiled in a long and Cold War-fuelled civil war, had long been seen as the mirror image of Angola. Mozambique's two-year peace process, culminating in elections in October 1994, was a triumph. As with the Namibian mission in the late Eighties and early Nineties it was a testimony to the benefits of allocating sufficient money and time, born of the West's early post-Cold War optimism. But the Angolan mission rapidly degenerated into a joke. Devoted officers like Major Kundalkar did oversee the disarmament of thousands of troops, but most of the best units from both sides stayed in the bush. Far from bringing Angola nearer to peace, the mission gave UNITA a chance for a breather to regroup and rearm. With a few honourable exceptions, the mission became little more than a chance for Third World soldiers to live the expat life by banking hard currency salaries and living off expenses.

The decline and fall of the mission was all too familiar to Angolans. Its predecessor had been appointed amid much fanfare to oversee the 1992 elections, but it was the Cinderella of UN operations. Margaret Anstee, the UN special envoy, was reduced to making fun of the Security Council Resolution 747 which had authorized the mission. She had, she joked, been given 'a 747 to fly with only enough fuel for a DC3'.[6] In time, Angolans altered the remark to 'only enough fuel for a car'. Anstee's complaint was valid. While the Namibian peace process of 1988/9 had a budget of $430 million and 10,000 UN personnel, Angola was allocated $132 million and barely a thousand personnel for a far more complex task. Tragically for Angola, penny-pinching was merely a symptom of a greater malaise.

The list of mishaps and mistakes was endless. The first error was the choice of the special envoy. Anstee was a highly experienced diplomat, but her appointment suggested that political correctness counted more in New York than realpolitik. To send a white woman to a chauvinist country like Angola was never going to work. Africa is the most sexist of continents. Neither Savimbi nor Dos Santos would take kindly to receiving instructions from a woman, as any African veteran could have told the UN headquarters staff. Anstee's colour and nationality also stood against her. In Angola the scars of colonialism are still unhealed.

Her successor, Alioune Blondin Beye, a Malian, argued that one had to understand that the West's 'bull in a china shop' approach would never work in Angola. 'An African understands as a [citizen of a] more developed nation might not, that a conflict that developed for years gathers many layers, all of which must be rooted out before peace can be built on a clean foundation,' he said, in an interview with the Associated Press, shortly before his tragic death in a plane crash in June 1998. His 'African solution to African problems' chimed very well with the West's disinclination to get involved, but as time passed with little progress his softly-softly approach seemed perilously close to subservience.

Still more disastrous, however, than the choice of the leader was the timetable. Under pressure from the three peace-brokers, Portugal, Russia and America, the UN pushed ahead with the election. Representatives of the troika were anxious to bring to an end their long and convoluted history of involvement. And so they ignored repeated warnings that Savimbi had not disarmed his principal forces. It was also patently clear that the UN had not had enough time to oversee a climate conducive to free and fair elections.

If the UN was to achieve anything, it had to be willing for a long haul. Angola needed a two- or three-year peace-keeping force to oversee an interim period before elections and then it needed adequate resources for a follow-up operation. Africa is littered with the debris of elections which were held without sufficient support. The classic example was Sierra Leone, where the West funded elections in 1996 to end military rule. The poll was a triumph. Images were duly transmitted around the world of happy lines of voters. But after years of chaos and civil war the new civilian government needed more than democratic legitimacy to stay in power. It needed money – and muscle – to defend the hard-won civilian rule and entrench democratic institutions and values. Within a year there had been a military coup and the elected president was in exile.

The fundamental problem was Third World fatigue. The crisis in Angola in 1992 was low on the list of the world's priorities in comparison to the war in the former Yugoslavia. I was in Bosnia in the winter of 1992 when Boutros-Ghali visited the besieged Bosnian capital, Sarajevo, and outraged its belea-guered inhabitants by declaring that it was far from being the most dangerous city in the world. Like many other correspon-dents I was angered by what seemed an attempt to deflect attention from the shortcomings of the UN's Balkan commit-ments. The UN was indeed then desperate to wriggle off the hook of responsibility for the carnage in the Balkans. But Boutros-Ghali was stating the truth. The people of Huambo, Cuito and other Angolan cities were in a worse plight than Sarajevans, but the artillery and planes that were shelling them were being fired in deepest Africa, and the Sarajevans were in Europe. During the crisis in the former Yugoslavia, advocates of Western intervention regularly argued that morality and a defence against barbarism had to start somewhere. But, as Africans repeatedly protested, that in itself is selective morality.

The UN's reputation in Africa reached its lowest point in Somalia and Rwanda. The Somalia mission began in a blaze of publicity in December 1992 when American marines stormed ashore before banks of waiting television cameras. Their task, code-named Operation Restore Hope, was to restore peace and order after two years of civil war and famine had killed several hundred thousand Somalis. But a series of humiliating defeats by Somali militias showed they had wholly failed to understand the nature of the problem they were facing. The operation reached its nadir in October 1993 when a plan to abduct the leading Somali warlord General Aidid, who had been identified by Washington as the main villain, went terribly wrong. Two helicopters were shot down and eighteen crack Rangers, who had been flown in specially for the task, were killed. It later emerged that their armoured vehicles were driven by Malaysian drivers who lost their way. One American was captured and shown on television. The dead body of another was filmed being carried through the streets of Mogadishu, the capital, by a Somali mob. The images brought back all the old Vietnam fears of body bags. The Somali mission effectively killed any desire in Washington for serious involvement in Africa. Fifteen months after their colourful arrival the Americans made an ignominious withdrawal, leaving a pared-down multi-national UN force. By the end, the UN forces were barricaded in their bases, spending all but a handful of the operation's billion-pound budget on merely staying alive. Kofi Annan, the then UN Under-Secretary of Peace-Keeping, remarked acidly: 'The impression has been created that the easiest way to disrupt a peace-keeping mission is to kill Americans.'

The Rwandan operation was even more of a disaster, or rather disgrace. When the genocide started in April 1994, there was a UN peace-keeping force in Kigali to monitor the recently signed peace accords. But they were forbidden by New York from intervening on the grounds that they had only a monitoring mandate. Even as mobs with machetes slaughtered civilians in the city centre, the blue berets were confined to their barracks. A patrol of ten Belgian soldiers was ordered to the house of the prime minister, Agathe Uwilingiyimana, a moderate Hutu opposed to the killing, to escort her to safety. When they arrived, they were surrounded by a mob baying for her and their blood. On radioing for instructions, they were told to put down their weapons. As soon as they did so, they were hacked to death. The Security Council ordered Boutros-Ghali to withdraw the troops. As the killing intensified, it backtracked and tried to raise an intervention force, but nothing happened. The UN monitors were left literally to pick up the bodies.

Major-General Romeo Dallaire, the UN commander, was later vilified back home in Canada for failing to act, but the blame lies with the Western governments for whom an African genocide was not worth risking any lives. I met Dallaire shortly after the genocide ended and he could barely control his anger at the Western powers for, he said, failing in their duties. When America finally did respond, they restricted their involvement to flying in tonnes of supplies to the Hutu refugees in the very camps that were sheltering the killers. Even that was a disaster. They delivered the wrong sort of food to the wrong place. I accompanied the first C-130 transport plane from Entebbe Airport, in Uganda, and watched the excited faces of the aircrew as they offloaded giant bundles of food into the sky. The next day, as recriminations reverberated from Washington, the airmen shuffled around the airport; they wanted to help but they just could not get it right.

The one positive development that emerged indirectly from these botched missions is that they encouraged a new spirit of self-sufficiency. The disastrous record of the West and the UN in Somalia, Rwanda and Angola stirred bitter memories of the partisan UN mission in the Congo in the Sixties and entrenched a deep cynicism in Africa about the morality and commitment of the international community. In a handful of African capitals the realization grew that the time had come for Africa to look to its own interests.

There are still plenty of voices arguing that the West has a debt to repay which requires it to intervene. But such an abdicatory philosophy has been waning steadily since the Sixties when it was in vogue. There are indeed signs of a growing wariness about Western involvement. The impetus for this new approach came from the Horn of Africa, where Eritreans and Ethiopians had learned the hard way that liberation only comes through your own efforts. The Eritreans fought a thirty-year war to win independence from Ethiopia. The Ethiopians simultaneously fought a long guerrilla war against the Marxist government which culminated in 1991 in the overthrow of the dictator Mengistu.

The philosophy of President Issaias Afewerki of Eritrea and Prime Minister Meles Zenawi of Ethiopia was simple. They argued that Africans had to learn to solve their problems. The corollary was that they should be left alone to get on with the job. Hopes that they were the forerunners of a new pragmatic breed were dampened in 1998 when they began a pointless war over a disputed strip of land. But the idea that the American 'cavalry' would not and even should not bale out Africa took root elsewhere, particularly in Uganda under President Museveni and in Rwanda, where the UN relief agencies and non-governmental organizations were regarded with open contempt by the RPF, who tolerated their charity only as long as it suited their ends. Aid workers were outraged when the RPF attacked the UN's Hutu refugee camps in Zaire in 1996 in an attempt to defeat the Hutu militias once and for all. The policy was tough and even brutal, but it worked. The bulk of the refugees returned to Rwanda, and the camps that had fostered enmities and sedition at the expense of the UN were finally closed.

As the twentieth century drew to a close, Angola badly needed a dose of this self-determinist vision. But this was never going to come from either of the feuding leaders. Dos Santos became fixated on crushing Savimbi and Savimbi had long since lost sight of everything but the quest for power. In January 1999 the UN acknowledged that its ten-year peace-keeping mission had failed and prepared to pull out. Such was the elemental force of Savimbi's personality that at the end of the century he was reported to be training a new generation of cadres to replace those that had defected, died or been purged. The loss of his Cold War allies had been a blow but it was surmountable as he was blessed by access to fabulous supplies of minerals – the modern key to the continent.

𐋀𐋀𐋀

On paper the rich mineral seams which criss-cross the continent should provide the bonanza to fund Africa out of its misery. But in reality they have proved the continent's bane. The deadliest faultline running through Africa at the end of the century is neither ideological nor tribal but geological. Far from financing development, Africa's minerals have fomented chaos, misery and war, leading many Africans to argue wearily that it would have been better if the continent had never seen a single diamond. The only exceptions are Botswana and South Africa where the minerals are out of the government's direct control.

The pattern started in the last century when the Witwaters-rand seam of gold was found in the Transvaal, one of the two then independent Boer republics. The discovery sparked one of the world's greatest-ever gold rushes around what is now Johannesburg. It also led to war between the hardy isolationist Boers, who viewed the birth of the licentious new city around the ever deepening mine shafts as a terrible curse, and the British empire, which was urged by Cecil Rhodes and other financiers to take control of the mines.

Shortly before the war began, Paul Kruger, the hirsute Boer leader, is said to have sat on his Pretoria *stoep* (veranda) gloomily contemplating the ruin that the gold had wreaked. Ironically, he was echoing the sentiments of a man he would have regarded as a primitive savage, Lobengula, the last king of the Ndebele, who frequently cursed his country's fabled and elusive mineral wealth which lured Rhodes to send a team of volunteers to invade his kingdom. The *cri de coeur* of these two very different men has been resounding through Africa ever since, although not, it has to be said, from the mouths of many leaders. Far from bewailing Africa's rich deposits, African governments have for the most part welcomed them as a quick way to fund exotic lifestyles and insure their futures.

Nigeria, the sprawling giant of West Africa, is the starkest example. It is the world's ninth largest oil producer and also has fabulous deposits of natural gas. But the oil that is drilled off-shore in the Niger delta literally stays off-shore, with the vast profits heading straight into foreign bank accounts. Nigeria reaped a 12.4 billion-dollar bonus from the 1990 Gulf crisis when oil prices soared. A few years later a state audit could account for barely 5 per cent.

Shortly after the report was compiled, I asked the British High Commissioner in Lagos where Nigeria had gone wrong. He gave a one-word answer: oil. 'If you are wealthy in bananas or groundnuts it makes it hard for the state to be too corrupt,' he said. 'But Nigeria suddenly got oil [in the Seventies] and no one sees it. It just disappears.'

Dr Mofia Akoba was Minister of Oil in the mid-Seventies,

the early years of the oil boom, when the depressing saga began. Two decades later he was an environmental activist in Port Harcourt, the principal city in the delta. He worked in a dilapidated old town house on the outskirts, brimming with books and paperwork, and reminiscent of the study of an absent-minded tutor. As I drove to meet him, dark columns of smoke rose from Ogoniland, the most exploited region, where fires were burning off excess gas. As the sun went down, the land-scape was lit up as if by a full moon.

'The people who live among this oil don't have anything to show for it,' he said. 'It's not like Saudi oil where the oil is in the desert far away from the people. There are six million people in the delta living among the pipelines and rigs. All they get is pollution of the air and the land. They are prepared to do without oil for two or three generations until a humane govern-ment is in place that uses the revenues in a responsible way.'

Dr Akoba was a close colleague of the writer and activist Ken Saro-Wiwa, who was, at the time of my visit in October 1995, imprisoned with eight other Ogoni activists awaiting trial for the murder of three tribal chiefs. It was patently a political case. A month later General Abacha, the hardline military leader, turned down pleas from Mandela and other Common-wealth leaders and executed Saro-Wiwa and his fellow activists. After a brief outcry, international outrage waned. All the while the oil-wells kept pumping.

Shell, which drilled half of Nigeria's 1.9 million barrels a day, gave me a sanitized tour of Ogoniland by helicopter, ending with a visit to a brand-new clinic they had funded in one of the poorest areas. At dawn the following morning a Catholic priest smuggled me into the restricted area in the back of his car for a very different view. Life in Ogoniland was an endless battle against repression, poverty and fear. Oil pollution was clogging up its creeks, making it ever harder for the fishermen in their dug-out canoes to keep their families alive. Hundreds of locals had been arrested, tortured and killed for daring to demand a share of the revenue. Blackened and deserted homes in village after village testified to the brutal ways of the state. Shell did later suspend its operations in Ogoniland pending increased government investment in the region, but only after increasingly violent protests.

The same harsh pragmatism pertains wherever there is oil in Africa. When drugged-up youths festooned in bandoliers and rocket launchers ransacked Brazzaville, the capital of the Republic of Congo, in July 1997, the scenes of burning boulevards pandered to all the old preconceptions of African anarchy. Nominally it was a war of revenge between the president, Pascal Lissouba, and his predecessor, General Denis Sassou-Nguesso, whom he had ousted in the Congo's first multi-party elections in 1992. But this was no random chaos; the real motivation for the war was control of the off-shore oil-fields.

Lissouba had made the fatal mistake of alienating France, the regional power broker and former colonial power, by renegotiating long-standing contracts with French oil companies and dangling them before American firms. For several years he had been a valued regional client of the Quai d'Orsay. But he had failed to appreciate that he was valued for only one thing – oil. French forces have a long history of involvement in their former colonies, but when several thousand paratroopers and foreign legionaries were sent to rescue expatriates from Brazzaville, the most striking aspect of their operation was their neutrality. Lissouba's hotline to Paris had been cut off and he was left to roam Africa in a fruitless search for support before he was forced into exile by his old rival. Lissouba had taken power by the ballot box and had been overthrown by the bullet and yet there was a marked lack of international condemnation for his successor. Western politicians pursue the same remorseless logic towards Africa as the Big Men: oil matters more than ethics.

Angola fits the tragic pattern but with an added twist: it is twice cursed as it has a treasure trove of diamonds as well as rich fields of oil. Adventurers in the nineteenth century thought that 'King Solomon's Mines' lay in what is now Zimbabwe. They were wrong. Angola is the El Dorado of southern Africa, or at least it would be, if it were at peace. By the mid-Nineties what had been the archetypal Cold War conflict had become a clash of minerals – the oil of the MPLA against the diamonds of Savimbi. In one of Africa's classic ironies, the richest oil-wells of Cabinda, an enclave separated from the rest of Angola by a promontory of the former Zaire, were operated in the Cold War by a subsidiary of the American company Chevron but guarded by Cubans.

After an abortive attack on the oil-wells in an attempt to bankrupt the MPLA and so win the war, Savimbi relied on his diamonds, a far more cost-efficient source of income for a rebel army. Unlike in South Africa, where the remaining deposits of diamonds are deep underground and can only be extracted at vast expense, in Angola they are alluvial and so can literally be plucked from the ground.

The scenes on the Chicapa and Cuanda rivers in eastern Angola bring to mind tales of the gold-panners in the Klondike. The banks are riddled with holes and populated by thousands of villagers digging away like termites. They work for a minimal wage as they have no hope of finding a market for the stones. Angola is the world's fourth largest diamond producer and Savimbi's control of the north-east guaranteed him between £220 and 300 million a year, four-fifths of the national trade. For UNITA it was the equivalent of a bottomless bank account. To the envy of Angolans, Mozambique moved effortlessly towards peace after its election in 1994. It had as bloody a recent history but it had no minerals.

♦♦♦♦

Nearly a hundred years ago, when work started on the Benguela Railway, it is said that for every labourer the contractors had to hire a second to carry water. Further inland, oxen could not cope with the climate and terrain, so camels had to be brought down from North Africa. Then came the threat of cannibals followed by the disruption of the First World War. It was an extraordinary story. The end of the Cold War so nearly provided a new chapter. The new breeze paved the way for a resolution of what was regarded as a far more intractable problem, South

Africa's white minority rule. A few weeks after my train ride I was to witness a potent symbol of the changing times when I came across a group of Afrikaner farmers trekking north through Zambia in search of a new life. But Savimbi was no F.W. De Klerk, the Afrikaner Nationalist who negotiated himself from power. The superpowers' premier proxy battlefield will be silent only when Savimbi is defeated or killed – and it is only when that happens that the Benguela Railway will have a chance of running again.

5

The Last White Patriarch

F.W. De Klerk – Whither the White Africans?

The Toyota *bakkie* (pick-up) was caked in thick red dust and its metalwork was pitted with dents and scars. It had already travelled more than 1,000 miles through southern Africa, but the worst part of the journey was still to come and the driver clearly had no illusions about the scale of the challenge ahead. He was a thick-set grizzled man in his early forties with a sparse beard. Switching off the engine he sat chatting to his two passengers, men of similar ilk, before sauntering over to a roadside farm-shop for a bag of biltong, the dried meat staple of the Afrikaner. It had kept the Boer commandos in the field for two long years at the turn of the century, much to the frustration of the 'khakis' of Lord Kitchener's British Imperial army. Now it was once again sustaining a spirit of adventure.

It was August 1995, and Dirk Kruger had been three days on the road since leaving his family farm north-west of Johannesburg. In the finest pioneering tradition he had stayed clear of towns and laid out his bedding roll at night by the side of the road. Now he was twenty miles north of Lusaka, the Zambian capital, within a day's drive of his goal, the rich untamed bush of the north. His dream of a plot of land was within his grasp. Only the newly painted signboard advertising fresh farm produce and biltong had persuaded him to take a break from the road.

With asphalt for at least some of the way and four-wheel drive for the gravel roads and thorn scrub, Kruger was undoubtedly having an easier time of it than his ancestors, whose ox-wagon trek through southern Africa last century was one of history's great feats of endurance. Fittingly he was reluctant to compare his endeavour with that of the *voortrekkers*.

'Lots of people would like to see this as a second Great Trek,' he said. 'I'm not so sure. It's economic circumstances that forced me to leave South Africa. That is all. South Africa is not an agriculturally friendly country. The drought there is so bad I probably wouldn't be able to farm my old place in a few years. Here the rainfall is good, as is the soil . . .'

After a growl of Afrikaans from one of his companions he broke off and they departed in a cloud of dust. But as they chugged in search of a new plot of land it was tempting to conclude that Kruger's forebears would have been proud of him. His farm, near Mafikeng, the small market town immortalized in British schoolbooks by the Boer War siege, was for sale. In return he hoped to buy 1,000 hectares of untamed bush. He would rent a plot of irrigated land while the authorities processed the 'investment licence' he needed to buy state land. His family were waiting for his word before joining him.

Kruger was in the vanguard of a extraordinary exodus. Under apartheid Afrikaners were reared to fear and deride the rest of their continent under black rule. From their earliest days the lesson was drummed home from the blackboard and pulpit: Africa was hostile, brutal and corrupt. And yet in an apparent contradiction that goes to the heart of the Afrikaner psyche, they saw themselves as Africans, the continent's 'white tribe', and despised the *rooineks* (rednecks), the English-speakers, who had a foot in Europe.

In reality most Afrikaners' contact with Africa was no more profound than bush hunting expeditions and romanticized fireside evocations of their rugged past. Afrikaners had little understanding of the rhythms and privations of African life, so it was all the more remarkable that after years of preferment under white rule Kruger and hundreds of others should head north of the Limpopo and confront arguably their darkest fears.

For many of the new trekkers Africa came as a terrible shock.

South Africa's white farmers were cushioned by fat subsidies under successive apartheid governments. Prospective trekkers were devastated to find their promised land was every bit as run-down as the old jokes about Africa had implied. Many lost their life savings in 1997 in the Republic of Congo, a favoured destination, after it erupted in a bloody civil war. Zambia, too, while stable, was to prove the nemesis of many a would-be pioneer. Some did an abrupt about-turn a few miles across the frontier after seeing the appalling state of the roads. As Dirk Kruger headed off on the final stage of the journey, Charles Harvey, the owner of the farm-shop, snorted in derision. His family has farmed in Zambia for most of the century, somehow surviving the economic blunderings of the country's independence ruler, Kenneth Kaunda.

> Hundreds of them have been pitching up here for advice, but the attitude of most of them is all wrong. If you want to live in the middle of nowhere you have to be a hell of a special guy. When your kid is sick it takes five hours to reach a doctor . . . You can't phone your granny on her birthday and you don't get any more money for your produce if it comes from the back of beyond. It's not easy: you have to start from scratch. Okay, you decide to set up in the bush, but how do you get your goods out?

There were fertile grounds for cynicism about the grandiose claims of the new *trekboers*. While their spokesmen maintained they were forging a new partnership between the Afrikaner and Africa, the prime motivation of many of them seemed to be just the reverse. Kruger, like many others, was not a natural 'new' South African. He came from a right-wing heartland. Just as his forefathers had trekked away from British suzerainty in the Cape, so he conceded he was keen to escape his new overlords, South Africa's first black government. Initially several African governments, most notably Zambia, Mozambique and Congo, welcomed the initiative. They hoped that in exchange for cut-price land Afrikaners would revitalize their devastated agriculture. But as the movement gathered pace in the late

Nineties, the hosts became concerned they had sanctioned the entrenchment of right-wing enclaves which were exploiting their cheap labour.

And yet despite its imperfections the new 'trek' did symbolize one of the more striking turnarounds in Africa in the late twentieth century. Since Jan van Riebeeck founded a way-station for the Dutch East India Company at the Cape in 1652, the Afrikaners had kept the rest of Africa at arm's length. Van Riebeeck formalized the division by planting a bitter almond hedge to keep the interior at bay. Over the next two and a half centuries Afrikaners forged through the hedge and fanned out across southern Africa, but it remained a heresy to consider that Africans had rights.

The alienation of the Afrikaner from the rest of Africa reached its height in the second half of the twentieth century when, far from modernizing their world view, South Africa's whites codified it in law. In protest at apartheid, white South Africans were barred from most of the continent. Planes flying to Johannesburg were banned from flying over black Africa and had to take a lengthy detour round the 'bulge' of West Africa. The Afrikaner Nationalists responded in kind, launching punitive raids into South Africa's neighbours against the governments that supported the then banned black liberation movements, the ANC and the more radical Pan Africanist Congress (PAC).

The end of white rule in South Africa brought that sequence to an end. The inauguration of Nelson Mandela brought liberation not just for blacks, but also ironically for many of South Africa's 5.3 million whites, even if many of them, particularly among the three million Afrikaners, could not see it at the time. In one stroke Afrikaners had been freed from the burden of their history and from responsibility for their tortured country. Theirs will not be an easy journey into the new millennium. The Afrikaner carries an immense burden of guilt from the past, which may in part account for Mr Kruger's Zambian trek. Many are also resentful of the present and fearful of the future: as each year passes they will face increased competition from blacks and will watch an erosion of their old world. But, contrary to outsiders' perceptions, there is no monolithic Afrikaner group. The end of apartheid meant that the way was at last clear for Afrikaners to play a more constructive role in Africa with their agricultural, commercial and industrial know-how and their financial and military might. Unlike the white settlers elsewhere in the continent, Afrikaners have nowhere to flee.

Even as Kruger rumbled across Zambia hundreds of white South African businessmen were moving north across the Limpopo, signing contracts and looking for deals. Maputo, the capital of neighbouring Mozambique, has been reinvigorated by South African investment. Locals sometimes muttered their opposition. The newcomers were not of course philanthropists. But Africa does not need charity; it has been suffocated by it over the years. Rather Africa needs business, and white South Africans, both as individuals and as leaders of Johannesburg corporations, may be among the few with the capital who are prepared to give the rest of the continent a chance.

A few miles down the road from Charles Harvey's biltong shop an unmarked track heads off into the bush. After bumping for eight or nine miles a low homestead ringed by a simple wire fence comes into view. With its tumbledown outhouses and dusty yard, Gerrit and Bernice Bronkhorst's 2,000-hectare farm is nothing like their former smallholding east of Pretoria. It has neither electricity nor a telephone. The week before I visited them a hyaena took one of their precious cattle. Even as we spoke a column of soldier ants was taking possession of the yard.

'It's tough,' said Bronkhorst, whose swarthy features and black grizzled hair suggested an African strain had entered his bloodline in the distant past. 'There are no luxuries. You have to be self-sufficient, but if you want to hear a hyaena at night you have to make some sacrifices. We're not European any more, we are African.'

As they sat on the *stoep* with their two small children, with the sun going down, that did not seem an exaggeration. The Bronkhorsts genuinely appeared part of their landscape. For this reconciliation they had to thank a bald-headed chain-smoking career politician, Frederik Willem De Klerk, the last of the Afrikaner patriarchal leaders.

✦✦✦✦

February 2nd 1990, the day that De Klerk stood up in parliament in Cape Town and announced the unbanning of the liberation movements and the release of Mandela, has been the subject of more conjecture and celebration than just about any other date in South African history.

With historical hindsight it is easy – and indeed increasingly in vogue as the years pass – to play down the significance of De Klerk's decision, on the lines that it was the inevitable step for him to take. Ever since the townships erupted in the mid-Eighties, white rule lurched from crisis to crisis: international pressure mounted; the economy shrank amid disinvestment and sanctions; logically something in Pretoria had to give if South Africa and the Afrikaner were not to slither into the abyss of civil war. Then, according to the glib version of events, in the nick of time world politics intervened: the collapse of world Communism removed the 'rooi gevaar' (red peril) which had sent shivers through many an Afrikaner nursery over the years, and thus the way was clear to reform.

De Klerk himself has always stressed that unbanning the ANC was a strictly logical step. He had had no blinding flash of light, he explained time and again to interviewers keen to profile the iconoclastic Boer. Falling back on his training as a lawyer he had weighed up the situation at his holiday home at Hermanus on the coast. He had balanced the conflicting imperatives of leading the *volk* and realized that, although they could fight on, he had no alternative if he really was both to safeguard their interests and to ensure their survival.

And yet, however obvious that may seem now, at the time it was far from clear-cut. While it was traditional for the opening address of a new session to sketch out the coming year's policy, all too often over the years since taking office in 1948 the Nationalists had used the occasion to tighten up rather than reform. After his inauguration as state president in November 1989 De Klerk had belied his conservative reputation by repealing some of the pettier and more absurd apartheid laws. The authorities had even given tacit approval to an anti-apartheid demonstration outside the parliament planned for the same day as his address. But few dared to hope that De Klerk would take the decisive steps avoided by his predecessor, P.W. Botha.

So secretive was De Klerk about his intentions that he had not even briefed his wife. On the eve of the speech Western diplomats cautioned the foreign press, who had gathered in droves, against expecting too much. It is easy to understand their caution. Although the security forces had by the late Eighties lost control of many of the black and mixed-race townships, the ANC was years away from being able to march victoriously into Pretoria. The party's armed wing, *Umkhonto we Sizwe* (Spear of the Nation), known as MK, had barely chipped the apartheid edifice. The repression of the township unrest was increasingly costly in money and lives, but the security forces felt under no real threat.

Years later De Klerk bridled when he felt history was being written without sufficient recognition of his role and, at a press conference held in October 1998, he said, 'The reality is that it was we ourselves who abolished apartheid, not primarily because we were forced to do so, but because we came to the realization that it was wrong and could not bring justice to all our people.' Most South Africans would dispute the idea that he was driven by morality and a desire for justice, but it is hard to challenge the logic of his opening claim. Even if MK had drastically stepped up its offensive, it was far from clear whether the Nationalists would have flinched. The Afrikaners, like the Serbs, take a positive pride in wrapping themselves in the past and defying the turn of history's wheel.

As an archetypal British writer of the late Victorian era, Sir Arthur Conan Doyle is an unlikely Boer hero. But during five years travelling in South Africa I lost count of the number of Afrikaner homes which proudly displayed a plaque with his testimonial to their doughty ethos:

Take a community of Dutchmen of the type who defended themselves for fifty years against all the power of Spain at a time when Spain was the greatest power in the world. Intermix them with a strain of those inflexible French Huguenots who gave up home and fortune and left their country for ever at the time of the revocation of the Edict of Nantes. The product must obviously be one of the most rugged, virile, unconquerable races ever seen upon earth. Then finally put a finer temper upon their military qualities by a dour fatalistic Old Testament realism and an ardent consuming patriotism.

By 1990 many Afrikaners had long since been urbanized. More than a million trooped into work every day in the civil service or public utilities before returning to their comfortable bungalows, many with swimming pools and maids. Although some seemed twenty years behind the prevailing fashion in the West, with safari suits, A-line skirts and even beehive hair-dos not out of place, they bore little relation to the hardy caricatures of Conan Doyle.

And yet tradition still ran deep in Afrikaner veins. For many it was a point of principle that the more the outside world criticized South Africa and lectured them on the need for reform, the more obdurate they would be. De Klerk, or F.W. as he was widely known, was steeped in such thinking.

In nature and nurture De Klerk was every inch the blue-blooded Afrikaner Nationalist. His brother Wimpie, a reformist commentator, later mused that F.W. was 'genetically predeter-mined to become a politician'.[1] Their grandfather, Willem De Klerk, a *dominee* (priest in the Dutch Reformed Church), was a friend of Paul Kruger, the Boer War leader, and played a leading role in forming the National Party in the Twenties. F.W.'s father, Jan De Klerk, was a Nationalist cabinet minister for fifteen years, and his aunt, Susan, was married to Hans Strijdom, 'The Lion of the North', South Africa's prime minister from 1954 to 1958.

The family pulpit reinforced F.W.'s orthodox strait-jacket. He was a 'Dopper', a member of the strictest branch of the

Dutch Reformed Church. Even if he had over the years displayed any liberal tendencies, the chances are they would not have lasted long over the breakfast table. Marike, his wife, who was his university sweetheart, made no secret of her strait-laced conservatism. Long after Mandela took office she was photographed in his presence, a picture of prim disapproval.

For much of F.W.'s political career Marike's views appeared to hold sway. He was known as a conservative in the turbulent and repressive Eighties. In 1985 he was reported to have been against the abolition of the Immorality Act, which prohibited sex across the colour line, one of the shabbiest of apartheid's phalanx of laws. He was seen as the most conservative of the three candidates who vied for the party leadership in 1989 when his predecessor, P.W. Botha, had a stroke.

Such was the track record of the man who revolutionized South African politics. Seven years after his fateful address, he recalled in a political speech made in January 1997 the heartache his decision had caused. 'The decision to surrender the right to national sovereignty is certainly one of the most painful that any leader can ever be asked to take. Most nations are prepared to risk total war and catastrophe rather than surrender this right. Yet this was the decision that we had to take. We had to accept the necessity of giving up on the ideal on which we have been nurtured and the dream for which so many generations of our forefathers had struggled and for which so many of our people had died.'

F.W. set a precedent for Afrikaner Nationalists. His predecessors had either died in office or resigned in the wake of scandal or a party coup. He, however, effectively negotiated himself from power, even if he did not mean to do so at the time. It was a turning point for South Africa and indeed the entire continent. It was no wonder that commentators searching for an explanation speculated lovingly, albeit it seems mistakenly, that he had had a Damascene conversion. For the first time since the days of Louis Botha and Jan Smuts, the Boer War commando leaders who made peace with the British at the turn of the century, a *volksleier* (leader of the people) had opted

to give ground in order to survive. The Afrikaners and their last
leader now had to prove they could unhitch their wagons and
adapt to the new order.

♠♠♠♠

Lost in the loneliness of the high veld, the vast plateau 6,000
feet above sea level which covers much of South Africa's
interior, the town of Koppies is an improbable place to go in
search of insights into the mind of De Klerk, let alone optimism
about the likelihood of the Afrikaner adapting to the new order.
One hundred miles south-west of Johannesburg, Koppies is the
quintessential conservative *dorp* (small town) in the heart of
the *platteland* (flatland), a repository of the bleakest side of the
Afrikaner soul.

With its trim green lawns the single street is as pristinely
starched as the surrounding landscape, which stretches for mile
after mile across open fields. The dried milk factory, once the
main source of employment, has long since closed. When the
sun goes down, the Hotel Friesland, a down-at-heel bungalow
with a dingy bar, fills with farmers downing brandy and Coke.
Fearful of change and of the future, the end of apartheid left
the 2,000 white residents on the brink of despair. Only on
Sundays does the town come to life. The Dutch Reformed
church, an angular high-pointed edifice as totalitarian in structure as in ethos, fills with congregants in suits and patterned
dresses. As soon as the service is over, they hurry home.

Across the railway track its twin town, the satellite township,
is the shambolic home to ten times as many blacks. KwaKwatsi
is just one mile down a dirt road, but for the white residents it
was an unthinkable journey before April 1994. There is a hang-
dog subservience to anyone over forty in KwaKwatsi that leaves
no doubt they have had to learn to know their place. On
Sunday afternoons hundreds of people cram into the community centre for choral competitions. The close harmony
resounds through the shacks and matchbox township houses,
and, on the few occasions I heard it, seemed all the more
striking and wonderful in the depressing surroundings.

Koppies' plight is mirrored a hundred times over in the South African outback. Here, more than anywhere, I found myself face to face with the extraordinary conundrum of conservative Afrikanerdom which has perplexed and infuriated outsiders for generations. How can such hospitable and God-fearing people be racist to the core?

I visited Koppies regularly to take the pulse of the interior. For my first few visits I stayed at the Hotel Friesland, where the elderly proprietress epitomized the apparent paradox. In the winter she would give me a hot-water bottle and cook homely fare. In the summer she would serve home-made fruit juice and chatter about her late husband. Her down-to-earth manner was refreshing after the smug double-talk of many suburbanites and British expatriates in South African cities who have merely learned how to mask their racism in sugary platitudes. It is estimated that in the 1987 all-white election, English-speakers contributed over 40 per cent of the Nationalists' votes. And yet the blunt approach of the *platteland* Afrikaner was racism at its most unrefined. After welcoming me fondly and asking after my family, in the same breath the proprietress of the Friesland would talk of the need to keep the 'smelly farm *kaffirs* on the *stoep*'.

A year later I had to find alternative accommodation after she was telephoned one day from London by an outraged reader of one of my despatches. I had described her apartheid house-rules, and this so incensed one of her fellow countrymen who was on holiday in Britain that he rang international directory enquiries for her number and vented a tirade of abuse through the ether. Thereafter I was one of 'them' and my access to her clientele and indeed her lodgings was at an end. My link with Koppies might have waned had I not already formed a bond with the local store-owner, whom I came to think of as the F.W. De Klerk of Koppies.

Charl Van der Merwe was of De Klerk's generation and he shared his politics. He was a rare Afrikaner Nationalist in a town dominated by ultra-right-wingers who were opposed to – and terrified of – the slightest reform. As the town mayor in the last days of white rule he had to be part diplomat and part dictator. His agonized stop-start relationship with the people of KwaKwatsi and his delicate dealings with his own tribe neatly mirrored De Klerk's attempts to come to terms with the 'new' South Africa.

⁂

Our first encounter was not promising. It was a bitterly cold morning in the winter before the election, and relations between Koppies and KwaKwatsi had reached a new low. The previous morning at 4.30 a.m. on a pre-arranged signal the white residents had swung into action in their bid to keep the township and the 'new' South Africa at bay. Frustrated by months of black boycotts of their shops they had decided to take the fight to the other side and had barricaded the township.

One unit took over the water-tower with its commanding view of the terrain. Another manned a side road, a third the main road and a fourth patrolled the surrounding fields. Within half an hour more than a hundred whites were in position, brandishing shotguns, side-arms and rawhide whips. Shots were fired at any black who had the 'impudence' to leave his home.

Van der Merwe was the spokesman for the 'Action Committee'. He had been delegated that unpopular task as he was the most moderate committee member and also the only one with a good grasp of English. He stared at me suspiciously across a trestle table at the back of the hardware store. Two young boys in the doorway waved the standard of the nineteenth-century Orange Free State Republic. Bakkies screeched to a halt outside, disgorging khaki-clad youths looking for instructions and dollops of hot soup from the womenfolk.

My faltering Afrikaans greetings had done little to break the ice. Van der Merwe conferred with his colleagues before agreeing to talk. It was at least to my advantage that I was a genuine *rooinek* and not an English-speaking white South African, the devil incarnate for the right wing. Van der Merwe picked his words with the precision of a lawyer, pausing between sentences to check his drift.

138

'We are not racist. We are just trying to stand up for our rights ... We too have rights ... How can you build an economy when you are dealing with endless strikes? Take my shop. For three months last year a group of blacks squatted on the corner outside and intimidated other blacks from coming in. My revenue went down 85 per cent and I am not the only one to suffer. We had to take a stand.'

From the other side of the barricades the Afrikaners' angst looked more like bloody-minded bigotry. KwaKwatsi's indignant residents were brimming with tales of how the doctor refused to serve them and how a black traffic policeman had been thrown out of the Hotel Friesland. I drove back to Johannesburg that night wearily convinced that Koppies was doomed to long years of confrontation.

Successive trips reinforced my pessimism until, more than a year later, several months after the April 1994 election, it became clear that just as no one had expected De Klerk to open the floodgates of reform, so Koppies was defying its typecast. Once again I interviewed Van der Merwe in his store but this time he wore a broad smile. The town's white council had just held its first joint meeting with the township council, in accordance with the constitution, and to his surprise but delight he had been asked by his new black colleagues to stay in charge.

'Strange to say things have normalized. Last Christmas (the last under white rule) I sent out a letter to all the white residents assuring them that it would all be all right. The right-wingers didn't like this and called for me to resign. I said that I would stand against them and their bluff was called. We've brought in five black councillors. The blacks, you see, nominated me and we thought if those guys are being so generous we will allow one of them to chair the management committee.'

It was a very De Klerkian tale. Van der Merwe's Christmas ultimatum to the local farmers echoed South Africa's whites-only referendum in February 1992 when De Klerk took on and trounced the right wing on the issue of whether to push ahead with reform. After the dramas of the Action Committee the year before, it seemed miraculous that Koppies should have reached any accommodation with KwaKwatsi.

The spirit of 'Afrikaner *contra mundum*' has always been offset by a desire to be liked in the outside world, and especially Europe. One of the major frustrations for fervent Nationalists was that the rest of the world 'did not understand' what they were trying to achieve. Van der Merwe seemed quietly pleased to have surprised me. It was as if he knew I had expected to hear tales of 'Koppies on the brink' and instead it, or rather he, Van der Merwe, had done the 'right thing' and embraced reform.

But the language he used to describe those landmark moments laid bare the pain it had cost him, and also the obstacles which would continue to hamper relations between the two communities. He clearly felt he had done the township a huge favour by 'bringing them in', blind to the reality that they were fellow citizens of South Africa and more pressingly that the law now dictated that the worlds of town and township should coalesce. He was still far from treating his new colleagues as equals. He closed with a revealing display of bewilderment about Koppies' new residents.

'The town swimming pool is now open to everyone but "they" are not using it. The church is open but "they" are not using it . . . And "they" are expanding at such a rate you do not know where they are coming from. A youth recently stood on my *stoep* and said we want power now. I said "Be realistic. Would I give my car keys to my son without teaching him how to drive . . .?"

'I have explained to the councillors that the old habit of being called *baas* [boss] just because I had a white skin was over. "I may be twice your age but you must call me Charl." We are still far more disciplined in terms of time. You go and listen to some of these guys and they just like the sound of their own voice. So I tell myself I must be patient. One guy was slouching in his chair in the first meeting and I said, "You must be disciplined. We don't want arguments . . ."'

As he spoke I could hear the voice of De Klerk addressing

Mr Mandela's cabinet in his post-apartheid capacity as deputy president. ANC government ministers muttered after the early sessions that the National Party leader still thought he was the *baas* and patronized them as inferiors. After one particularly intemperate early cabinet Mandela accused him of addressing ANC ministers in the manner in which 'white men used to speak to blacks'.

Neither Van der Merwe nor De Klerk, I suspect, consciously wanted to upset their black peers. They genuinely thought they had embraced the new order. But it was beyond their powers to discard the assumptions of their upbringing. No amount of dissimulation could hide the fact that they had been reared to believe that whites were superior to blacks. Their body language, their intonation, their choice of words gave them away. Theirs was the world of the compilers of a "Teach Yourself Zulu" course I briefly used in which the first dozen or so sentences were either commands to black employees such as 'Come here Joe. Come here I say' or critical asides like 'Joe smokes a lot.'

Van der Merwe did try to lower his guard. In the countdown to South Africa's first all-race local government elections in November 1995, I came across him pinning up electoral posters on a telegraph pole on the road to KwaKwatsi. I was driving two of the new ANC councillors back home. We stopped and the three South Africans chatted and teased each other about their electoral chances. Van der Merwe was trying to do his bit in an echo of De Klerk wearing traditional African costume and campaigning in Soweto in the campaign for the general election. The soft evening light enhanced the harmonious impression. But it was a fleeting encounter and such gestures neither meant nor counted for much.

'I just don't trust him [Van der Merwe],' Charles Masibi, one of my passengers, muttered as we drove on. 'He plots every word he says . . .' I had first met Masibi, a young teacher, during the 'Action Committee' showdown before the election. He raised his eyebrows when I recounted Van der Merwe's account of the swimming pool. 'Of course we don't go there! The first time a group of school-children went there from KwaKwatsi two of them were beaten up by white racists . . .'

In Van der Merwe's defence his was a thankless task. Just as De Klerk was reviled as a traitor by many Afrikaners who accused him of betraying their interests, so Van der Merwe risked isolation in Koppies, an uncomfortable position in such a small town, particularly when your family's well-being depends on regular customers. As the changes began to affect Koppies with the inevitable shift of government spending priorities and the onset of positive discrimination for blacks, so Van der Merwe returned to the white *laager*. He resigned from the council and helped to found an anti-ANC alliance of local Nationalists and right-wingers. Ironically this was formed just as the town started to liberalize. The doctor ended the old practice of making blacks queue at his back door and allowed them instead into his front waiting room. There was even the odd discreet fraternization in the Hotel Friesland. But Van der Merwe had had enough. He was a dispirited figure by the end, just like De Klerk when he too came to resign.

'There's no magic wand to be waved here,' Van der Merwe told me. 'There is a bridge between the two communities but no one dares to cross.'

⁂

In the early Nineties it became a journalistic commonplace to compare De Klerk with the other celebrated but flawed reformist of the late twentieth century, Mikhail Gorbachev. On my arrival in South Africa I thought the analogy unfair on the Afrikaner. While the Soviet leader proved incapable of adapting his vision and so was ultimately subsumed by it, De Klerk kept modifying as he went along. In February 1990 he had no intention of negotiating the whites from power. His sights were set on a limited democracy with an enforced coalition entrenching white interests. He even talked of setting up a rotating presidency to share power. As time passed, however, so, albeit reluctantly, he altered his ideas and gave in to ANC pressure, ensuring that in 1994 he could at least hold up his head and say he had not been defeated. As head of the second largest party he became one of two deputy presidents. He would, he insisted, be able to steer the Afrikaner into a safe haven.

Within three years of Mandela's election, however, the Gorbachevian cap fitted the Afrikaner all too well. Just as the last Soviet president was lauded abroad and vilified at home, so De Klerk too led a schizophrenic existence. He was lionized on the international speaker circuit as the midwife of South Africa's democracy. He had, after all, shared the 1993 Nobel Peace Prize with Mandela. But in South Africa he was a tired and embattled figure stirring deep resentment among, ironically, both blacks and whites.

For black South Africans, De Klerk's image was fatally damaged by his apparent hardening of heart post-1990. By releasing Mandela and unbanning the black liberation movements he had caught the ANC unawares. For the first time in the National Party's forty years in power, blacks had a reason to applaud their head of state. But those anticipating Afrikaner capitulation had to think again. After his fateful announcement, the influence of his granite predecessors came to the fore and he focused his attention on the *volk*.

Subtlety has seldom played a part in African politics. It is a continent where all too often power is all that counts – and members of rival tribes have to look to themselves. In the bloody four-year period between De Klerk's February 1990 speech and the election, elements in the apartheid security forces did all they could to undermine the transition.

De Klerk himself has always denied knowledge of the hit-squads who waged an underground war in the countdown to April 1994, fomenting fighting between the ANC and Chief Buthelezi's Inkatha Freedom Party. He angrily rejected the findings of the Truth and Reconciliation Commission, which was set up after the election to expose human rights abuses committed by both sides between 1960 and the end of white rule, and which linked him to the 1987 bombing of an anti-apartheid centre in Johannesburg. The commission was a crucial part of the post-apartheid settlement. Intended as a halfway house between Nuremberg and amnesia, it offered perpetrators amnesty for political crimes in return for confession. In a series of public hearings all over the country it also gave victims the chance to tell their stories of suffering. Supposedly the victims would be appeased, the oppressors humbled and the country could then move forward to a brighter future, purged of its past. But politics inevitably mired this bright design. On the eve of the commission's final report De Klerk's lawyers said they were contesting the findings, and, much to the outrage of the commissioners, had his name excised from the report, pending the case.

The secret policemen who controlled the shadowy 'Third Force' had frequently in the Eighties operated as autonomous units. In the final days of apartheid there was no shortage of disillusioned police and army commanders who could give orders without seeking political approval. In some instances indeed the 'Third Force' may have been motivated as much by a desire to discredit De Klerk as the ANC, given that he was seen in reactionary circles as a traitor.

However, in an authoritarian society like South Africa, his plea of ignorance is unconvincing, and critics suspect that 'Tricky Frikkie', as he was dubbed, was playing a double game during the transition in an attempt to reduce the ANC's vote. As president of one of the world's most centralized and autocratic societies, they assume that he must have known of the Third Force, and must have been able to stop it. He himself concedes in his autobiography that his relationship with the security forces was like a man who is given two watch dogs who has to decide whether to try pulling on their leashes and 'choke them' or risk letting them 'slip their collars and cause pandemonium.'[2] Mandela never forgave his co-Nobel laureate for the violence. More than 10,000 people died in political violence in the transition, mainly between supporters of the ANC and the largely Zulu Inkatha, as the ANC and the Nationalists negotiated the post-apartheid future.

'It is impossible to defend him [De Klerk] in our communities,' Mandela said as he prepared to receive the Nobel Prize. 'In his view their [black] lives are cheap ... that is the most serious problem for us as far as the violence is concerned.'

The ANC was also incensed that De Klerk refused to apologize for apartheid. For many who had suffered imprisonment or torture or lost relatives in the fight against white rule, it stuck in the throat that the closest he came to an apology was to concede that excesses had been committed in apartheid's name. He bridled when challenged on his failure to apologize, and insisted he had. But his 'apologies' were always hedged with conditions and the insistence that all sides had sinned in South Africa's 'struggle', an assertion which was undeniable but which equally was missing the point.

It was, however, always improbable that De Klerk would issue a whole-hearted *mea culpa* for the simple reason that to do so would be to undermine his and his party's world view for the previous forty years. Apartheid required a continual self-deception. Nationalists had to keep deluding themselves that their system was pinned on firm moral foundations – namely, the need to allow 'nations' to develop untainted by others. Maintaining this required considerable contortions, moral, religious and linguistic. For many Nationalists the world view changed because of a simple but profound meeting with a black South African in an unaccustomed role. Inevitably, in the aftermath of the 1994 election it was impossible to find anyone who had voted for apartheid. But there were still very few former Nationalists who were prepared to concede that it had been actually wrong.

The Truth and Reconciliation Commission pricked the bubble of self-righteousness. While scrupulously condemning ANC abuses, the process proved a damning indictment of how during the last years of apartheid South Africa had developed into a police state, as former agents and policemen laid bare their complicity in atrocities, many already well documented but some which were previously unknown. But even amid the avalanche of revelations most Nationalists, including De Klerk, found it impossible to concede that their philosophy had had a rotten core.

De Klerk was prepared to admit that specific acts of repression had been beyond the pale. But as for the philosophy of apartheid itself he could never go beyond conceding that it had ultimately been proven misguided and unworkable. As Lourens Ackermann, an Afrikaner writer, explained: 'He had no sense of the rightness of apartheid and yet also had no sense of its wrongness. What apartheid was on the one hand and what it pretended to be on the other hand has completely seduced him – he believes only in the latter.'

The furthest De Klerk was prepared to go in acknowledging the misery of being black under apartheid was to admit that the planners 'forgot that human beings and not planning statistics were involved.'[3]

Even after the end of white rule, De Klerk still saw politics in an ethnic prism. In his speeches and interviews he would harp on about 'group' rights. Those who had expected otherwise had made the mistake of assuming he was a new model Afrikaner when in fact he was an old model. Not only was De Klerk motivated by conservatism, as his critics supposed, but also duty ran deep. He was doggedly determined not to abandon his party. He had promised to lead the *volk* into the new era and he would do so. The irony is that the more he dithered and agonized over which way to go, the more he was pilloried as a turncoat by the very people he was meant to be leading.

♦♦♦

Six months before he was to resign, I had an intriguing behind-the-scenes peep at the final days of De Klerk's National Party. It was a balmy Cape evening after a typically gorgeous southern summer's day. The day's debate in parliament had just ended and the tree-lined avenue outside Sir Herbert Baker's classic, colonial parliament building was packed with MPs of all races and creeds chattering like school-children after a long and disputatious day. It was a reminder of how South Africa had changed. Once, however, I turned off the avenue and headed for the Nationalists' parliamentary offices I found myself back in a very different era.

The chambers were wreathed in smoke from a dozen cigarettes. They were also filled with grey-suited middle-aged Afrikaner males. These were the rump of the parliamentary caucus who had survived the shock of the election when they shrank from having a comfortable majority of seats to barely a fifth. De Klerk was at the centre of a conspiratorial huddle in one corner, busily defending himself against a recent attack on him by the Afrikaans press, while absorbing praise for his combative performance in the chamber a little earlier.

Starved of the publicity of the apartheid era when the world's press followed their every move, the MPs welcomed the focus of a foreign correspondent. The chief whip took me to one side and assured me that within a decade he would be a cabinet minister. 'You wait. Once the Mandela glue goes we will get 30 or 40 per cent of the vote . . .'

His arguments and insights were as outdated as the heavy three-piece suits of the party founders whose portraits covered the walls. His naivety did, however, help to explain why De Klerk remained in politics as long as he did, one of the conundrums of my time in South Africa.

As each month in the post-apartheid era passed, so De Klerk's prestige and authority declined. He was one of six Nationalist cabinet ministers in line with a clause in the interim constitution which granted cabinet seats to parties that secured more than 10 per cent of the vote. As second deputy president he was the third most powerful man in the country. But his aides complained that he had minimal influence on policy and that his deputy presidency was little more than a sinecure. He was, they said, at best expected to act as South Africa's ambassador at large, travelling around the globe and addressing investors as the reassuring white face from the new black government.

With the Truth Commission's revelations chipping away at his reputation it was a humiliating routine for a man who had once commanded the world's attention, and yet still he soldiered on as party leader. But as the chit-chat of his parliamentary colleagues in their Cape Town offices made clear, his party lived in a time-warp and had blinded itself to the reality of politics in a mainly black country. De Klerk himself was convinced, one confidant went so far as to suggest, that he still had a good chance of being re-elected, that the people would turn back to him for reassurance once Mandela had stepped down.

A reformist wing recognized this was patent nonsense. The only way they could see the National Party playing a significant part in national politics again was with a new name, new leadership and a genuine commitment to multi-racial membership. Before the election the Nationalists assiduously and successfully courted the Coloureds, people of mixed race who made up the majority in the Western Cape province. Fearing they risked once again being the wrong colour – they had been too black in the old era and now feared being too white – two-thirds of South Africa's three million Coloureds voted for De Klerk in the 1994 election, ensuring that the National Party won control of the Western Cape provincial government. Afrikaans helped to bond the partnership of Coloureds with their old oppressors, as it is the first language in most Coloured communities. Emboldened by its success, the National Party even set its sights on winning black votes and opened a branch in Soweto.

But the non-racial 'crusade' was unconvincing. The party leadership remained dominated by Afrikaners. De Klerk was too clear-sighted a politician not to appreciate that if Afrikaners were to play a political role in South Africa's future they had to be part of a truly non-racial party. But he was, it emerged, a one-match wonder. He had crossed one Rubicon but could not do so again. When his reformist lieutenant, Roelf Meyer, who had been the Nationalists' main negotiator in the constitutional talks, broached the idea of disbanding the party, De Klerk balked. Party insiders suggested that after being branded a traitor by one wing of Afrikanerdom for ending white rule, he did not want to go down in history as the man who had destroyed the National Party – even though that was what he had effectively set in motion in 1990.

For his critics both within and without Afrikanerdom it was easy to be impatient. But the final stage of South Africa's revolution had been astonishingly swift, and psychologically many Afrikaners inevitably lagged far behind the political changes. The evolution of Nationalist thinking post-1994 was reminiscent of the agonized stop-start ideological development of former Communists in Eastern Europe post-1989. Bar a few diehards, most recognized that the values of their old world had failed and yet they still had to be prised from their former beliefs. In the same way, Afrikaner Nationalists knew that white rule was doomed and yet still found it hard to renounce the past, particularly given that, as in Eastern Europe, the new order was far from perfect.

The agonies and confusion of this process were starkly apparent at the first public session of the *Broederbond*, the secret society which in the Twenties and Thirties masterminded the Nationalists' rise to power, and then underpinned white rule. Under apartheid you had to be a member of the *bond*, or at least to know one, to get anywhere in South Africa, whether in the government, law, church or civil service. At the *bond*'s fiftieth anniversary congress in 1968, H.J. Klopper, the first chairman, boasted they controlled South Africa. 'Do you realize what a powerful force is gathered here tonight between these four walls?' he said in a speech later leaked by a defector. 'Show me a greater power in Africa. Show me a greater power anywhere even in your so-called civilized world?'

How mortified Klopper would have been by the hunched shoulders and defeatist expressions of the *broeders* a mere twenty-eight years later as they filed into the University of Bloemfontein. The meeting had been billed as the *bond*'s 'coming out'. It had been renamed the *Afrikanerbond* and, supposedly, had its first non-white and women members, although I saw only a handful of white women amid the ranks of Afrikaner males, and the only three blacks were the parents of children singing in the multi-racial choir that self-consciously opened proceedings.

The *bond*'s information officer, Cobus Rossouw, was clearly delighted with his radical new responsibilities. 'Quite a few guys are itchy about the publicity,' he joked. 'It's not long ago that we checked for helicopters flying overhead and photographers in hot-air balloons.' It could have been the annual general meeting of a London club, an analogy which the new chairman, Tom de Beer, was keen to promote. 'I joined when I was a student,' he reminisced. 'I found members from different churches, different groups. I enjoyed the divergent views.' That was a whopper of an obfuscation even for a country which prided itself on ambiguous language – 'Ministry of Plural Affairs' was the old South African department that was responsible for Africans. But I let it pass because I was more interested in the present than the past. I was looking for signs of change, for an indication that the former Afrikaner powerbrokers might be willing to provide leadership for the confused and bewildered bulk of Afrikanerdom.

In the Eighties the *bond* was an important player in secret talks between the ANC and the Afrikaner establishment. Long before the government could openly consider forging links with their enemies, the *broeders* were sending out feelers to the ANC. But by the mid-Nineties they appeared to have retreated back into their shell: the *laager* mentality prevailed; the old victim mentality of the apartheid era was intact; far from looking out, they seemed more insular than ever. Their reluctance to face up to the past was frustrating but inevitable, but their inability to face up to the future was more damaging if the Afrikaner was to take his place in the new South Africa.

De Klerk was not at Bloemfontein. In the old days all cabinet members were in the *bond*, but post-1994 it would have been political suicide for a Nationalist MP to attend a meeting. However, many of F.W.'s friends and soulmates were present. These were not horny-handed farmers from the *platteland*. These were the lawyers, the judges, the academics, the thinkers who had provided the moral and intellectual platform for white rule. If they were finding it difficult to adjust to the new order, it seemed hardly surprising that De Klerk, too, was struggling.

There is an old Afrikaans expression '*die boer is soos n kakiebos*' (the Boer is like the kakie weed, a particularly dogged plant which is deemed almost impossible to kill off). Under South Africa's new multi-racial democracy De Klerk proved remarkably obdurate. His catchphrases were 'politics is not for sissies' and 'cowboys don't cry'. Month after month he slugged it out with critics from the right and the left. But in typical Afrikaner fashion it was an attack from within the ranks that proved the most wounding.

Since the first ox-wagons headed off into the interior the Afrikaners have proved past-masters at fissiparous politics. In Afrikaans the phenomenon is called *broedertwis* – brother fighting brother. After the 1994 election it threatened to tear the National Party apart between reformist and reactionary wings. Caught in the middle, De Klerk was criticized from both sides. Conservatives accused him of having flunked the pre-election negotiations with the ANC and of having betrayed the Afrikaner. While recognizing that his telegenic style made him easily the party's best vote-winner, reformists argued his past was a brake on their attempts to attract new supporters. Following the retirement of R.F. 'Pik' Botha, his veteran foreign minister, he was the last of the old guard. As a scandal loomed over his private life, he belatedly decided to step down.

On the day he announced his resignation from politics the South African Broadcasting Corporation led its nightly television news with a report on the collapse of a scaffolding in Johannesburg's northern suburbs. Three people were killed and fifteen injured in the accident, hardly an explosive story in a country where some 30,000 people were murdered each year, and yet it eclipsed the political obituary of the world's best-known Boer. The editorial decision said something about the politically correct priorities of the 'new' SABC. It also highlighted how De Klerk had shrunk in the public eye.

His departure was not mourned. He left whites struggling to see if they could adjust to the changes with any more success.

⋀⋀⋀⋀

There is no shortage of depressing case studies of Afrikaners who have failed to make the grade in the new South Africa. The tale of Benjamin de Kok is a classic case. For over a decade he ran a successful plumbing business until shortly after the April 1994 election when his bakkie was stolen with all his tools. With his experience he was swiftly taken on as a plumber's mate, but the job did not last because his face or rather skin did not fit. Four years after the 'rainbow revolution' he was to be found each night outside a café just round the corner from my Johannesburg home, parking cars for a few pounds a day as part of a thriving new security co-operative for the unemployed.

'As soon as the darkies took power I knew things would change. But I didn't know how quick it would be. My boss needed more black faces to win the right contracts. He could also pay them less. What chance did I have?'

De Kok's story had resonance across white South Africa as Mandela's government started to try to redress the divided past. Day in day out his gaunt unshaven face hovered in the shadows. A few months before I met him his wife had been made redundant after twenty-five years as a bank clerk. He said he could not afford a night off if they were to pay their rent. His humiliation was absolute.

'And it is so embarrassing. I see on the street people I went to school with, with nice houses and cars. And here I am walking the streets. I hide my head and hope they don't see me.'

There have always been poor whites in South Africa. One of the misconceptions about Afrikanerdom was that all whites became rich under apartheid and joined the middle class. Many blacks freely admit how shocked they were to see poor whites, until they reminded themselves that they had been brainwashed by the 'system' to assume whites were rich and blacks poor. But under apartheid if you had a white skin it was hard not to thrive. For many there was a job for life. The National Party implemented the ultimate 'affirmative action' scheme for Afrikaners. The deal was simple. You voted 'Nat' and you joined the club. If there was no room in the civil service or the post office you could try the railway. If you tired of the army there was always room in the police. Horrified as they would have been by the parallel, the Afrikaners were merely behaving like other dominant élites in the rest of Africa. But post-1994 the boot was on the other foot as the ANC introduced its own far-reaching programme to uplift its own supporters.

There is a reassuring precedent for the Afrikaners. In the aftermath of the Boer War they looked doomed to a shadowy life as inferior citizens under British rule. They had lost the war. More than 20,000 women and children had died in British concentration camps. Their farms had been razed to the ground. Even their culture and language were under threat from English. The tale of Afrikaner boys standing in corners derided as dunces because they could not speak English resounds through the collective Afrikaner memory.

And yet the spirit of the *kakiebos* won the day; the Afrikaners learned to adapt and then counter-attack. The British aided the recovery by opting for magnanimity rather than triumphalism. In the post-war settlement which led to the Act of Union of 1910 the Afrikaners were accorded the same citizen rights as the smaller group of English-speaking whites. But the main factor in the Afrikaners' fightback was the perseverance of their leaders, a burning community spirit and a determination never again to be humbled.

Once in power in 1948, the Nationalists took pride in bringing hundreds of thousands of their people into the cities, where they were educated and rescued from the poverty and discrimination their forefathers had faced. This was in tune with the communitarian spirit of the continent. Just as the *voortrekkers* had circled the wagons until trouble passed, so black township residents rallied together to survive the worst of apartheid. Many Afrikaner civil servants still beat their breasts

about being the first generation away from the breadline. 'Pik'
Botha, who was the world's longest-serving foreign minister,
told me that winning a place in the foreign service as a young
man was one of the proudest moments in his long career.

During the years of apartheid's cosseting, however, the Afrikaners' sense of community seems to have waned. On the
outskirts of Johannesburg's city centre lies the domain of the
white-collar poor. Shabby bungalows jostle dingy apartment
blocks. It is here that you can find Florida Park caravan site. In
the heyday of white rule it was a stop-off for Afrikaners on their
way from the veld to the coast. Post-1994 it became a permanent home for poor whites. Amber van Wyk took up residence
there when she finally gave up the battle to pay the £200 a
month rent for her flat. For twenty years she had worked as a
supermarket supervisor. She resigned when her husband retired
to live off his pension, but he died a few months later and she
could not find work. She smiled when asked why her two sons,
a security guard and a mechanic, did not help. 'They are too
busy with their own families and you know what daughters-in-
law are like . . .'

Everyone knows everyone in Johannesburg's teeming black
townships, but in Florida Lake shame and suspicion hold sway.
'I don't know my neighbours,' added Mrs van Wyk. 'We tend
to keep ourselves to ourselves.' Sheltering behind a rickety
caravan I came across Sara, who was unwilling to give her
surname, sunning herself on a white plastic chair outside her
new home. 'I am always here,' she chuckled. 'It's nice, don't
you think?' Her Jimmy had been made redundant four years
earlier after more than thirty years on the railways. 'He was
such a hard worker. He never took off one day. He's just fifty-
one and he may never get another job. It's been a terrible
shock.' She broke off to call him to put his own case. There was
a pause followed by a mumbled reply. 'If you don't mind, he'd
rather not see you,' she explained. 'He seldom goes outside.
He's so ashamed.'

It is easy enough to paint a fairly bleak picture of life for
whites in the future. The suburban nightmare of maids and

gardeners walking through the front door and demanding the keys to the car soon faded as blacks proved, as they had always insisted, that they were not seeking revenge but merely wanted a fair chance. As the months have passed, however, so inevitably the old white certainties have crumbled amid a dawning realization that a revolution has taken place.

A far-reaching programme of reverse discrimination threatens the job prospects of future white generations. The spread of South Africa's appalling levels of criminal violence from the black townships into formerly white areas has led to a siege mentality in suburbia. White farmers were among the worst hit: 400 were murdered in the four years after De Klerk handed over power. Official statistics indicated the national rate of murder dropped slightly after the end of white rule, but that was no consolation for those living in terror of every knock at the door. The rule of law does not run far in much of the continent; Africa at the end of the twentieth century is as prone to eruptions of unrest and war as it ever was. The violence that blights South African society has rekindled the old white fears that black equals barbaric and bad. According to official statistics about 10,000 whites a year, mainly professionals, emigrated during Mandela's presidency, but many more are thought to have left unannounced. The inevitable temptation among the vast body of whites, and not just those who voted for apartheid, is to wallow in defeatism and blame the ANC.

Wilhelm Verwoerd, the grandson of the architect of apartheid, Dr Hendrik Verwoerd, is profoundly depressed about the Afrikaner mindset. He is a philosophy lecturer at Stellenbosch University, which was once the intellectual home of Afrikanerdom. He is married to an ANC MP and is not on speaking terms with most of his family but still has close contact with the traditional wing of the *volk*. We met during the honeymoon period of the first two years when many whites were still congratulating themselves on having avoided the abyss. But Verwoerd was already convinced that many Afrikaner Nationalists were willing the new South Africa to fail so their doom and gloom prophecies could be proven right.

'It's foolish, misguided and offensive but understandable because if the new order works then their vision is finally undermined. Afrikaner culture is more fluid than the right-wingers like to make out. If people can move out of their skins, experiment, take risks, then there is hope. But just as trekking is a prominent part of the Afrikaner myth, so is the *laager*. If you can't trek, you huddle behind the wagons, and that is what they are doing.'

For many whites the solution is clear: it is back to the days of the bitter almond hedge. With its temperate, very 'un-African' climate and its European feel, Cape Town is increasingly being seen by whites as a last bastion. Throughout the Nineties there was a steady stream of whites moving south from Johannesburg back to the very city whence many of their ancestors had first trekked.

The geographical symbolism was stark: Cape Town clings on to the toe of the continent just as the end of white rule left whites feeling they were scrambling to maintain a foothold in Africa. When the city was making an abortive bid for the 2004 Olympics, a powerful anti-lobby warned of the dangers of blacks heading south from all over the continent looking for jobs.

'The Cape is to South Africa what Belgium was to the Belgian Congo,' one senior Nationalist MP confided. It was an analogy that he would not have dared to make before the April 1994 election.

𝀝𝀝𝀝𝀝

The post-colonial history of Africa does not make positive reading for South Africa's white tribes, at least not for those who want to play an active part in political life. If South Africa is to develop the robust democracy the ANC says it wants, then it has to be prepared to let white politicians and critics have their say. But with memories of apartheid's injustices so recent and racial inequities so starkly apparent, the race card will for the forseeable future play well with voters. The road may even lead to Zimbabwe or Kenya, where, as Richard Leakey knows all too well, whites are expected to stay out of politics unless they are prepared to take the government line. Three years after he founded the opposition party, Safina, he returned to his old job as director of Kenya's Wildlife Service, tacitly acknowledging that he could do more for Kenya in conservation than in politics.

Ian Smith, who led white Rhodesia into its unilateral declaration of independence, readily concedes that his old enemy, President Robert Mugabe, has to be congratulated for swallowing his resentment at the dour old white reactionary whose intransigence prolonged the civil war at a cost of thousands of lives. He resides in a nondescript bungalow with the front door always on the latch, alongside – of all ironies – the Cuban Embassy. But whenever there is a political or economic crisis, 'Smithie' and other whites are the first to face Mr Mugabe's spleen. It was seen as no coincidence that Smith's farm was one of those earmarked for confiscation in the first draft of a controversial land reform scheme to transfer property to landless blacks.

The ANC attests the liberal sprinkling of whites in its National Executive, the party's inner circle, as a riposte to critics who claim that the days of white politics are over. Three of the most important ministers in Mandela's government were white ANC members. But it is hard to see a white holding one of the top government posts in the first few decades of the twenty-first century. There is a defensive current in the party that fears that appointing a white to a key ministry would be an admission of defeat. Moreover, the real test of the ANC's commitment to non-racial politics will come in its attitude to white opponents.

As the euphoria of liberation faded and the problems inevitably mounted for the ANC, some of them followed the hoary old tack of other newly independent African states and started to brand white criticism as racist, reactionary and *ergo* irrelevant. Outside the Western Cape, where it controlled the provincial government, the National Party required little kicking as its plodding style, born of years in government, was easily brushed aside. Under De Klerk's successor, Marthinus van Schalkwyk, a colourless party hack, the National Party plummeted from

20 per cent of the vote in 1994 to 6.9 per cent in 1999. The handful of MPs from the Democratic Party, the Nationalists' old liberal rival from the days of white-only politics, assumed their old role and became the ANC's most trenchant critics. The DP was repeatedly repudiated as élitist and white, in a sign that its attacks had hit home. Tony Leon, its pugnacious leader, relished the cut and thrust, and, at the expense of the Nationalists, increased the DP's share of the vote from 1.7 per cent in 1994 to almost 10 per cent in 1999. But with its white 'European' image the DP may never be able to break out of the suburbs and win enough non-white votes to become a genuinely national party.

And yet the gloomy and paranoid views to be heard from both Afrikaners and English-speakers do not always reflect the reality. The white man in Africa may be destined for an apolitical role, but that does not mean he is doomed. For most whites, life five years into the 'new' South Africa was little changed. As De Klerk says in his autobiography: 'The golf courses [in Pretoria] remained busy with peak activity on Wednesday afternoons and over the weekends. In the country-club lounges the ladies continued to play bridge and sip tea and sometimes gin and tonic.'[4] Beyond the paranoid dinner table talk in white households, there are tentative signs of a metamorphosis unfolding as many whites are slowly adapting. It is, in the words of a prominent Afrikaner academic, or at least can be, 'surrender without defeat'.[5]

Tim du Plessis, the deputy editor of *Beeld*, the leading Afrikaans newspaper, is wrily confident the Afrikaner will not only cope but may even prosper. He believes there is a spirit of subservience that runs through the Afrikaner psyche that may help them to adapt more easily than white English-speakers, many of whom hoped to go on living to the same rules as their relatives and friends did in Western Europe – a perfectly justifiable but wholly unrealistic expectation.

'Once we Afrikaners can overcome racism and bigotry we will slip easily into the African way of thinking,' he told me. 'The Afrikaners are used to defending corruption and bigotry in the old government. They will easily adapt to the inefficiencies of the new.'

When a group of right-wingers launched a white 'homeland' east of Pretoria they claimed that kindred spirits would come flocking from all over the country. The headquarters was a farm called 'Loneliness'. In the valley below, just visible through the trees, was a cemetery of Boers, mainly women and children, who died in a British concentration camp at the turn of the century. The founding ceremony was brimming with Old Testament rhetoric. But it was very much the soft underbelly of separatism. The 'homeland' was a 400-acre co-operative whose modest aims showed how aspirations for a homeland had withered. The founders shied clear of talk of independence. Taxes would still be paid. Most of the members would be weekenders.

'A republic? Oh no,' said Andries Campher, a bearded farmer who organized the project. 'This is a place for like-minded people.'

The Rand Afrikaans University (RAU), a modern red-brick sprawl on the edge of Johannesburg's city centre, epitomizes new Afrikaner pragmatism. The university was founded by the *Broederbond* as an Afrikaner academic beachhead in the English-speaking world of mines and business. Professor J. C. van der Walt, the university's post-apartheid rector, is determined RAU will retain its Afrikaner ethos, but to do that he is convinced it has to embrace the new order, that in order to survive it has to learn when to fight and when to give ground.

Defying precedent and the advice of some of his colleagues, he travelled to Soweto and forged a link with the township's premier football club, the Kaizer Chiefs. When America's black Howard University sent a delegation to South Africa looking for a twin, the delegation's ground rule was to ignore Afrikaners. They had not reckoned with the rector, who intercepted them midway in their schedule, gave them a guided tour of his campus and ended up signing a twinning agreement.

'You see the image of the granite Verwoerdian is not correct,' he said. 'We Afrikaners are very adaptable. The coming of the new dispensation has for many of us been a huge relief.'

On the other end of the social spectrum, Frans Campher long ago stopped expecting government largesse. He started work with Ben de Kok as a freelance security guard soon after the 1994 election. His scarred and short-cropped head hardly mark him out as a man of enlightenment and yet his experiences suggest that a new co-operative spirit can take root.

'Soon after I came here, this guy Alan dumped a whole load of blacks here and told them to park cars. We had to fight them and we did. We chased them off. But then they started to come back in ones and twos. Last night there were three of them in my street desperate for work. I told them I don't want to fight. So we divided the street in two and we each took one side . . .'

Most whites who matured under apartheid will probably never again feel that South Africa is their country. The new black élite will be tolerated but despised. The first decade or so of the twenty-first century will probably be marked by racial disputes as Mandela's spirit of reconciliation gives way to a more confrontational administration under his successor, Thabo Mbeki. Four years into the 'new' South Africa he gave warning that whites and blacks were two separate nations, accused whites of having done nothing to redress the situation, and warned them of a growing 'rage among millions of people'. But as long as the ANC is prepared to curb its frustration at the 'lack of white reciprocity' and the racism which still underpins most whites' world-view, and as long as it resists the temptation to use whites as scapegoats for its own mistakes, a new generation of white South Africans may emerge who feel part of their country.

Nearly 300 miles west of Johannesburg, the small town of Vryburg is tailor-made for an Afrikaner backlash. White free-booters founded it as the capital of a short-lived republic in the mid-nineteenth century. Two years after the high school uneasily opened its doors to non-white pupils, armoured cars were trundling through its streets to keep the peace, and it was tempting to conclude that little had changed since those anarchic times. The trouble began when scores of black pupils demonstrated to protest at the expulsion of five classmates who had been sent home for disrupting classes. For the white parents that was enough, and they set upon black pupils with rawhide whips. It was ugly confrontational politics, reviving memories of the bad old days. Brendan Gous, the head boy, was, however, unconcerned, relations would improve.

'The past still runs deeply through us. We don't mix. We don't want to be friends; we don't want to be enemies; we just don't want contact. But my little brother will be fine. Young children don't have memories.'

⁂

Not all Afrikaners felt able to leave the *laager*. Some opted to confront Africa as in the early days of whites on the continent, although with mixed results as I was to see in a small town court where Eugene Terre'Blanche, the white extremist, was sentenced for attempted murder. But one who it seems has been liberated is the man who brokered the end of white rule in Africa, F.W. De Klerk. He disappeared from view after his resignation for five months, until unexpectedly he issued a statement to the South African news agency. Coming from such a strait-laced and conventional man, it made extraordinary reading. 'I have fallen in love with another woman. It all started a number of years ago. Both of us tried to prevent the present situation. Part of this was not to see or even talk to each other for a period of years . . .'

The statement hinted at a Titanic struggle within his Calvinist soul. There were echoes of a favourite theme of white South African novels – forbidden love. In this instance, however, the passion was not for a woman of different race but for a foreigner: De Klerk's paramour was the wife of a Greek shipping magnate.

To traditionalists Elita Georgiades was hardly a fitting match for a leader of the *volk*; the admission of adultery was beyond the pale. But modernizers were able to hail this as another step away from the past. The last of the Afrikaner leaders had been able to shed the hypocritical morality of his upbringing and come clean.

6

White Man's Magic

Eugene Terre'Blanche – Militants and Mercenaries

The Mercedes skidded to a halt in the centre of the amphitheatre. The doors swung open and four young white women in
neatly pressed designer khakis threw themselves on the ground.
In the moonlight you could just see their faces taut with anger
and fear. In a flurry of Afrikaans commands two went down on
their knees behind the passenger doors and pointed their revolv-
ers into the shadows. Their muzzles quivered in the direction of
the squat totalitarian outline of the Voortrekker Monument,
Afrikanerdom's holiest shrine; their imagined black attackers
were at bay. The clear night air resounded to the cheers of the
spectators who had gathered in their thousands in the amphitheatre in the lee of the monument to have their myths
reinforced and their ardour fuelled. They would not go home
disappointed.

There are few more emotive images in Africa than the white
man with his gun. For Africans it stirs barely healed memories
of subjugation and fear, conjuring up stories of Henry Stanley
shooting his way through the Congo jungle for King Leopold of
Belgium, or Cecil Rhodes' pioneers annexing the lands of the
Shona and Ndebele. Ever since the battle of Blood River on 16
December 1838, when the muskets of a band of trekkers and
their black retainers annihilated a vastly superior Zulu army, the
message has been clear: the white man's magic will win the day.

If you are white, however, the image has a very different
resonance. The gun has long symbolized safety and civilization,

it is all that keeps the barbarians from the gate. Stanley and Rhodes were dogged and determined adventurers who let nothing stand in their way to open up the continent. The battle of Blood River was a victory of right over wrong, Christianity over barbarism, avenging the fate of their leader Piet Retief and some seventy fellow trekkers who were impaled at the royal Zulu enclosure as they tried to wheedle a concession of land. The savagery of Retief's end represents starkly the fear that many whites continue to live with in Africa. The victors handed down from father to son the tale of how King Dingane, Shaka's successor, uttered the fateful words 'bulala abathakhathi' (kill the wizards). Zulus, however, remember Retief as a confidence trickster who came seeking their land and was only just kept from annexing a chunk of their kingdom by a timely spilling of blood.

The myth of the white man with his gun endured even as Africans displayed astonishing bravery in defying the logic of science, or more pertinently the bullets of the Martini Henry rifle and the Maxim gun. At the battle of Isandhlwana in January 1879 Zulus armed with spears, rawhide shields and phenomenal courage outmanoeuvred and annihilated an entire British column in one of the Empire's heaviest defeats in the Victorian era. Zimbabweans still mark the Ndebeles' victory over Major Allan Wilson's advance patrol across the Shangani River. The Ashanti fought long and hard to keep the British at bay in the Gold Coast in the 1890s. But these successes were short-lived and hard-won.

The tide turned a little in the twentieth century as Africans proved able and willing to take on the white man, and latterly with his own weaponry too. The Mau Mau rising in Kenya in the 1950s, the anti-colonial wars in the Portuguese colonies and the rape and murder of white nuns in the Congo in the Sixties, and most of all the liberation war against the white Rhodesian government in the Seventies, shifted the balance of fear. Successive waves of white refugees fleeing to South Africa from black rule in the rest of the continent, the Belgians from the Congo in the Sixties, the Portuguese from Angola and Mozambique in

the Seventies, and Rhodesians from Zimbabwe in the early
Eighties, reinforced the convictions handed down from the Boer
trekkers. But the symbol of white might was still pre-eminent.

South African forces supporting Savimbi were checked in
Angola in the Eighties only when they met a superior Cuban
force. France regularly sent troops to former colonies to support
its allies and puppets. Belgian and American forces at different
times restored the status quo in Mobutu's Zaire. In the starkest
example of all, in nearly thirty years of the 'struggle' the ANC's
armed wing inflicted barely a pinprick on South Africa's white-
led army. It was with such memories and traditions at the back
of their mind that the four Afrikaner Amazons were practising
their 'anti-ambush' routine.

Built as the totem of Afrikaner Nationalism to mark the
centenary of Blood River, the Voortrekker Monument is white
Africa's equivalent of a Roman triumphal column. Its stark
profile is visible thirty miles away across the veld. The marble
friezes which line the interior are as uncompromising as the
rocky hillside on which it stands looking out over Pretoria. The
panels show trekkers heading into the unknown with their
ox-wagons, the slaughter of Piet Retief's advance party, the
massacre of their women and children at Weenen, the place
of weeping, and finally the whites' revenge at Blood River with
mounds of dead Zulus lying in front of victorious Boers giving
thanks to God.

Under apartheid, every 16 December thousands of Afrikaner
Nationalists gathered at the monument to mark the 'covenant'
that the victors at Blood River were said to have made with
God. In its early years the occasion had a religious intensity that
hinted at the Afrikaners' need for historical props for their
young nation, and also at the tortured complexity of their
emotions for Africa, a love-hate relationship for a continent
which they felt part of and yet which they also feared and
despised. The climax comes on the stroke of midday when a ray
of sunlight arches through a specially designed hole in the roof
and comes to rest on the holy of holies, the trekkers' cenotaph.

By the early Nineties the 'Day of the Covenant' had been

hijacked by the militant white right wing in their desperation to turn back the clock and rekindle the spirit of the days when whites ruled Africa and blacks knew their place. The ceremony became an opportunity for a crude display of white supremacism and militancy by the neo-Nazi *Afrikaner Weerstandsbeweging* (Afrikaner Resistance Movement). As the 'Valkyries' skidded across the grass stage of the monument's amphitheatre on 15 December 1993, the eve of the last 'Day of the Covenant' under white rule, the AWB leaders were determined to send a message that white power was not a spent force.

Buoyed up by the spectators' full-throated applause, the four 'armed avengers' were heading for the shadows when their car stalled. Keen to prove their versatility they jumped out and started to push, with the exception of the most buxom of them, who got stuck in one of the doors. She was still straining to join her companions when the car lurched into life and spluttered into the shadows dragging her, half in and half out, in its wake.

The AWB had struggled to be taken seriously ever since its foundation in the basement of a garage in 1973. With its eye-catching uniforms and clownish units, including an Underwater Commando and an airborne squadron, it smacked more of pantomime than paramilitary politics. Even the *Ystergarde* (Iron Guard), its most disciplined unit, was hard to take seriously. They marched into the amphitheatre after the women had departed, with military precision. With their black uniforms and cap badges they had unpleasant echoes from Europe in the 1930s; their namesake, Romania's pre-war fascist movement, led bloodthirsty pogroms of Jews. But many of the sombre traditionalists in the audience struggled to remain straight-faced as the *Ystergarde* began a display of high kicks and mock karate chops. These were not the descendants of the white pioneers who had hacked their way through the bush. They were the usual rabble of social outcasts and misfits who are seduced by fascism – some indeed were neo-Nazis from Europe – and their cameo display was patently light entertainment intended for the television cameras.

But a hush descended on the stadium when the *leier* (leader) strutted into view. Consummate performer that he is, Eugene Terre'Blanche, founder head of the AWB, gazed around him at the packed benches. Then, without notes, he launched into an apocalyptic diatribe about the 'horrors' of black rule. He had long contended he was born for war. He was christened Eugene Ney after the Napoleonic general whose reckless bravery so nearly won Waterloo. He closed with a choking pledge to fight black rule, with, if necessary, the last breath in his voluminous body.

'Mandela does not want peace,' he bellowed. 'He wants war. If he wants war, he'll get it. No government can govern without the Boers. No government can govern without God. The Afrikaners have been asked: who would you rather have? Jesus Christ from Blood River or Barabbas from Robben Island? The people have chosen Jesus Christ . . .'

Throughout his career Terre'Blanche had been regularly written off as a loud-mouthed bully and buffoon. He fell off his mount, a large black stallion, at one public rally, shattering his pretensions to be the heir of the brilliant horsemen of the Boer commandos. He had a high-profile affair with a white newspaper columnist in a blow to his quest for the support of the Calvinist Afrikaner mainstream. And yet, even though his rants had little contact with reality, he posed a threat to a peaceful end of white rule in Africa.

With his flowing beard and powerful oratory he had an extraordinary presence. His fighting talk inspired right-wingers and confused conservatives all over South Africa. His voice ebbed and flowed with a sensitivity that was all the more remarkable given his bully-boy appearance. You had only to shut your eyes and ignore his racist vitriol to be swept away by the poetry of his language. I could understand how his admirers claimed he could read a telephone directory and bring his audience to tears.

⚱⚱⚱

In the best tradition of his Boer War idols, Terre'Blanche is a farmer's boy who can trace his origins back to early Afrikaner stock. His family is said to be descended from an Etienne Terre Blanche from Toulouse who is believed to have emigrated to South Africa in the 1760s as part of the Huguenot diaspora which infuses Afrikaner genes. The white supremacist sentiment for which the family is now best known may date back to this time, since the Terre'Blanches pointedly did not simplify their name to Terblanche, as did many others of the clan. Instead they treasured the distinctive 'white earth'.

Contrary to popular belief, the invocations of a heroic past which pepper Terre'Blanche's speeches do have a historical foundation. Terre'Blanche's grandfather was one of the 'Cape rebels', the Afrikaners who fought with the Boers in the Anglo-Boer War despite not living in one of the two Boer Republics. After the war he settled in a farm at Ventersdorp, a typically drab souless Transvaal small town, eighty miles north-west of Johannesburg. It was there that he raised Terre'Blanche's father, who was to become an army colonel, and it was there that E.T., as the AWB leader is known, was born in 1941.

E.T.'s interest in politics is said to have started at an early age in Ventersdorp, where he was chairman of the high school debating society, founded his own cultural organization, *Jong Afrikanerharte* (Young Afrikaner Hearts), and was also captain of the school's first rugby fifteen. The combination of leadership roles, academic, cultural and sporting, was a sure route to success in the heady era of Afrikaner nation-building. In those days of jobs for each and every Afrikaner it was merely a matter of deciding which ladder to climb, and Terre'Blanche opted for the police, a fruitful soil for his incipient right-wing beliefs.

He soon rose to serve in the bodyguard of John Vorster, South Africa's hardline prime minister between the assassination of Verwoerd in 1966 and 1978, when he had to resign in a political scandal. Terre'Blanche's aides play down the claim that E.T. had high-level connections and say he merely served with the special cabinet protection unit. Whatever, by the time E.T. left the force in the late Sixties he would have made some useful contacts for his later career.

Terre'Blanche was also chairman of what many South

Africans would regard as the ultimate oxymoron – the Police Cultural Group. He acted in many police dramas. He tried his hand at writing poetry and historical plays, including one that was briefly a set text in white schools. He is even said to have won three awards from a conservative Afrikaans cultural foundation. These threads infused his rhetoric and style from the start of his career: as with so many extreme nationalist organizations, culture and history were the oxygen for the AWB. His supporters' sometime defence that he was merely a poet gained him little sympathy from any who had been following the Balkans descent into chaos: Radovan Karadžić, the leader of the Bosnian Serbs, was a published poet who long before the Bosnian war wrote an apocalyptic poem about Sarajevo in flames, a vision which his supporters were later to bring hideously to life.

The right wing's gain was the stage's loss. Terre'Blanche's sense of timing and his ability to vary his delivery make him a natural actor. From the moment he founded the AWB in the basement of a suburban garage his story took on the dimensions of a low-brow farce. His affair with Jani Allan, a leggy Johannesburg journalist, titillated South Africa when it emerged that they had been caught by the police late at night trying to break into the Paardekraal, another of Afrikanerdom's totems. The colourful details spread to Britain in 1992 when Channel 4 successfully defended a libel case against Ms Allan. Terre'Blanche became synonymous with his 'holey green underpants', which one of the witnesses told the court he had spied through a keyhole.

As Terre'Blanche blundered through these colourful episodes it was tempting to dismiss him as a Falstaffian character were it not for the vicious racist attacks by his supporters against blacks which had marked his rise to prominence, and also that South Africa was all too fertile ground for his ideology. Afrikaner Nationalist extremists had long flirted with fascism. The *Ossewabrandwag* (Ox-Wagon Fire Guard) movement, which originated in the 1938 centenary commemoration of the Great Trek, openly backed Hitler in the Second World War. The support was partly motivated by anti-British feeling but also by an empathy for the Nazis' search for racial purity, anti-Semitism and quest for *lebensraum* (living space). Many OB members were interned by the government of Jan Smuts, and then went on to play an important role in National Party politics, among them the future prime minister, John Vorster. The AWB's clowning and violence were abhorred by the Afrikaner Nationalist mainstream, but the organization's views were shared by a significant white minority, even if few would have voted for them at the polls.

According to AWB mythology, E.T. and the six other founding members met on 7 July 1973. The date – the seventh day of the seventh month in the seventh decade of the century – is significant. The organization likes to claim that its sinister mock swastika symbol is in fact a cross of three sevens designed as the ultimate Christian symbol to counter the triple-six sign of the devil. The rationalization is typical of the schoolboy ethos of the organization. It did little but bicker and dream until 29 March 1979, when it exploded to the forefront of right-wing politics.

The spark was none other than the 'Day of the Vow'. By 1979 there was a growing strain of revisionist Afrikaner thinking which maintained that the vow was not a binding covenant but had been artificially revived at the turn of the century when Afrikaners were looking for an identity. Professor F.A. van Jaarsveld, a historian at Pretoria's University of South Africa, was the leading advocate of this thinking, and in March 1979 published an article arguing that it was illogical to claim divine intervention in wars. He also proposed the question that Afrikaners should ask themselves whose side God had been on when the Zulus massacred Piet Retief and his trekkers.

A few days later the professor was elaborating the ideas at a lecture in the university when Terre'Blanche led more than twenty young men through the hall to the podium. Taking the microphone he said the 'Boer' people could never stand by and

watch the desanctification of a holy day. His men then threw a
bucket of municipal tar over Van Jaarsveld and coated him in
feathers.

The horrific incident resounded through white and indeed
black South Africa. The belief that the white man could still
have his way in Africa had won a new lease of life. The AWB
claimed in the Eighties a membership of thousands. Despite
their caperings, no one dared dismiss them as a spent force.
They were known to have sympathizers in the upper ranks of
the army and police, as became starkly clear in June 1993, when
hundreds of them rampaged through the World Trade Centre,
the conference hall outside Johannesburg where politicians were
negotiating the post-apartheid settlement.

Spearheaded by an armoured vehicle which crashed through
the building's plate glass façade, they took over the negotiating
chamber. Police stood by and watched, awaiting instructions
that never came as delegates took refuge in a locked office. It
was a meeting of the old white-run Africa with the new, of
country and town, of reaction with reform. The escalators which
moments earlier had been thronged by dark-suited politicos
were packed with men in khaki and hobnailed boots, crunching
broken glass, singing triumphal chants. They clearly felt they
had done nothing wrong, on the grounds that they were white
and the law did not apply to them. Laying down their weapons
they reached for their picnic bags and celebrated their triumph
with a barbecue in the conference hall grounds.

Their bubble burst only just before the April 1994 election.
It happened in, of all places, one of the tribal homelands which
were an integral part of the apartheid dream.

⋔⋔⋔

I missed the last skirmish of white Africa by a few minutes. It
was 11 March 1994 and a force of several thousand white right-
wingers had assembled at an airport hangar on the outskirts of
Mmabatho, the capital of Bophuthatswana. The homeland was
as absurd in its layout as in its name. With its disparate chunks
of territory scattered in the north-west of South Africa it

looked as if an apartheid cartographer had thrown ink at a map. Mmabatho made no more sense, with its giant floodlit stadium, a parliament and a shopping centre in the middle of the bush. But there was nothing farcical about the countdown to the battle of Bop, as the last 'stand' of the white right became known.

The right-wingers had been invited by Lucas Mangope, the president of Bophuthatswana, to shore up his crumbling pseudo-state against the escalating street protests of thousands of his subjects, many of whom were demanding immediate incorporation into South Africa and the right to campaign for the election. Officially the right-wingers would bring Mangope's capital under control before retiring across the 'border' to the farms and small towns whence they had come. But their mission posed the greatest threat to the 'new' South Africa since the release of Mandela four fraught years before. Many of the right-wingers were experienced soldiers or members of the citizen commando, South Africa's territorials. If they decided to stay in Mmabatho, South Africa's negotiated settlement risked falling apart. The officer corps of the South African army abounded with right-wing sympathizers. It is far from clear that they would have moved against their former comrades. Their loyalties would have faced an even greater test if General Constand Viljoen, the right-wingers' commander, had urged them to stand aside: he was not only a soldier's soldier, he was also an Afrikaner's Afrikaner.

A latterday Cincinnatus, the retired Roman senator who returned from tilling his fields to save his embattled republic from barbarians, Viljoen had been called back from retirement on his farm to lead the Afrikaner *Volksfront*, a group of right-wing parties that included the AWB. His presence added a much-needed gravitas to the white right. The silver-haired diminutive general was a legendary former commander of the South African Defence Force who was famous for leading his men from the front in the bush war against the Cubans in Angola. In 1978 he joined a Parachute Battalion raid into an enemy outpost 160 miles inside Angola and had to be rescued by helicopter while the air force kept off encircling Cuban tanks. Two years later he was blown through the hatch of his armoured personnel carrier by a Soviet mine and walked away with a bad headache. His straight-talking ways and piercing blue eyes could and did win over the most ideological opponents to apartheid. Mandela himself always said he had a far better rapport with Viljoen than he did with De Klerk. They were more obvious soulmates as both had entered politics for a cause rather than as a career, but, notwithstanding all the talk of mutual admiration, both Mandela and the old Afrikaner war-horse forged the link as much because of strategy as sentiment and respect.

For Viljoen's followers the Bophuthatswana mission was just like the old days. Douw Steyn, a veteran of Angola, was to mobilize a force and assemble it at Mmabatho Airport. Then Colonel Jan Breytenbach, a former special forces commander with a reputation for daring exploits, would take over. He would link up with Mangope's small but well-equipped Bophu-thatswana Defence Force and restore order to the homeland. There was only one problem – what to do with the AWB?

When Mangope made his appeal for help he is said to have warned that his soldiers would mutiny if Terre'Blanche's racists took part. Viljoen himself had long ago left no doubt of his disdain for the AWB's fake decorations and racist bluster. He warned Terre'Blanche to keep his men out of the homeland. But it was too late. As soon as Mangope's request for assistance reached the *Volksfront* headquarters eager AWB members were broadcasting to their colleagues on the farm radio networks and telling them to mobilize.

As dawn broke on 11 March more than a hundred AWB diehards were cruising through the back-streets of Mmabatho and its satellite town, Mafikeng, in bakkies, trucks and family cars, hell-bent on trouble. They had driven through the night from farms and dorps all over South Africa. In their fevered minds the invasion of Bophuthatswana was in the spirit of the *bittereinders*, the Boers who went on fighting the British long after their leaders had surrendered. It was a stand against the ungodliness and Communism of black rule. It was also an excuse to get their own back on the new order. They would shoot a few blacks before returning home in time for a *braai*, too many beers, a drunken reminiscence and a long sleep before church the next morning. As *Beeld*, the main Afrikaans newspaper, reported with heavy irony the next day, for the AWB it was a '*kaffirskietpiekniek*' (a *kaffir*-shooting picnic).

Garbled reports that the AWB were on their way met scepticism in the casino where I was staying. In the heyday of apartheid, 'Bop' served a vital function for Afrikanerdom. As an 'independent' state it was free from the Calvinist prohibitions on gambling. Every Friday night the roads north and west from Pretoria would be clogged with civil servants going 'abroad' for a quick flutter. The Mmabatho Sun was built to cater for this demand. Little more than a swimming pool and a giant casino, it symbolized the tawdry reality of the grand apartheid vision. Indeed, the flashing lights of the one-armed bandits and the cheap fittings were, like the very concept of the homeland, intended to insulate visitors from reality. So the pre-dawn rumours of a right-wing invasion that roused me and other journalists from our beds seemed to many of us just another element of fantasy in a surreal half-world. But by dawn a band of thick-set white men with guns was visible at the front gate. A mile down the road in Mafikeng battle had already been joined.

The AWB were not expecting any serious resistance. They arrived assuming that the protesters would cringe and flee as, over the years, had so many of their farm-workers in their presence. In the process they would be taught a lesson they would never forget. Graeme Williams, a photographer friend, followed one breakaway convoy of a dozen vehicles and watched as a man in the rear car took careful aim at a black woman and shot her dead. Nothing epitomized more clearly the out-and-out cowardice of the AWB and the difference between them and professional soldiers like General Viljoen. Graeme was spotted, chased, beaten up and had his cameras smashed. He was lucky. If he had been black, he would almost certainly have been killed.

A few miles away on the outskirts of Mafikeng I was following a second AWB convoy when three troop carriers jammed with soldiers of the Bophuthatswana Defence Force rumbled past. They had, it seemed, mutinied against Mangope and were intent on repelling the AWB. On impulse we abandoned the second convoy and followed the armoured cars in the direction of the airbase on the edge of the town, where the right-wingers had assembled. And so it was that we missed the final showdown.

I gleaned the background to the swirl of events an hour or so later in, of all places, the Mmabatho Sun's poolside bar. The Africa of Evelyn Waugh's novels remains an astonishingly accurate guide to how the continent works. In the most chaotic of situations there is often a businessman or spy, monitoring and manipulating events, and privy to the inside story – just as in *Scoop*, where a mysterious financier provides a chapter-and-verse account of the upheaval in the fictional Ishmaelia. The challenge is to find such characters and persuade them to talk.

The key to the Mmabatho imbroglio was a British-born Bophuthatswana intelligence officer who had left London for Africa in the Sixties in search of adventure after seeing an advertisement for Rhodesia's British South Africa Police, and never returned. He lived in a small suburban house in the backstreets, a slight greying professorial figure. He was known to old friends as the 'Plato of the *platteland*' as he liked to read philosophy in his spare time. Mmabatho was his last post after more than three decades monitoring regional security matters for various bosses.

In the measured tones that he no doubt used for post-mortems of his wife's latest hand of bridge, the obsession with which she whiled away long hours in southern African towns, my source explained that Mangope was cowering in a country estate on the border with Botswana, Terre'Blanche had backed down, the AWB were on their way out of town, the main body of the right-wingers was leaving Bop following the mutiny of the Bop soldiers, and South African units were preparing to take over the homeland. Everything he said that afternoon was later proved accurate. The only insight I had to 'trade' was a second-hand account of the critical encounter of the day. It was not much of a swap. A few hours later it was on the national television news.

Even as I had decided to follow the armoured cars of the Bop Defence Force, the AWB were pulling out of the airbase bound for home following a bitter argument with General Viljoen's commanders. One of the convoys of about twenty vehicles made a final foray through the back-streets, and as it sped past Mafikeng police station shooting broke out. It is not clear who fired first. But the final car in the convoy, a light blue Mercedes, slewed to a halt in a volley of shots.

The front passenger door opened and the dead body of Nic Fourie, an AWB 'general', slithered to the ground. The driver, Alwyn Wolfaardt, a mechanic from the conservative northern town of Naboomspruit, was the caricature Boer of schoolbooks, six feet five inches tall, with a flowing brown beard. One of his ancestors, Pieter Jordaan, had been impaled with Piet Retief. He had been raised on an undiluted diet of anti-Communist rhetoric and Boer nationalism. Now his worst nightmares had come true. He lay face down in the dust pleading for an ambulance as his close friend, Fanie Uys, lay propped against the side of the car bleeding from his hip.

An angry crowd gathered screaming *'bulala amabhulu'* (kill the Boers), in a subconscious echo of the fateful command uttered by Dingane. As journalists interviewed the two Afrikaners, a young black policeman strode through the throng and shot Uys in the head. Swivelling, he walked up to Wolfaardt and shot him twice. Then he thrust his rifle in the air in triumph and kicked the dead bodies. This time there would be no Blood River.

The 'ifs' of history are manifold in a country with a past as littered with murders and assassinations as South Africa. Would apartheid have moved in a different direction if Verwoerd had not been stabbed to death by a deranged parliamentary messenger? Would Steve Biko, the inspirational black consciousness leader, have led South Africa if he had not been killed in police custody? Would Chris Hani, the charismatic Communist Party leader, have inherited Mandela's presidency if he had not been gunned down by a Polish right-winger in April 1993? These are questions for historians, but the last high-profile killing of the 'old' South Africa gave rise to no such debate.

With his three shots the Bop policeman had spun the old legend on its head. He was the *baas*. He, the black man, had the gun and it was the turn of the white man to cringe in the dust. The lingering remnants of the white man's African fantasy had been laid to rest.

The incident had been captured on camera and the news spread across the veld like a forest fire. I gave an Afrikaner teenager a lift back to Johannesburg. His father had taken part in the assault and he had briefly 'gone along for the ride'. He said the farm radio network was humming with tales of dozens of dead Afrikaners and that local hospitals were brimming with their wounded. His stories I later ascertained were untrue. The hospitals were full but with blacks, of whom as many as fifty were killed, not whites. The only Afrikaners to die were the three at the crossroads. But my young hitch-hiker believed the rumours and was appalled. He would not dabble in insurrection again.

Ironically, if Terre'Blanche had managed to keep his cadres out of the homeland, the end of white rule might have been far bloodier. But the AWB's behaviour and the bloodshed appalled many of the conservative and God-fearing Afrikaners who were still allied to the right-wing cause. A few hours after the fateful shots General Viljoen formed a splinter movement of the Afrikaner *Volksfront* and registered for the elections as the Freedom Front, recognizing that the only hope for the *bittereinders* lay in dialogue, not war.

Four days before the polls were due to open, Joy Brady, my

office assistant, was just starting to play the organ in Johannesburg's St Mary's Cathedral when a massive explosion shook the building. A bomb had exploded outside the ANC's headquarters a few streets away, killing nine people and injuring ninety-two. Ten more people were killed the following day when a bomb exploded in a taxi rank in the city's suburbs. Two days later, on the second day of voting, another bomb, potentially the most deadly of all, exploded just outside Jan Smuts International, as the city airport was then called.

The bombing campaign was a tragic postscript to white rule which reminded South Africa how close it had come to the abyss. In the heyday of white rule the bombers might have expected to reach a deal with sympathetic police officers. In a fascinating insight into the workings of the apartheid old-boy network, Koos Botha, a reformed right-winger who post-1994 'found' his black brethren and ran a housing project in a black squatter settlement, told me how in the early Nineties, after he exploded a bomb late one night in the deserted premises of a multi-racial school as a protest at the changes, the policeman appointed to investigate the case was an old school friend.

He met me at Jan Smuts airport as I flew in from Cape Town . . . And I said, 'Hey, Chris, what brings you here?' And he muttered that he had come to give me a lift home. And we were chatting away and I could see something was wrong, so I asked him what the matter was. He paused and said, 'Something terrible has happened, Koos. I have been asked to investigate you.' And I said, 'Oh don't worry. I don't mind a bit. Of course I did it.' And a huge smile spread across Danie's face and he slapped me on the back. 'You did? Ah. That's fantastic . . .' So we drove together to my home to work out what we were going to do.

Such was the old order. But a few hours after the airport bomb, as voters disregarded the threat and streamed to the polls, the police swooped and arrested more than thirty right-wingers including members of the *Ystergarde*. The days of white preferment were over as even Terre'Blanche would have to accept.

⋀⋀⋀⋀

'The *leier* will see you at Klerksdorp this weekend. Drive to the showground and wait for him there. He knows you are coming. He will make a sign when he is free.' Liaising with the AWB had long been a cross between dealing with a second-rate secret society and a royal court. Plans changed depending on the mood – and sobriety – of the *leier*. Terre'Blanche was the prima donna of white politics and had to be feeling like putting on his show. This time, however, the AWB spokesman was adamant. Terre'Blanche was due to address a rally to mark the 'Day of the Vow', which much to the AWB's outrage had been renamed the 'Day of Reconciliation'. He had, the spokesman insisted, an important message.

More out of curiosity than conviction that Terre'Blanche had anything to say, early that Saturday morning, eighteen months into the 'new' South Africa, I found myself parking my car beside half a dozen horses tethered to the stands of the Klerksdorp showground. The rapt expression on the face of the two lookouts left little doubt that E.T. was in full flow. In their late teens and wearing pale blue and grey camouflage shirts and khaki trousers they were staring through the stands with all thoughts of their duty forgotten.

As ever, he looked like a cross between an Old Testament prophet and a Boer commando leader. His booming voice was thundering warnings of the coming apocalypse as in his heyday when his rallies drew several thousand heavily armed supporters. But this was more like a weekend cultural get-together. The stands were less than half-full. There were barely 300 people, mainly farmers with pinch-faced wives and blue-eyed blond children in khaki drill. A few bourgeois types stood around uncomfortably in jackets and ties. The only enthusiasm came from the horses. Saddled up and ready for action, as if for a Boer War costume drama, they pranced up and down. As the final indignity, a storm broke halfway through Terre'Blanche's speech and his audience ran for cover.

At the height of his fame in the late Eighties E.T. was nicknamed 'Ramboer' when he jettisoned his beige safari suit, the *platteland* uniform, for designer fatigues. The sartorial shift came on the advice of his one-time lover, Jani Allan. Shortly before she was found with him trying to break into the Paarde-kraal she wrote about being impaled on 'the blue flames of his blow torch' eyes. Those fires were still blazing as I was ushered into his presence in December 1995. My strategy was simple. I would allow him a few minutes for the usual guff and then would ask him straight out whether it was not time for the AWB to stop its threats of war, and whether Mandela's recon-ciliatory approach had led him to modify his views on race. I never had a chance.

> You are not from Africa or South Africa. There is always silence before the storm. We are heading for total destruc-tion. If you know the history of Africa, a year or two after the black takeover comes the second revolution . . . and the reason is that Mr Mandela can never give all those beautiful things he promised to his electorate. We are organizing right now to meet that onslaught. We don't want to run as penniless refugees as white colonists did in the rest of Africa. Out of the chaos of smoke and disaster we will take a part of this land and keep it as a Third Boer Republic where we will reign and try our utmost to live in peace with our neighbours. The reins are falling out of Mandela's hands and the stallion is bucking harder and harder . . .

And so the stream of consciousness flowed on and on for more than twenty minutes, starting in a low growl and climaxing with a Pavarotti bellow. He broke off mid-sentence as he reached the 'historic' role of the Zulu. Rising to his feet he strode out of sight, muttering in Afrikaans to his colleagues. It was, explained one of his generals – a cheery fellow in a boiler suit who had come all the way from the Cape – the end.

I sat there for a few minutes pondering South Africa's good

fortune that Terre'Blanche's magnetism and oratory were inspired by bigotry and not more of a brain. It may be that the Afrikaner, for all his love of strong leadership, does not have the sentimental and romantic streak which allows a leader like E.T. to win votes. But it is easy to forget that he was for a time a player on the national stage. He was a buffoon, but then so, too, Hitler and the Nazis in their early days were derided by many Germans because of their thuggery and silly rituals. By moderating his aims and methods E.T. could have whipped up white conservatism into a potent force. As it was, however, in one of many ironies hastening the new era, it was Terre'Blanche who finally shattered the myth of the white man with his gun once and for all – or almost.

Against my expectation, just three weeks passed before I was next embroiled in a heated talk with men in khaki about the Voortrekker Monument. But I was several thousand miles from Klerksdorp in the heart of Sierra Leone, where a band of Afrikaner hired guns were fighting for a diamond concession. It was a scene that could have been lifted from the previous century and yet it also hinted at a way forward for Africa in the years ahead.

⋔⋔

'Jesus, Jesus, be a fence all around him every day. Jesus, we want you to protect him as he travels on his way.' The nine pupils at the Koidu Mission school kept their eyes fixed on the ground as they sang their haunting farewells to their headmaster. It is always sad when a much-loved teacher leaves a school, but the wrench is even harder when your school lies in the middle of a war and your only teacher is taking up a new post. I had had a dispiriting journey from Sierra Leone's capital, Freetown, a hundred miles to the west. I had come via the second town of Bo, where scores of villagers had had arms and legs chopped off in random attacks by armed bands. So it was all the more inspiring to see the schoolboys lined up and singing to their teacher in front of a blackboard, even if the timetable was months out of date.

The Catholic Church has a controversial record in Africa. Most notoriously priests in Rwanda exhorted the Hutu mobs in their slaughter of Tutsis. But in Koidu, a war-ravaged mining town in the heart of Sierra Leone, Father Andrew Mondeh was doing all he could to provide hope to a community which had plumbed the depths of despair. Since 1991 when Sierra Leone was invaded by a shadowy rebel movement led by a former corporal, Foday Sankoh, Fr Mondeh's pupils had sought refuge in the bush more times than they could remember, as rebels and government soldiers ('sobels' as they were dubbed by the war-weary population) took turns to loot and kill the very people they were claiming to liberate or defend.

Whenever the fighting slowed, Fr Mondeh led his flock from the bush and started again, as did the thousands of villagers who were lining the road in from the airstrip on my arrival, naked to the waist, digging with picks, shovels and their bare hands in the hope of finding the stone which would change their lives. Koidu was the capital of Kono, one of the richest and deadliest regions in the continent, a fifty-mile-square patch of bush where diamonds literally seeped from the soil.

I arrived on Fr Mondeh's last day. The following dawn he was due to catch a flight to Kenema, a southern town, on one of the dilapidated Dakotas owned by the Lebanese traders who controlled the diamonds. He wanted to say goodbye to his friends, so we walked down the rutted path from the mission towards Koidu's dilapidated main street, where we rejoined Simon, the town's taxi driver, who had brought me in from the airstrip in a doorless chassis held together by wire and string.

Fr Mondeh had an eclectic group of friends. We started with Abdul Karim Hassan, one of the leading diamond dealers, whose family had been in Sierra Leone since the 1950s, when his father joined an exodus from Lebanon to West Africa. Cross-legged in dark silk pajamas serving sweet flavoured coffee as if we were in the Levant, he was as incongruous as a colonial officer in a solar topee. But the Lebanese had lasted longer than the British because they had stayed out of politics and focused on business instead.

'We've been here for donkeys' years,' he said. 'Africans can't live without us and we can't live without them. You get used to their ways, the cassava leaves and palm oils and all that. There are risks, but we like it. It is our Phoenician blood.'

The Lebanese are bitterly resented in West Africa, like the Asian traders in East Africa, but they offer a vital service. In the Liberian capital, Monrovia, there are Lebanese who have lost a fortune several times in the cycles of chaos since war erupted in 1989, and yet still they come back. In Kono every morning, soldiers, lowly officials and villagers lined up outside the Lebanese stalls to haggle over the value of their latest find. Fr Mondeh was a regular visitor but he had other matters on his mind. He had the drive and enthusiasm to bring peace, but he needed the Lebanese to pay for it, and they did, weaving deals with the soldiers to keep the town and their businesses alive.

Major Augustine Kamara, the commander of the Koidu garrison, was next on our tour. His command post was more of a prison than a barracks as the people of Kono had successfully pleaded with him to keep his drunken soldiers off the streets. It took much of the afternoon to talk our way first in and then out of his gate, so the sun was setting and the Lebanese generators were roaring into life as we spluttered up the rocky outcrop that overlooked the town for the final call.

The car could not manage the incline so we walked the last few hundred yards to the compound of sturdy stone buildings that lined the hilltop. The British district commissioners had lived there in the colonial era. It required little imagination to picture them sipping their sundowners on the veranda with its magnificent view of the surrounding bush. After independence in 1961, it became home to expatriate staff from the Standard Bank. Now it was once again the headquarters of a 'governor general', or at least that is what expatriates in Freetown had dubbed the new man in charge.

We had come to see Fr Mondeh's 'African brother', a man who was worshipped as a saviour all the way to Freetown. He was known in Koidu as 'Colonel Rudolph', or more simply 'Sahr', the local name traditionally given to a first-born son. On the eastern horizon close to the border with Guinea you could just make out a granite pinnacle. It was the final post on an ancient diamond-smuggling route through the jungle. The Sierra Leoneans had long venerated it as a cradle of voodooism. As the shadows lengthened, it was just a smudge. But in the early morning its stark outline dominated the view. For Colonel Rudolph and his men it meant only one thing: they had dubbed it the Voortrekker Monument.

Colonel Roelf van Heerden – Rudolph was his nickname – was a wiry man with a close-cropped beard. Sitting on the veranda, leafing through papers and sipping a cup of tea, he was more than happy to admit the irony of his position. He had spent most of his adult life fighting to defend white minority rule. His CV read like a roll call of apartheid's special forces. In the Eighties he fought in *Koevoet* ('Crowbar'), the counter-insurgency unit, which spearheaded a ruthless anti-guerrilla campaign in Namibia and Angola. He also served in the Civil Co-operation Bureau (CCB), the military intelligence unit which specialized in political assassinations. The end of apartheid, he conceded, had left him high and dry: 'We were not very popular in the new way of thinking. The new guard wanted us out of the way' – not that, he added firmly, he had any regrets for what he did.

And yet the new era had also liberated him. He still did the same work, but financially, and in his view spiritually, his post-apartheid life was the most rewarding time of his career. Colonel Van Heerden was a mercenary, or rather, as he put it, a consultant. He was, he explained carefully, the senior operations commander for Executive Outcomes, the ultimate new-age security firm.

The end of the Cold War and the eclipse of white rule in South Africa spawned a new breed of African mercenaries. These are not the 'Dogs of War' of the days of Bob Denard and 'Mad' Mike Hoare. Instead they call themselves consultants, talk of contracts and the law and tout their trade in brochures from air-conditioned offices. Men like Van Heerden shudder at the thought of being the inheritors of the tradition of

Terre'Blanche. But in the iconography of the continent that is what they are. They are white men with guns using superior education, training and firepower to have their way over Africa. The only difference is that they are motivated not by ideology nor duty but by a bottom line.

Executive Outcomes was by far the most successful of these new outfits. Founded by South African veterans in 1989, EO began as a counter-intelligence consultancy, but developed into Africa's premier private army. It could call on a limitless supply of veterans following the end of apartheid. Not only did these include some of the world's most experienced bush-fighters but they also had a healthy incentive to do their job. With their backgrounds many would have spent their lives looking over their shoulders if they had stayed in South Africa. EO swiftly gained a reputation for going where no one else dared – and for winning its battles.

Legend has it that EO first came to the attention of Sierra Leone's government in November 1994, when Valentine Strasser, the young military ruler, read about them in *Newsweek*. The American news magazine had published an article about EO's success in Angola, where they had led the government forces to a series of victories against UNITA. The bumptious Strasser is said to have been hooked by the tale. He had taken power inadvertently in 1991, when as a young army captain he marched into State House with fellow junior officers to protest against the government and the head of state fled into exile presuming it was a coup. Since then Strasser had proved as incompetent and corrupt as his predecessor and had failed to halt the rebels' advance after their invasion in 1991, so when Western mining companies followed up the *Newsweek* article and promoted EO he was easily convinced. In May 1995 EO's first men arrived in Freetown, guaranteeing to restore order. In return they were to be given more than a million dollars a month and a fat mining concession in Kono for sister firms.

One hundred years ago EO's Sierra Leone contract would have passed without comment. The British Empire was effectively founded by the private armies of merchant adventurers.

When Robert Clive won much of India, he was fighting on behalf of the East India Company, not Whitehall. Cecil Rhodes' British South Africa Company operated in a similar way. He recruited a force of 'volunteers' to take over what was to become Rhodesia.

A hundred years later, however, a very different morality prevails. The word 'mercenary' conjures up images of the drunken Brits fighting in Angola under the incompetent and brutal leadership of Costas Georgiou, a Greek Cypriot former British army sergeant who posed as 'Colonel Callan' and was executed by the Angolan government in 1976 having been found guilty of murdering fourteen of his fellow mercenaries. As for white South African mercenaries, their background brands them as beyond the pale. Indeed, there was outrage in the West and in South Africa when the news leaked out that Van Heerden and his men were waging war in Sierra Leone. The South African parliament passed an anti-mercenary law prohibiting private security groups from basing themselves in South Africa, but unsurprisingly it had little effect. Sitting under the thatched canopy over his veranda Van Heerden ventured that the criticism was a little unfair.

'For me it seems our mission has been a great achievement,' he said. 'When we came, the rebels were five kilometres away and everyone had fled into the bush. Now the place is back to normal. Police work is not the main purpose we are here; we are here for business. But if we were not here where would all these people be – dead or in the bush? Last Christmas the government was struggling to pay our contract and a delegation of chiefs and businessmen came to see me and said they were busy collecting money and they would foot the bill. Why do people call us mercenaries? We are soldiers in a contract with a legitimate government. A mercenary is someone who supports whoever pays him. Definitely we do not do that.'

Fr Mondeh nodded vigorously throughout this short speech. After rolling back the rebels from the gates of Freetown in May 1995, EO's forces had turned their attentions to Kono, which was funding the rebels' war effort. With their overwhelming fire-power they swiftly drove the rebels into the bush and repulsed three counter-attacks at the cost of hundreds of rebel lives. Since then South African music had become Kono's unofficial anthem and could be heard blaring from tinny battery-powered ghetto-blasters along the main street. People waved and cheered as the colonel's jeeps rumbled past.

A few hours before my visit Van Heerden had been due to stand down as chairman of the Kono Community Committee, the unofficial town council, but in a public gathering chiefs, business-men and hundreds of residents had begged him to stay. In his taciturn way he was clearly pleased to be hailed for once as a saviour. 'They say we are fellow Africans who have come to save them – it is good to be putting something into our continent.'

It is right to be cynical about Van Heerden's hazy idea of post-apartheid redemption and his vision of a 'new African order' as was glossily trumpeted on EO brochures in its Pretoria headquarters. He and his kind do what they do best: fighting dirty bush wars. Scores, maybe hundreds, of civilians were killed in their helicopter attacks on the rebels' bush positions. All that matters is money, or rather minerals. EO's operations in Angola secured oil concessions for Heritage Oil and Gas, a British-owned company with close links to the South Africans. In Sierra Leone the beneficiary was Branch Energy, a Hampshire-based affiliate of Heritage. The firm regularly denied links with the mercenaries but its vehicles drove around Kono escorted by EO soldiers. Van Heerden readily conceded that Branch Energy was their partner.

Sierra Leone is a classic case of a state being run as a business. King Leopold of Belgium patented the idea with the Congo. Now the pattern is re-emerging in West Africa, where govern-ments are making ruthless calculations about the net worth of its people. EO's humanitarianism in Sierra Leone stopped abruptly at the fringe of the mineral areas. Even as the diamond mines churned out stones in Kono, the rebels were continuing to terrorize villages twenty miles away. 'It was a pact with the devil,' an anthropologist in Freetown explained to me. 'Every-one prospered bar the ordinary Sierra Leoneans.'

As for the South Africans' pious claims that they only work with 'legitimate' leaders, such talk is meaningless in Africa, where many governments are legitimate in nothing but name. Van Heerden was one of the key figures in a mercenary rescue package which was drawn up to prop up Mobutu in his last days by turning back Kabila's forces from the gates of Kinshasa. A week before Mobutu fled, a contact in his entourage tipped me off that a South African advance party was on its way, but they were wrongfooted by the speed of Kabila's advance and never deployed.

And yet with the UN unwilling and the OAU unable to intervene in the continent's many wars, 'private armies' do fill a gap. It is a depressing indication of the depths into which much of Africa has sunk that governments have to rely on mercenaries for law and order. The flowering of new-age mercenaries at the end of the millennium sparked considerable hand-wringing in the West. But a country as devastated as Sierra Leone requires dispassionate assessment. The Nigerian-led regional peace-keeping force which the West was keen to promote, looted Monrovia (the capital of neighbouring Liberia) more thoroughly than the feuding warlords, before it was eventually brought under control. For the people of Kono EO had at least brought stability for the first time in several years. Diplomats, politicians and even some aid-workers in Freetown made flattering comparisons between EO and the cost and track record of the UN in Africa.

EO's importance to Sierra Leone's stability was cruelly illustrated in 1997, just over a year after it held its first democratic elections. Bankrupted by the excesses of his military predecessors, President Kabbah, the newly elected civilian leader, cancelled EO's contract shortly after he took office. He made his decision after the IMF made clear that its loans, the economy's prop, could not be used to foot the South Africans' bill. He was renegotiating a contract when junior army officers, who had formed an alliance with, of all people, the rebels, took power in a coup.

For a year Freetown and Kono were subject to a reign of

terror until the junta was overthrown by a regional peace-keeping force advised by none other than EO and a British firm of 'consultants', Sandline. Regional diplomats were convinced the coup could never have happened if EO had been retained in its proposed role as national security advisor.

The role of mercenaries in Sierra Leone developed into a major scandal in Britain when it emerged that the British High Commissioner, Peter Penfold, had liaised with Lieutenant-Colonel Tim Spicer, the head of Sandline, a former Guards officer, in trying to bring down the junta. The left took their chance to attack the Foreign Office and accused it of reverting to old-fashioned gunboat diplomacy. The right saw it as a chance to attack the Labour government over its pledges to introduce a new moral foreign policy.

Afflicted by the myopia of its critics, the government pledged to root out the culprits. Only after several days on the defensive did it appreciate the most important point of the 'Arms to Africa' affair, as the Sandline/Sierra Leone controversy became known, namely that the 'good guys' had won.

Sierra Leoneans, however, had no such difficulty. They demonstrated in the streets of Freetown in their thousands in support of the embattled high commissioner and indeed for Sandline. History repeated itself six months later when the rebels, this time backed by Liberia, once again took Freetown before once again being bloodily repulsed by the Nigerians. When Penfold toured the city, he was cheered by residents who saw the criticism of him as the height of Western hypocrisy and arrogance. They were convinced that if he had been allowed to work with Sandline the city would never have fallen for a second time. Of course, they would love to be bound by the same stringent laws and principles of a Western liberal democracy, but they know that that is a fantasy for the forseeable future, and so they calculate accordingly: if sanctioning mercenaries is a compromise, then so be it.

♦♦♦♦

So is Africa heading back to the interventionist ethos of Cecil Rhodes? The echoes of this 'new' white involvement are unpalatable to some in the West, and unsettling to many Africans. EO officially disbanded on 1 January 1999 shortly after South Africa passed the law banning mercenary activity by its nationals. But it was widely believed that EO had merely shifted its assets and personnel, in search of a lower profile. In the twenty-first century the chances are that there will be groups of khaki-clad Afrikaners toasting granite pinnacles all over Africa as stand-in Voortrekker monuments, as private security companies and mercenaries expand their business and turn chaos to capitalism. Often they will be propping up brutal and corrupt regimes. All will be motivated by profit and their arrival will coincide with an outpouring of oil, diamonds or gold. But ironically, with the West washing its hands of Africa, it may be that in the future the flowering of private armies will not be seen as a blow to the idea of an African renaissance but rather as a factor that helped to bring a crude stability to the continent.

While the 'security consultants' and mining companies inevitably attract the colourful and controversial headlines, the neo-colonial phenomenon is not all as exploitative. There are also white professionals earning the gratitude of ordinary Africans, as in Mozambique, where the customs service is run by a team from Crown Agents, the former agent general for British Crown Colonies, who were in 1995 commissioned to reform one of the world's more porous frontiers. It was not a conventional aid project as the initiative came from the authorities. It was a partnership which the government would never have considered when Mozambique became independent twenty-five years before, and yet which showed how the old colonial powers could work with, and assist, Africa.

General Viljoen, one of the few South Africans who had the charisma and standing to have led a last white stand, had an instinctive understanding of the parameters of this new world. He was one of the instigators of the movement to send Afrikaner farmers around the continent and he travelled around Africa meeting government ministers to smooth the way for the Boers. His bluff soldierly ways adapted well to parliamentary politics. When I last saw him in his office in Pretoria he was still talking of the need for a homeland for Afrikaners, but the decline of his party's vote by two thirds to less than 1 per cent in 1999 made clear that the dream was over, whether he was prepared to admit it or not.

His one-time ally, Terre'Blanche, however, found the 'new' Africa, not to mention the 'new' South Africa, far less congenial. His reputation imploded once and for all in a magistrates' court in Potchefstroom, a university town west of Johannesburg once seen as a cradle of Afrikaner thinking.

E.T. was in court to be sentenced for attempted murder after he assaulted a black employee with an iron bar, leaving him with permanent brain damage. As he sat in the dock in a beige suit, the scene behind him must have been reassuring. Whites occupied the front three rows of the gallery, while blacks were crammed into the back. But his supporters watched in silence as the magistrate branded Terre'Blanche 'a violent man motivated by a hatred for blacks' and jailed him for six years. He had to sit in the cells as court officials counted the three sacks of coins delivered by his supporters as bail money. As a black crowd danced triumphantly outside the court, several AWB members had to ask for police protection to reach their cars.

The old deferential attitudes, however, took rather longer to die than E.T.'s enemies had hoped. His appeal was still pending for more than eighteen months after his sentence. It was almost as if no one could quite bring themselves to turn the key – not that this seemed to matter to E.T., who was, of course, in his mystical make-believe world, rooted in the 'old Africa', oblivious to the fact that these days even tribal chiefs are starting to adjust to the modern era.

7

A Very Zulu Chief

Chief Mangosuthu Buthelezi – The Rebirth of Traditional Leaders

The first to boo was a portly chief with a leopard-skin head-dress. Sweating profusely, he cleared his throat and emitted a low growl of dissent. His neighbours in the packed public gallery of the Zulu legislative assembly chamber, an eclectic riot of patterned cotton gowns, traditional Zulu wear and grey suits, glanced down at their leader as if for reassurance that the time was right. Mangosuthu Buthelezi, the traditional prime minister of the Zulu nation, was staring ahead of him, but with the tiniest hint of a smile. The rumble turned into a roar. A matronly Zulu in a painted cotton dress jumped to her feet with an ululatory shriek. The circular hall echoed to the stamping of feet.

Utterly outmanoeuvred, the guest speaker, a bespectacled white judge, spluttered, shuffled his papers and temporarily abandoned his speech. Judge Johann Kriegler, one of South Africa's most respected liberal judges and head of the electoral commission for its first all-race vote, had come to tell the chiefs of Zululand to step into line, to bow to the will of central government. As if in a Johannesburg courtroom he wagged his finger for emphasis. He should have known better. No outsider lectures a Zulu chief on his home ground, least of all in Ulundi, the old Zulu capital, where since time immemorial nothing has happened without the say-so of the traditional leaders.

King Goodwill Zwelithini, direct descendant of Cetshwayo, whose *impis* humbled the British at Isandhlwana in January

1879 before finally being crushed on a plain a few miles from the chamber, sat to the right of the judge. He wore a dark Nehru suit and clutched a sceptred staff. Not a flicker of emotion passed his face, not even when a priest recalled his ancestors' deeds and prayed that he too would have 'strength, courage and wisdom . . . at this time of great trial.' But he was in those days little more than a puppet. Beside him sat Buthelezi, his uncle and mentor, the Richelieu of Zulu politics. He was – of course – the model host.

'The judge is only the messenger,' Buthelezi chided the hecklers. 'If you don't like the message, don't hit the messenger.' But the crowd knew their man. They hummed their support for his every word. When the judge tried again, they drowned him out. His appeals for fair play were shouted down. His hectoring tone and loss of temper met scornful laughs.

After the meeting I bumped into Prince Vincent Zulu, one of the more thoughtful members of the Zulu royal house. He could barely control his contempt. 'He came down applying his glib Western democratic values as if we were in Cape Town or Johannesburg,' he said. 'He had no idea. This is what happens if you dare to criticize a chief.'

A newcomer to Zulu politics might have been tempted to conclude it was a classically South African black/white contretemps. The sight of the white official coming to give orders to proud tribal leaders was steeped in colonial imagery. If you blurred your vision and blotted out the suits, the judge could have been an emissary of Sir Theophilus Shepstone, the Secretary for Native Affairs, in the late 1870s, warning Cetshwayo either to submit or face war, or an agent of Cecil Rhodes, a decade later, trying to wheedle his way into the affections of Lobengula, the last of the Ndebele kings.

But the Zulus' fury was founded on something far more profound than historical or racial gripes. The acrimonious scene was part of the giddy final countdown to South Africa's April 1994 election. Buthelezi had won another victory in his bid to wield absolute power in Zululand. He had also won the latest round in one of Africa's longest-running battles – the clash of Western liberal democracy with traditional leaders, a dispute that went to the heart of the continent's predicament in the late twentieth century.

I was given a vivid and improbable reminder of the judge's humiliation two years almost to the day later when the proud and puissant Zulu chiefs gave short shrift to another grey-haired luminary from Pretoria. But this time the visitor should have known the form as he had spent his formative years in a chief's homestead – he was none other than Nelson Mandela.

The world's most famous former political prisoner had been in office for nearly two years, and he had made an unprecedented journey to the royal palace at Nongoma to urge the chiefs to accept that the days of untrammelled feudal authority were at an end. His magic was then at its most potent. The most diehard right-wingers were still falling for his reconciliatory charm. But the Zulu chiefs would have none of it.

In a deliberate snub he was kept waiting for over an hour as they and their *indunas* (headmen) gathered under a vast marquee. The whistles and catcalls began even as he opened with a judicious condemnation of the two main regional political parties, his own African National Congress and Buthelezi's Zulu-dominated Inkatha Freedom Party, whose followers since the mid-Eighties had been engaged in a murderous low-level civil war. He gamely plodded through his prepared speech but his fury was tangible. His mouth was set in a scowl usually reserved for public appearances with his estranged wife, Winnie. Finally he could take no more and he left his text.

'It's people who think through their blood, not through their brains, who are creating the problems,' he said. 'I don't hide from speaking the truth anywhere in South Africa. You can shout until you are blue in the face . . .' And that is exactly what they did through a long and fractious afternoon until he rose in frustration and left.

It was a Friday night and a feast had been prepared. Chuckling with delight, the *amakhosi* (chiefs) settled back to enjoy themselves before returning to their villages to crow over their leader's famous victory.

♦♦♦♦

If you believe the idealists, there was a time when Africa had a baronial democracy that was second to none. 'Then our people lived peacefully under the democratic rule of their kings . . .' wrote one African politician in 1984, with a yearning reminiscent of Virgil recalling a more glorious and simple past. 'Then the country was ours in our name and right . . . All men were free and equal and this was the foundation of government. The council of elders was so completely democratic that all members of the tribe could deliberate in its deliberations. Chief and subject, warrior and medicine man, all took part and endeavoured to influence its decisions.'[1]

The longing in this instance is forgivable, as the author was Nelson Mandela and he was writing in 1984, his twentieth year in prison, with no end in sight. Mandela was echoing the language of black liberation politicians from the first half of the century when talking up that pre-colonial history was vital for inspiring the future. But in these confused and troubled times for Africa it is as destructive to talk up the past as it is to deride it. Over the last century or so both Africans and outsiders have been guilty on both counts. All the while traditional leaders have fallen further into limbo.

After years of partisan scholarship there is now a rough and ready consensus that in the middle of the last century when the trickle of colonial traders and missionaries penetrating Africa turned into a flood, most of the continent had a working social structure under traditional leaders. It was superstitious, hereditary and often inhumane. There were plenty of barbaric tribes who neatly reinforced European stereotypes about the 'Dark Continent'. But contrary to the widely held perception in Europe at the time, many chiefs did run their tribes along well-established lines. If you were a chief, you had to consult the elders and allow the people their say in assemblies before making major decisions. If you defied the rules, you might get away with it. A handful, like Shaka, the warrior founder of the Zulu nation, broke the customary compact and forged a military dictatorship. But there was always the danger of being 'de-stooled' if you were too oppressive. Chiefs were seen as the repository of ancestral spirits. It was a brave man or woman who chanced their wrath by breaking the rules.

This system, which had lasted for hundreds of years, stood in the way of the colonists as they started to make inroads into Africa. Initially the newcomers masked their disdain and respected the authority of traditional leaders. But the portly African leader with a few necklaces of beads, a gourd of liquor and an out-of-date musket soon became a stock figure of fun. When the Great Powers decided to carve up Africa at the end of the last century, chiefs were widely dismissed out of hand. The British proved more canny than their French, Portuguese and Belgian counterparts. For the British, the chiefs were useful local partners, albeit of an unequal status. But any colonial officer would, of course, have been shipped home in a trice if he had dared to suggest a parallel between the House of Commons in Westminster and the popular African custom of holding tribal assemblies under the central village tree, or a link between councils of elders and meetings of the cabinet.

The arrival of the colonists began a period of relentless decline for chiefs. In one of many ironies of independence, many of the leaders who had endlessly talked of returning Africa to the Africans proved the most abusive of chiefs. In the 1860s Dr James Africanus Horton, a prominent African academic, had drafted a constitution for an independent African state. Taking into account tribal diversities he suggested a confederacy with a parliament composed of two houses, one with traditional leaders, the other of elected delegates. But his counsel went by the wayside in the heady days of independence in the Fifties and Sixties. 'Presidents for life' – possibly the most odious coinage of independence – trumpeted the hereditary rule of Africa's chiefs to justify their own permanence in office. But on the ground chiefs were treated as colonial stooges and relics of a conservative past. At odds with the Marxist and modernist dreams that were the fashions of the time, in swaths of the continent they were stripped of their authority, doomed in some cases to become little more than Scottish clan chiefs, relying on baubles to re-create their forefathers' glory.

It will come as no surprise, however, to anyone acquainted with the tragic failure of the modern African state, that many chiefs survived even if their powers had been curbed. A glance at the map shows that a rigid centralized government would be doomed to fail in most of the continent. The distances are too huge and the physical and climatic obstacles too severe to expect central directives to achieve their goal. Respect for chiefs has dwindled in cities as urbanization has dismantled traditional social units. But in rural areas, home to an estimated two-thirds of sub-Saharan Africa's population, traditional leaders are a way of life. Buttressed by Africa's creaky infrastructure and poor communications, chiefs have continued doing what they have always done, applying customary law, resolving land, marital and livestock disputes while leaving politicians in distant capitals to pontificate on the need for reform.

Every day all over Africa clans and communities gather before their chiefs, usually under a village tree, to discuss their troubles. Some are generals, others perform the service of social workers, magistrates and much more. It is all very fine to talk of individual rights in air-conditioned offices in capitals. But even South Africa, by far the richest and best administered sub-Saharan state, lacks the means to implement its modernizing message. Indeed, after the trauma of colonialism and independence, many Africans in rural areas are turning back to their chiefs as a bedrock in a chaotic and confusing world.

When Sierra Leone's central government collapsed in the early Nineties, who did the villagers turn to for guidance but their chiefs? They resurrected a rag-tag militia of tribal hunters, known as Kamajors, a buccaneering lot who dressed up in colourful uniforms and went on patrol draped with bandoliers, bows and arrows and automatic rifles. The Kamajors consulted witch-doctors for spells to ward off bullets. They swore primitive oaths. Their re-emergence was condemned in many quarters as a retrogressive step. A prominent American academic wrote a millenarian article entitled 'The Coming Anarchy', published in February 1994 in *Atlantic Monthly*, in which he presented Sierra Leoneans' reliance on traditional authorities and 'ju-ju' warriors as a sign of West Africa's social and moral decay. Sierra Leonean friends and indeed Kamajors themselves shook their heads indignantly when I put this theory to them. 'He (the academic) should have been here before the mobilization of the Kamajors,' they muttered. 'That was when we had real anarchy.' It was the modern state that had failed them. The Kamajors may have been little more than an African Dad's Army but they and the chiefs were protecting the people from their own soldiers.

After a clumsy attempt at social engineering in many parts of Africa, notably Mozambique, there is a tacit recognition that the attempt by independence governments to abolish chiefs was too doctrinaire, and they have been reallocated carefully defined roles. In Uganda King Ronnie of Buganda has restored the monarchy of his father, the late King Freddy, who was forced into exile in 1966 after a vicious assault on his palace led by Idi Amin, the then army commander. After studying at Cambridge, where he did not finish his degree, and a stint as a double-glazing salesman, the Kabaka, as the king is known, argues he can work with the government to contribute to Uganda's development. He has only ceremonial powers but believes the institution can help to blend tradition with modernity.

The challenge is to work out how to keep traditional leaders in check. In Zululand the struggle is particularly intense.

ᚚᚚᚚ

South Africa's traditional leaders weathered the twentieth century's vicissitudes better than their peers north of the Limpopo. Settlers and colonists had always had a soft spot for chiefs and so white rule cushioned them from the storms to the north. The Afrikaner Nationalists saw them as integral to their warped social and ethnic vision and gave them greater powers than they had enjoyed under the previous more liberal governments. This reached a climax in the Seventies when they were promoted as leaders of ten tribal homelands as part of the 'Grand Apartheid' vision of separating tribes.

Their authority crumbled, however, in the Eighties as the white minority government spluttered to a close. Discredited by their associations with apartheid, they were seen as legitimate targets by the youths who were pushing for change under the banner of the United Democratic Front (UDF), the surrogate for the ANC, which had been banned and in exile since the early Sixties. The social revolution if anything gathered momentum after the ANC was unbanned in 1990. Chiefs were criticized as autocratic and outdated. Most in the ANC were adamant: the chiefs had to go.

Heading the ANC's hate list was Chief Buthelezi, the chief minister of KwaZulu, one of the ten homelands, a patchwork quilt of land which included most of the old Zulu kingdom but not, of course, the richest farmland in the region which had been reserved for the whites. He had led KwaZulu from its foundation in 1970 and had stubbornly resisted the white government's pressure to accept a nominal independence, correctly arguing it was a sham which merely served whites' needs.

When KwaZulu was founded, the Zulu chiefs were a shadow of their historical selves. While nominally imbued with the traditional authority granted to them by the British a century earlier, they were formulaic placemen who could be appointed and dismissed by the white government in Pretoria. Their glory days of the last century which had culminated with their destruction of Lord Chelmsford's central column at Isandhlwana were a hazy memory to be replayed over pots of sorghum beer. The British refused all peace overtures in their determination to avenge the shame of their defeat, and crushed the Zulus at Ulundi and sent Cetshwayo into exile, plunging the royal house into a Macbethian saga of ambition and betrayal which sparked far bloodier battles than Isandhlwana. The sorry tale reached its denouement in 1906 when a minor chief, Bambatha, led a short-lived rebellion against a poll tax. He and more than 2,000 followers were killed. The humiliation of the Zulu chiefs was complete. Since then youths have been drifting from the valleys to the big towns in search of work in ever increasing numbers, an agonizing exodus powerfully portrayed in Alan Paton's Cry, *the Beloved Country.*

Buthelezi changed all that, converting the chiefs from an apathetic bunch of greybeards to a potent political force to further his quest to control the levers of power in the province. The KwaZulu government provided the key to the chiefs' loyalties as it controlled the purse-strings and allocated their stipends and perks. Zulu nationalism provided the glue. As the ANC's feud with Buthelezi intensified in the early Eighties so the chiefs were sucked into politics and ultimately a low-level civil war.

At least 15,000 people were killed from the mid-Eighties to the mid-Nineties in fighting between supporters of Inkatha and the ANC before a peace accord in 1996. The conflict was dubbed 'low-intensity' but it seemed intense enough in the valleys of Zululand and in the burgeoning squatter settlements outside Durban and Pietermaritzburg, the region's two main cities, where membership of the 'wrong' party could be a death sentence, and where thousands of Zulus had to flee their homes.

Latterly the conflict became a turf war for votes: KwaZulu was the one densely populated black area in South Africa outside ANC control. The fighting was also crudely primed by a 'Third Force' of apartheid security forces who backed Inkatha to sow confusion and undermine the ANC during the transition from white rule. The bloodiest clashes were in the townships around Johannesburg where it spread in 1990 as Buthelezi sought to make Inkatha a national political force. But politics was not the only contention; this was also a clash between two very different worlds. The political feud between the ANC and Inkatha fuelled a conflict of cultures between city-slickers and country bumpkins, or as often reignited an ancestral feud over cattle, women or land, the three burgeoning issues for a red-blooded traditional Zulu male.

The chiefs of KwaZulu were the old order coming up against

the new. It was inevitable that most of them backed Buthelezi. Not only did he control their purse-strings in Ulundi, the centre of the KwaZulu homeland government which paid the chiefs' stipends, he was also a champion of tradition against the modernizers of the ANC with their calls for social reform and downgrading chiefs. Further, Inkatha touted itself as a force of stability standing for education and the status quo when the ANC was calling for boycotting schools.

In the early days of the civil war Buthelezi won sympathy in international conservative circles. He was seen as holding the dyke against the more radical message of the ANC, the like of which had proved so destructive to rural Africa further north. But by the late Eighties opinion was shifting as KwaZulu had become little more than Buthelezi's fief. Touring the valleys he stoked the fires of Zulu nationalism with long impassioned speeches invoking the glorious past and calling for a return of the old Zulu kingdom. It was a dangerous game which threatened the very fabric of the state. It was also an object lesson in the potential absolutism of traditional chiefly power – and Ulundi was the belly of the proverbial beast.

⋀⋀⋀⋀

When a party of early white settlers travelled to see Shaka in 1824 to pay their respects, they were disconcerted to find he knew of their every move. Henry Francis Fynn, the party chronicler, recorded that messengers intercepted them every few hours on their journey to report on their progress from Port Natal, as Durban was then known.[2] During their stay, the Zulu Napoleon left little doubt he had installed the late nineteenth-century equivalent of an elaborate bugging system. Fynn was quizzed by Shaka personally after he made an unscheduled visit to a distant part of the kingdom. One hundred and seventy years later, as I travelled from Johannesburg to Ulundi for an audience with Buthelezi, it was as if little had changed.

In the best 'Big Man' tradition the visitor entering Ulundi is under no illusions as to who is in charge. Leaving the Mangosuthu Buthelezi Airport on my right, I drove along the Buthelezi

Highway and checked in at the Holiday Inn, reputedly the smallest in the world. Bypassing the Buthelezi conference rooms I bumped into the maid who had just finished cleaning my room. By now it came as no surprise to find she was called Precious Buthelezi. When I mentioned my host's name in the bar the other occupants looked into their drinks and froze. There was no need to ask for directions to the KwaZulu legislative assembly where the interview was to take place. In the old days Ulundi was a collection of huts and cattle pens clustered around the royal enclosure. Only the building materials have changed. Instead of the cattle kraals there is a tiny shopping centre and garage. Instead of the royal homestead there is a totalitarian complex which houses the KwaZulu assembly.

South Africa's first ever non-racial democratic constitution had just been approved. The elections, which would end white rule, were set for six months hence. On paper South Africa was well set to bid farewell to its tortured past. There was however one major problem: the chief was unhappy with the way things were going.

I had come to ask him why as head of Inkatha, the country's second largest black party, and as the 'third man' in South Africa after Nelson Mandela and the then president F.W. De Klerk, he was opposed to the poll. As I waited in his ante-chamber a convincing answer was to be found on the coffee tables and walls, which were adorned with the photographs of Western leaders shaking his hand.

Reagan, Thatcher, Bush, Kohl, the collection would have been the envy of many a head of state. They were a testimony to Buthelezi's record in the Eighties when he had been the darling of the West. As a free-marketeer opposed to the 'armed struggle' and sanctions, he was the black opposition leader the West could and did support. In his youth he had been a member of the ANC Youth League. His forthright anti-apartheid stance had led to his expulsion from Fort Hare University, the cradle of black nationalism whose alumni included Mandela and President Robert Mugabe of Zimbabwe. He accepted the chief ministership of KwaZulu in the early Seventies only after consultation with the ANC. Thereafter he was lionized by many blacks for his dogged defiance of the hard men of the National Party, and for his insistence that there could be no negotiations about the end of white rule until Mandela was released. It was not just his courtiers who whispered in the Eighties that he was in the running as a possible compromise first black president. Even the *Broederbond* was believed to be considering him in that light.

But those days were long gone as I waited for my summons. Buthelezi fell out with the ANC in 1979 when they accused him of turning KwaZulu into a personal power base. The West continued to back him as a black counterweight to the then Soviet-backed ANC. He maintained support in white liberal and business circles because of his opposition to the 'armed struggle' and his repudiation of calls by ANC radicals to boycott schools. But as relations continued to worsen between him and the ANC in the late Eighties so his principles appeared to become subsumed by a lust for power.

His nadir came in 1991 when he was forced to admit that an apartheid slush fund had financed two Inkatha rallies and a pro-Inkatha union movement. In the wake of disclosures that the white government had trained Inkatha hit-squads – which he always insisted were bodyguard units – his credibility crumbled outside the valleys of Zululand among all but a few conservative and Zuluphile businessmen. Although his constitutional stance remained an important check on the ANC, his judgement and principles faltered, to the ill-considered glee of his opponents, many of whom had no interest in allaying the chief's concerns and instead were set on crushing him, whatever the cost to South African stability. Friendless, he ended up forging an alliance with white right-wingers, the very people he had campaigned so long and hard against. The doors of the world's statesmen closed. Far from shaping up as a potential national leader, he was regarded even by many of his old allies in white business and foreign embassies as at best a nuisance and at worst a threat to South Africa's stability. He was regularly denounced in the South African media as the spoiler. Looking at his photograph collection I had no difficulty making a glib psycho analysis. This was a man whose pride had been badly tweaked. He had lost the race. He was at bay.

An aide ushered me into the cabinet room. Circular and devoid of windows, it reminded me curiously of politburos in the old Eastern bloc. My ensuing encounter was unsatisfactory inasmuch as I came no closer to understanding Inkatha's strategy. But I did gain an insight into the chief's dual ethos. He was in Western politician mode, in an immaculate dark grey suit, and talking the language of constitutions and liberal democracy. He seemed, in the jargon of consultants, a micro-manager. He gave the impression of having perused every paragraph of every paper that had passed his desk. Every question elicited a reply based on such and such a sub-clause in such and such a document.

And yet in the best chiefly traditions form was all important. Every greeting, every slight over the years had been logged. He recalled with obvious bitterness Mandela's failure to take up his invitation to meet soon after his release from Robben Island when regional ANC diehards dissuaded him from the idea, arguing that to meet Buthelezi would serve no purpose beyond boosting the chief's image.

Buthelezi is a pastmaster at using protocol as a pretext for obstruction. He boycotted the first set of constitutional talks after the unbanning of the ANC on the grounds that King Goodwill, who was then effectively his pawn, was not allowed a separate delegation – a manoeuvre that would have given the chief increased voting powers. But it would be wrong to dismiss his traditional hankerings as a political gimmick. He, and indeed Ulundi, had a foot in two worlds. KwaZulu was an adminstrative and financial centre for a large chunk of Africa's most developed state. It was also the nerve centre of Zulu politics, whose feudal complexities had changed little since the last century. Buthelezi as much as anyone personified the apparent contradiction. As we discussed his difficulties with the constitution, I could have been sitting in Brussels or Bonn. But the next time I saw him addressing a rally of rural Zulus and headmen, clad in leopard skins, wielding a sceptre and delivering a fiery two-hour historical speech, he was every inch the African chief.

His opponents mocked his chiefly credentials and trappings. Inkatha rallies did sometimes smack of pantomime. I was sitting in a Soweto stadium as thousands of bare-chested young Zulus bounded into the centre waving ox-hide shields and spears. At their head was an *induna* in full leopard-skin regalia. With the muscles on his arms and calves rippling and gleaming in the sun he cut a magnificent figure. Then he suddenly checked himself and lifted up a flap in his loincloth to reveal a pager tucked into a black leotard. It was a reminder of the play-acting that underpinned the glorification of the old Zulu ways, but no one could deny Buthelezi's brilliance at playing – and if necessary playing up to – traditional politics.

⋀⋀⋀⋀

The chief is not known for soundbites. In 1994 he entered the *Guinness Book of Records* for the world's longest speech after he spoke for an average of two and a half hours on eleven of the eighteen days of a session of the KwaZulu Legislative Assembly the previous year. He is also legendary for his pedantic pursuit of a line of thought. So I was startled when he suddenly broke off from a venture into the arcane recesses of South Africa's constitutional history and asked: 'Where is your wife? She must join us for lunch.'

Sophie, my wife, had indeed driven down with me and had dropped me off at the entrance to the legislative assembly, but I was not aware her presence had been logged by the sentry, let alone that it had reached the ears of my host. I muttered that she had gone sightseeing. The chief summoned an aide, whispered in his hear, and sent him out. Sophie was in the Ulundi museum and had just asked the young Zulu deputy curator a delicate question about political freedom in Zululand when he suddenly fell silent. There was a long shadow in the doorway. It was Buthelezi's aide. 'You are having lunch with the chief in ten minutes' time.'

The answer to Sophie's question never came. Given the deputy curator's agonized face she wondered, as she was driven to the legislative assembly, if he would have to answer for her candour. The stories of the chief's autocratic style are legendary. He is one of Africa's most prickly politicians and seems to expect unquestioning obedience. Over the years a series of lieutenants who appeared to show too much initiative fell from favour or 'retired'. At a press conference in Cape Town in February 1995 attended by dozens of diplomats he became almost inarticulate with rage when I asked him to justify one of his positions. I was apparently guilty of thinking like a white man and failing to understand the African mind, an argument beloved by African leaders when put on the spot by foreign correspondents. 'It amazes me, the mentality of the Caucasian people . . .' he raged. 'What is necessary in their minds . . . what is necessary in our black minds . . .'

And yet the chief also had a dazzle and charm. Not for a moment did he condescend to us over lunch even though we were less than half his age. With the rancour of his political obsessions out of the way, he was witty and entertaining. It was easy to see how he cut a dash in conservative circles in London, where, for backers like John Aspinall, the British gambling entrepreneur, zoo-keeper and wildlife conservationist, Buthelezi was a link to a nobler, more honourable past. This was a man after all whose ancestors had fought the British in the Zulu war. He even acted in *Zulu*, the Michael Caine classic film about the defence of the Rorke's Drift mission station by a tiny British garrison against overwhelming odds on the evening after Isandhlwana.

Ever since those battles, the Zulus have had a heroic and mystical appeal. The stereotype of the noble warrior imbues the international image of the Zulu. In the valleys small boys still play with sticks rather than footballs. The martial tradition is maintained in Johannesburg's township hostels, barrack-like dormitories which are home to tens of thousands of Zulu men. Under apartheid so-called migrant workers were forced to live in hostels as a temporary workforce for the mines in exile from their wives and families. Their conditions were Spartan as was their discipline – and their wartalk was not all bluster.

Shortly before the April 1994 election I watched from a balcony in central Johannesburg as thousands of Zulus went on the rampage in a central square. They were marching to show their opposition to the elections and, after attacking suspected political rivals, were fired on as they marched into town. As the rally descended into chaos two men were shot dead below my perch and another two a hundred yards away on the other side of the square. And yet amid volleys of gunfire many of the young men proudly refused to throw themselves on the ground and continued to prance the classic Zulu war-dance in a display of the spirit which inspired the suicidal charges against the British at Rorke's Drift and which also immortalized the Zulus' cult status in London.

Mr Aspinall once entertained the chief in the dinosaur chamber of the Natural History Museum. He also regularly attended Inkatha rallies following his declaration in 1991 that he was a 'white Zulu'. Dressed in a dark suit he told a crowd of 40,000 Inkatha Zulus that he had vowed in his childhood to base his values on those of the Zulu ancients. The Zulu ancestors 'gave me a model of how a life should be lived and also how somebody should die,' he said. He elaborated his vision to me on a scorching afternoon several years later when he and his family were the guests of honour at a rally in Durban on 20 August 1995. Flushed with excitement, Aspinall introduced me to David Ntombela, one of Inkatha's most notorious warlords, much to the latter's discomfort.

'Have you met this man? He is an *induna*. Tremendous chap. He has killed loads of people.' Mr Ntombela, who has been linked to several murders, muttered something about being a man of peace but Aspinall would have none of it. 'Nonsense. I tell you he has killed lots and lots of people . . . and I would think the worse of him if he hadn't. You should go and visit him one day. He'll give you a fantastic welcome.'

With the dust swirling, the sun beating down and the air reverberating to the humming of excited warriors it was indeed a dramatic sight. But there was of course nothing glorious about the battle over chiefly politics in Zululand. It was brutish and mean and utterly unlike what British Zuluphiles would like to believe.

⋔⋔⋔

It was a gruelling but magnificent haul to the home of Chief Siphiwe Mazibuko. In a vast natural amphitheatre on the fringes of KwaZulu, his valley of Loskop is Africa at its most serene. As I turned off the main Johannesburg-Durban highway on to the final stretch, herdboys with long sticks skipped past whooping like birds. The sky was diamond-bright against the deep purple outline of the distant Drakensberg hills. It was easy to understand why a loose translation of KwaZulu is 'in heaven'.

The chief was an Inkatha traditionalist in the midst of a rural war zone. I had decided to visit him to try to go beyond the rhetoric of party politics to understand the problem. As I descended further into the valley the sun lost its warmth and the whooping faltered. Three women with bright scarves quickened their pace when I asked the way. A queue at a hand pump stopped and stared. Only the local *induna* stood his ground.

Alpheus Mazibuko was wheeling a battered old bicycle. With his chestnut tweed cap he could have been a county squire doing his rounds. He was, it transpired, a kinsman of the chief, but now it seemed he was a little upset. It was a difficult time: in the previous ten days nine people had been killed in Loskop and many houses had been burned down. The *induna*'s account was a masterpiece of evasion. The trouble had started over an ancestral feud. Some said it was a cattle dispute, others a land battle. When the sun went down people headed for home. If villagers heard a knock at the door, they stoked their fire and prayed for dawn.

'Yes,' he added warily, the ANC and Inkatha were involved.

'And the chief?' I asked. The *induna* raised his *dondolo* (walking-stick) from his handlebars and pointed to a cluster of whitewashed huts on a distant hillside. Then he jumped on his bike and pedalled away.

It came as no surprise that the chief, Siphiwe Frazer Mazibuko, to give him his full name, was waiting for me as I rounded
the last bend. He was staring into the middle distance in the
direction of the neighbouring valley, the heartland of his
opponents, a rival clan including an outcrop of Sothos in a Zulu
sea.

The chief leaned his elbows on his fence. A plastic bag gusted
between us and settled in the sheep wire beneath his ample
tummy. Behind him a young man in a dirty white T-shirt was
tinkering with one of about half a dozen cars, all of which were
in chronic need of repair. The chief did not, it seemed, intend
to invite me inside. I coughed politely and cast my mind back
to a meeting that morning in the local town, Estcourt, just
thirty miles east and yet in a different world.

Frustrated by months of feuding, five of the chief's villagers
had taken the extraordinary step of taking their grievance to the
'white man's world'. According to custom they should have
gone to the tribal court, which was responsible for community
disputes. But that would have meant coming up against the
chief, and he was the very man they wanted to bring to book.
By chance they were sitting in the ante-chamber of the town
hall, talking to a local councillor, when I arrived. With its
wooden walls, besuited clerks and mountains of paperwork, the
setting was cosily familiar, but their tale seemed more at home
in the pages of the novelist Sir Henry Rider Haggard.

'He should never have been the chief,' ventured one of the
villagers. 'His mother was the old chief's third wife. He was the
third choice and one of the conditions of succession was that
he had to marry one of the daughters of the immediate family.'

'And then he sold a piece of land without consulting the
elders . . .' continued another.

'The Amangwane [the rival clan] had had enough,' interrupted a third. 'There were some deaths in a faction fight over
the *dagga* [marijuana] trade and they complained that he failed
to do anything about it. The Amangwane thought he was
behind it . . .'

'And then there was the massacre . . .' There was a long

pause for effect punctuated by loud exhalations. 'It happened at about four in the morning. The killers hid behind the trees and blazed away. The bodies were everywhere. To escape we hid behind the trees. And after that the Amangwane boycotted the tribal court and set up a rival chief, a distant cousin.'

Zulu storytellers are not to be hurried. An hour of colourful history later I had only the haziest idea of the plot. It would have taken a day of cross-questioning to draw up an accurate picture. But later I was able to confirm some of the episodes, including the massacre. What was clear was that to some at least of his people the chief was a tyrant whose overthrow was long overdue.

With hindsight it was remarkable that Mazibuko agreed to see me. His ancestors had been chiefs in Loskop for generations. His word was literally law. Once a week, like tens of thousands of chiefs all over Africa, he went to his tribal court, one of the few brick buildings in his territory, to dispense justice according to the customary law. Land, livestock, *lobola* (bride price), inheritance disputes, in short the important things in life, all came under his jurisdiction. He drove one of the few privately owned cars in his valley. His sullen stare gave nothing away. He was a man at the peak of his powers and yet he was all but under siege.

'I don't understand it. I was chosen to be chief in 1966 when many of my opponents had not been born. Now they are growing up and they want someone else. Last week they burned down my tribal court and they shot dead a friend of mine driving my car thinking it was me. One of my houses was burned down last July.

'They say I am not the rightful chief. But if that is the case how come the whole community paid a bride price for my wife? Would they have done that if I was not the chief? My house was paid for by the community's money. No one said we will build your house but you're not a chief . . .'

Leaving him to his lonely vigil I drove back to the main road, stopping on the way at the local police station. In the wake of the recent fighting it had been fortified with new rolls of head-high razor wire. There were at least twenty policemen milling around their prefabricated quarters. Indians, whites, blacks, they all seemed miserable in their remote posting. They could have been a Roman garrison posted to a far-flung province. They were desperate to know what I thought was going on in their area of responsibility but too terrified to leave the compound unless in an armoured convoy. I shrugged and headed back to the twentieth century.

For the ANC in the region the situation in Loskop was very clear-cut. The party's regional leader, Harry Gwala, was a self-avowed Stalinist and as ruthless a warlord as any of the Inkatha chiefs. I met him late one night in his township home outside the regional capital, Pietermaritzburg. His arms were flapping at his side as he suffered from motor-neurone disease. Half a dozen teenagers in T-shirts and tatty jeans mounted a star-struck bodyguard. In his string vest he would not have been out of place in a meeting of the Socialist Workers' Party circa 1930. Indeed, he quoted at length from a range of European Communist Party texts. His uncompromising stance fostered his cult among the disenfranchised youth in the informal settlements that mushroomed in the mid-Eighties as apartheid's restrictions began to collapse.

'We have liberated our people from white tyranny,' Gwala explained. 'Now it is time to free them from rural oppression. There is no ANC branch in Loskop. Every time we march forward they [Inkatha and the chiefs] retaliate. But we shall not fail.'

His certainty smacked of the interventionist approach of many of the post-independence governments to the north. Gwala was clearly an expert on dogma, particularly the history of European Communism. But it was equally clear that he had failed to study Communism's unfortunate record in Africa. In that respect he was as guilty as the colonists who tried to impose their own vision on the continent in smug disregard for the realities on the ground. Loskop's villagers were unhappy with their chief, but they looked blankly if you asked whether they would prefer to live without one.

Eugene Terre'Blanche, leader of South Africa's neo-Nazi AWB movement, in full apocalyptic flow in 1994 shortly before the collapse of the extreme Right-wing.

Above: Chief Mangosuthu Buthelezi, leader of South Africa's mainly Zulu Inkatha Freedom Party, at the annual Reed Dance with his nephew, King Goodwill Zwelithini. Buthelezi has encouraged Zulu traditions to bolster his political support.

Above right: A Zulu induna (headman) addresses an impi of Zulu men at a rally of the Inkatha Freedom party for the 1994 election. The mix of modern dress and traditional weapons reflects Africa's complex blend of values.

Right: Det Supt Douglas Campbell and Det Insp Jim Marshall of Scotland Yard in the Botswana village of Mochudi, on a mission to investigate a ritual killing. Murders for body parts for traditional medicine blight modern Africa.

Above: King Mswati of Swaziland, Africa's last absolute monarch, during an interview with the author in 1996.

Left: King Mswati in his traditional warrior costume at his enthronement ceremony. Somehow he has to marry Swaziland's traditions with the modernising imperative of progressives for democracy and reform.

Right: Huddled in a blanket and head-scarf the Rain Queen, Modjadji V, of South Africa, cuts an obtrusive figure during an interview with the author in 1997. Her dwindling devotees believe she has magical rain-making powers.

Above: Winnie Madikizela-Mandela at an ANC rally in 1994. A convicted kidnapper, she has been linked to more than a dozen murders but retains a devoted following among South Africa's poor.

Left: On taking office, Nelson Mandela turned his revolutionary instincts to South Africa's fashion. Mandela's shirts – flowing, knee-length, jazzy but not jarring – became one of his trademarks.

Left: President Jerry Rawlings of Ghana in a characteristic intense pose. Since taking power in a military coup the former fighter pilot has been hailed in the West for his economic and political reforms.

Below left: Thabo Mbeki, President of the ANC and President Mandela's chosen successor. His diminutive frame has to carry Africa into the next century.

Below: President Yoweri Museveni of Uganda has overseen a remarkable transformation of Uganda and earned widespread praise for his economic reforms. The West sees him as a model for a new Africa but his autocratic style is controversial.

I had little sympathy for Mazibuko. He reminded me of the caricature medieval robber baron of school history books. On a later visit I encountered him outside his tribal court. A long line of clansmen was queuing up for his services. He was sitting on the bonnet of his car snootily indifferent to their needs.

And yet elsewhere in the continent and indeed South Africa there were 'good' chiefs whose style of leadership suggested that if there was peace in KwaZulu, Buthelezi's traditional ways of government could be brought into line to play a constructive role.

♦♦♦♦

If anyone can support such a thesis it is Paramount Chief Linchwe II of the Bakgatla tribe. Indeed, were Africa's chiefs ever to decide to invest in public relations, they should pay a call on his village of Mochudi, thirty miles north of Botswana's capital, Gaborone. I met him there early one morning as the locals made their way to his presence for a tribal assembly. Most squatted on the dark red soil under the shade of a giant jacaranda, rubbing their hands against the pre-dawn chill. A few had brought deck-chairs. The odd pith helmet and golfing umbrella lent an exotic touch to the display. All rose respectfully when the chief appeared, but he did not stand on ceremony for long. The moment of truth had arrived. He had come to present two guests to his people. He had called on Scotland Yard to solve a ritual killing that had traumatized his tribe. It was time for the *kgotla* (tribal council) to assess what these latterday Solomons had to offer.

The sight of Detective Supterintendent Douglas Campbell and Detective Inspector Jim Marshall standing up before the *kgotla* lent itself to satire. With a purple silk handkerchief in his breast pocket and a spotty bow tie fanning from his collar the former cut quite a dash. He drew appreciative murmurs when on cue from the chief his thick Dorset burr negotiated a formal greeting in seTswana, the local language. Not since the *kgotla* had met to seek an end to the long recent drought had its members been so entranced.

The men from the Yard threw themselves into their task, promising confidentiality if anyone came forward, and assuring the people that they had no axe to grind. But the real hero of the hour was the grey-suited chief, a former ambassador to America, who had led the tribe for more than thirty years. When a group of schoolgirls had found the mutilated corpse of one of their colleagues the repercussions shook the entire country. First the village tried to lynch a suspect. Then, when the police released three suspects whom locals believed to be the killers, Gaborone, one of the few African capitals with a peaceful record, erupted into the worst riots since the British ceded independence in 1966. Into the breach stepped the chief.

'The last ritual killing here was in the Forties,' he said. 'So when the body of Segametse Mogomotsi was discovered everyone went mad. My duty was to control the people to tell them that there is a law that must be obeyed. I said the police must investigate. But I was misunderstood. People said I was protecting the murderers. We came to address the people and people started screaming at me.

'So I said we will call in professionals, either FBI or Scotland Yard. After consulting councillors and political leaders we settled on Scotland Yard because we are a former British colony, and we sent a delegation to the British High Commission to see what they could do . . .'

The detectives eventually left none the wiser. After thirty-five years in the force, DS Campbell willingly accepted the humorous side of their assignment. 'Most people think we come from a yard in Scotland, and that's not much of a compliment seeing how they keep their yards.' He chuckled as he recalled walking into the home of a *sangoma* (soothsayer). 'It would have taken the Yard's top forensic team ten days to do that house, just two rooms but all those herbs, jars and potions . . .'

The case was unsolved, but it did not matter. With his understanding of the old and the new Africas and his acceptance by both, the chief had defused the situation. His great-grandfather, Linchwe I, had evaded the Boers in the last century and led his people to Mochudi. He had, it seemed, a worthy descendant.

Inevitably, it was not always so easy for traditional leaders. But Linchwe was convinced that as long as chiefs steered clear of politics they had a vital role to play in Africa. Only they, he said, could be an authoritative bridge between the traditional and the modern. They could also, he added wistfully, be the link to the mystical past that African leaders are so desperate to find.

⋀⋀⋀

It was never going to be easy to achieve that balance in the 'new' South Africa. In the countdown to the April 1994 election, far from steering their people away from trouble, Buthelezi and his KwaZulu chiefs seemed determined to lead them into it. His firebrand Zulu nationalism threatened to plunge the region into ever more intense warfare, making visits to Zululand a depressing routine of chronicling massacres until two vital turnarounds occurred. First, Buthelezi at the eleventh hour agreed to take part in the poll, the very pledge Judge Kriegler had tried in vain to secure from his jeering chiefs. Second, and possibly as significant for the region's future, as the dust settled after the election the ANC subtly changed its tune on chiefs.

Buthelezi's decision to take part in the election, the last piece in the post-apartheid jigsaw, bore all the hallmarks of a chief clinging on to the remnants of his pride and trying to hold out until the last possible moment. The breakthrough came just ten days before polling when he listened to a last-minute proposal from a Kenyan mediator, Washington Okumu, who had stayed on in South Africa after the collapse of a delegation led by Lord Carrington and Dr Henry Kissinger. Buthelezi later claimed his climb-down was the work of God, that shortly after taking off to Ulundi from Johannesburg's Lanseria Airport an instrument failure had forced him to return to the terminal, where the Kenyan was waiting for him. It is in keeping with his touchy ego that he would be more likely to listen to a fellow African than a Briton or an American. But as credible an interpretation is that he had always intended to take part but had wanted to strut the stage and keep the world guessing. On the night of his climb-down, Inkatha's presses started churning out election material, hardly the work of a last-minute change of heart. Whatever, the first crucial step had been taken towards peace. A month later the chief assumed his seat as minister of home affairs in Mandela's first cabinet.

There were still many obstacles to be overcome before the new and the old could be brought together, as Mandela found out when he was humiliated by the Zulu chiefs in the royal plain outside Nongoma. The new constitution effectively fudged the role of chiefs. Nominally it accorded them a role in the new dispensation, but the ANC assumed that they would have only a token authority. As, however, the ANC came to grips with the realities of power, so some of its leaders grew to appreciate that their dream of transforming the socio-political landscape overnight might have to be moderated and they might instead have to reach an accommodation with the chiefs, until, over time, their powers withered away.

There were three main factors in their change of heart. The first was the failure of their attempt to woo the Zulu chiefs through King Goodwill. The Zulu king is not known for his political perspicacity but he commands a devotional respect in rural areas and even urbanized Zulus are reluctant to insult him. In a conspiracy worthy of the days of Shaka, who was murdered by his half-brother, the ANC plotted to destroy Buthelezi's rural support base by winning the king over to their side. They made their move in September 1994 just before the annual celebrations marking Shaka's death. The first public signs of trouble in the royal house came over protocol. To the outrage of Buthelezi the king invited Mandela to the Shaka Day commemoration without consulting him in his capacity as traditional prime minister. Then one morning it was noticed that there had been a change of the guard at King Goodwill's palace. Inkatha-aligned policemen were no longer at their posts but had been replaced by men from central government. The rift was formalized when Inkatha youths rioted outside the palace and stoned the windows.

The ANC were cock-a-hoop. With the king on their side

they thought Buthelezi was finished. But they had underestimated their rival's skill at Zulu politics. Not for nothing had a Buthelezi always advised the Zulu king.

Buthelezi was in Cape Town to meet John Major, who was in South Africa to cement British ties with the new government. The chief was a model of charm when he met the British delegation, but his mind was hard at work dealing with the far more ticklish problem in KwaZulu-Natal, the post-apartheid province encompassing the KwaZulu homeland and Natal. The Westminster press pack was somewhat nonplussed when Buthelezi slipped into traditional mode and explained to them he had sent a special head of cattle to the king as a peace offering. Buthelezi probably appreciated the cattle would not win back the king from the ANC, but he knew the form. The way was clear to tell his people that he at least had behaved by the book. Within days he held a Shaka Day rally without the king. His speech was couched in his usual careful wording: the king's absence was a source of sorrow; he would of course always be respected and welcomed back into the fold, but in the meantime he had been inveigled away by traitors in the royal house.

Belatedly the ANC realized that to win over the chiefs they had to court Buthelezi himself and they moved from confrontation to flattery. Mandela and other ANC leaders embarked on a concerted attempt to woo the chief, culminating in the masterstroke of appointing him as acting head of state when Mandela and his deputy, Thabo Mbeki, were out of the country. Buthelezi could barely restrain his delight when he was accorded this honour. Indeed, in the last two years of Mandela's presidency, Buthelezi frequently forsook the role of political rival and endorsed the ANC's record, particularly when it came under attack from white parties.

The second factor in the ANC's softer stance on chiefs was political pragmatism. Chiefs influence millions of rural voters whose support could prove vital in elections in the twenty-first century as the inevitable apathy and disillusionment with the post-apartheid order grows. A series of protests linking the Zulu *amakhosi* with chiefs from the Transkei, the home of the Xhosas and a traditional ANC stronghold, made clear that the issue transcended party politics. Moreover, in many rural areas as well as townships, the youths who had led the 'struggle' were no longer held in high esteem as residents watched them prancing around with high councillor's salaries and cellphones, patently far less efficient at building up an order than they had been at pulling one down.

The third factor in the ANC's shift of stance went to the heart of African identity and culture. In the days of the anti-apartheid battles, progressives viewed African tradition with deep suspicion as part of the white government's attempts to divide South Africa. But as the 'new' order developed, many Africans in the ANC appreciated they had more in common with chiefs than they had previously been willing to accept. Although Buthelezi's feudal policies remained beyond the pale, his fusion of Western and traditional African styles was recognized as a part of the quest to break from the 'old' South Africa and find a 'middle' non-European way. When Winnie Mandela, the arch-populist, started to espouse the chiefs' cause it became clear that Buthelezi's traditionalist vision was no longer on the fringes. Indeed his West African garb became mainstream chic for many of the intellectuals who were trying to articulate a new South African identity.

The power of chiefs is a huge obstacle to democracy and also to land reform, one of the most pressing issues in post-apartheid society. ANC activists rightly argue that liberation from white minority rule means little when millions of people are still subject to a medieval system of land tenure. But dealing with the chiefs and their powers is a long-term issue which requires sensitive handling. On paper, democracy and accountability are entrenched at all layers of authority, from Mandela's office in Pretoria through central and provincial governments down to the most isolated local council. Chiefs are relegated to an *ex officio* capacity on the councils; 'adapt or die' was the ANC's warning to the chiefs in the campaign for the first democratic local elections in 1995. But without ever officially changing its policy the party began to acknowledge that chiefs are a part of the landscape. Hundreds of chiefs and headmen will continue to be paid irrespective of their merits. To liberals this is a shabby compromise. But the tacit assumption is that, provided they do not abuse their power, they are there to stay.

Khaba Mkhize, the regional manager of the South African Broadcasting Corporation (SABC) in Durban, is in his image and outlook as far as you can get from the caricature Zulu of British folklore. In his former capacity as assistant editor of the *Natal Witness*, South Africa's oldest independent newspaper, he was for many years one of the most prominent and outspoken journalists in KwaZulu-Natal. He is one of the last people in the region you would expect to espouse a traditionalist's view, and yet four years after the election that is exactly what he seemed to be doing. Sitting in his glistening corporate office, he explained that he was going so far as to back plans for a controversial 140-foot Shaka statue in Durban harbour in order to help the region and Zulus come together.

'Just a year ago things were so bad that the ANC had its own Shaka Day, but now the young guns are growing up and embracing tradition. There is a Zulu saying that when a king farts it's not his fault, it's the poor man's fault. We Zulus have to unite together to confront the difficulties of the transition from white rule.'

His closing call for unity has delicate ramifications for the 'new' South Africa. The appeal is understandable given South Africa's troubled past. Mkhize argues passionately that to move away from the recent discord Zulus have to emphasize everything that they have in common. But the risk of stressing African tradition is that it will encourage black nationalism and anti-white sentiment, which could be disastrous for South Africa's hopes of entrenching a vibrant democracy. Speculation among senior ANC and Inkatha leaders of a long-term partnership exacerbated such fears, although an alliance would at least entrench peace. Traditional leaders, however, see the boosting of old ways in a much more straightforward light.

Bhekezizwe Luthuli, a descendant of the Nobel Peace laureate ANC leader Chief Albert Luthuli, and the fourteenth head of the Emathulini clan, is a busy young chief on the southern coast of KwaZulu-Natal. He is quietly confident that despite the hullaballoo over chiefs, his son and grandson will in due course assume his responsibilities. He was elected to the Cape Town parliament in April 1994 as an MP for Inkatha. But he loathes the sedentary existence of backbench life. There are no telephone lines in his valley so he guided me to his home on his mobile phone, the latest in breast-pocket design with a mock mahogany case. I was travelling with my sister and brother-in-law and their two-year-old son. The chief insisted on inviting us all in and and having a three-way chat. It was, he explained, little different from his usual routine.

'Early in the morning my people come here and I allow them to talk. Being an *nkosi* [chief] means you have to accommodate others. You foreigners love to say we are undemocratic. But if you want to see democracy you should come to see our tribal courts and our assemblies. There is a whole lot of reading I have to do before I pass judgement. I have to use my brain. And we are very fair, we never charge more than two goats. Things are different here, you see. It is not London and England.'

To prove his point – not that the last remark needed proving – he whisked us into his Mercedes for a guided tour of his domain. Stopping on a rise we gazed over an expanse of rolling green hills as he outlined his development plans.

'Over there I am building a supermarket for my people. And that spot there is to be a stadium.' Sensitized by the Western school of environmental protest, we found it hard to repress a murmur of concern at the thought of this beautiful unspoilt wilderness being straitjacketed in concrete, but we were of course missing the point.

𝍇

More than four years after my audience with Buthelezi in Ulundi, I attended a briefing he was giving in Cape Town on his ministry's legislative programme for the forthcoming year. Top of the agenda was a new identity card system to counter the tidal wave of illegal immigrants flooding into South Africa. It was worthy nation-building stuff, but about as far from his old obsession with chiefs and kingdoms as you could imagine. At the end of his talk he read out a list of countries whose citizens had outstayed their welcome. When he reached the United Kingdom and the Kingdom of the Netherlands he stopped and laughed. 'I have a soft spot for kingdoms . . .' he explained. The chief was tamed, but it is not always so easy to marry the old and the new, as I was to find across the border in Swaziland in the court of the former British public schoolboy who runs Africa's last absolute monarchy.

8

From Sherborne to Swaziland – The King of the Clouds

King Mswati of Swaziland – Magic, Ritual and Rite

From a distance the gathering looked like a typical village meeting in the African bush. Heads down, the villagers filed along the rutted pathways between their huts making for the barren stretch of ground at the top of the hill which doubled as schoolyard and local parliament. They could have been discussing the peanut harvest or the lack of rain. It was only when they started speaking that their grim purpose became clear. The people of Sekororo in South Africa's Northern Province had come to decide the fate of Johannes Baleaga, an 81-year-old cripple who had fled his home a few days earlier after being accused of being a witch. As the sun set over the distant northern Drakensberg Mountains, the people bowed their heads and mumbled a prayer. The trial could begin.

The 'evidence' was to be found in the corner of the schoolyard, a misshapen tree with a blackened branch. No one was hurt when the lightning hit, but in the remorseless logic of the region, a 'witch' was responsible. In remote communities all over Africa Christianity ends at sunset and anything out of the ordinary, a flood, the failure of a harvest, a financial bonanza, a chance encounter with a baboon, has people reaching for their money to send for a soothsayer for advice. Lightning is particularly ominous, even in regions where electrical storms are commonplace. Baleaga stood accused of causing the schoolyard strike. If found guilty, he faced exile or death.

Baleaga's misfortune had been to 'hobble' on the wrong day.

The day after the tree was hit, a group of villagers had sent a delegation to a local *nyanga* (a thrower of bones), who decreed that one of the 'witches' walked with a limp. The delegation recorded the verdict on tape and played it at the next village meeting. When Baleaga woke the next morning and tottered as usual to the nearest standpipe for his morning pail of water he became a pariah. He had spent all his life in Sekororo but suddenly people whispered in his presence and passed by with downcast eyes.

Somehow he made his way to the nearest police station more than twenty miles away. He was lucky to escape with his life. More than a hundred people, mostly elderly, had been lynched as suspected witches in the Northern Province in the previous year in a horrific sequence repeated daily all over rural Africa. After three miserable days sheltering in the cells Baleaga's family brought him home to see if he could ever live there again. Colonel Ferdi Jansen, the local Afrikaner police commander, had guaranteed his safety. The colonel however was the first to concede that his side of the bargain might be hard to keep: Sekororo had neither telephones nor electricity.

'Belief in witchcraft here is like Father Christmas is for children,' he explained as I set out for Sekororo with one of his black sergeants, a plain-clothes detective sporting jeans and a tatty straw hat, who was said to specialize in witchcraft. 'All we can do is push through dockets.'

Standing beside the scorched tree trunk, the school science teacher, Abram Saishago, explained that every household had contributed to pay the *nyanga* to identify the 'witch'. Saishago was young and well-educated and seemed an obvious confidant. So how, I asked hesitantly, did he reconcile the community's belief in witchcraft with his scientific training and what did he teach his children? He was as baffled by the question as a teacher in the West would be if someone queried the existence of gravity.

'I tell them that witchcraft exists. We have all seen plenty of evidence of that.'

Not for the first time in rural Africa I felt like a wraith. I was travelling with an American colleague in the heart of Lebowa, a former tribal homeland seldom visited by whites. As we passed by, the word *mlungu* (white man) skipped ahead on the wind preceding our coming. People spoke to us when addressed but otherwise we were ignored. All the while the witch-sniffing business drew to its numbing conclusion.

Saishago directed us to Baleaga's homestead, although he shrank from the risk of being tainted by entering the gate. Two low clay houses, three rounded huts and a cattle kraal joined by a earthen wall encircled a smooth clay yard. Baleaga sat in one corner by himself, little more than a bundle of bones and skin. Three women squatted to one side rocking on their haunches. The community meeting had not yet begun but all seemed resigned to their fate. For several minutes no one spoke. Then their fears and frustrations poured forth in a torrent. It was clear that if anyone else had been fingered they would have been in the thick of the crowd baying for blood. It was not that the community was wrong in looking for a 'witch'. It was just that the old man was innocent.

A very human motive for Baleaga soon emerged – it just happened that he was a successful farmer. His main accuser was a young smallholder whose crops were not doing well and who would stand a good chance of taking over the Baleaga plot if the family was banished. I had heard the argument many times before. A friend who ran a community group was accused of witchcraft by local youths when her market garden flourished. Sensibly, rather than hiding away, she confronted her denouncers, brought them to her home and taught them the merits of trench planting. 'Go home and do this,' she told them. 'Then you too can be witches.' Unfortunately no one seemed willing to listen to the Baleagas' defence.

'We were never given a chance to respond,' said Harris, the old man's youngest son. 'We wanted to put our side of the story at the first village meeting. We were shocked, but when the others saw we were a relative of someone pinpointed as a witch we were told to sit down.' There was little to say. We stammered our sympathies and left.

In the old days the chief could have stayed their eviction.

But his authority had long since been swept aside in the clamour for change in the closing years of apartheid. The youths had taken charge and in good revolutionary style had reintroduced summary justice in the name of progress: the days of the chief's shilly-shallying were over; witches were to be burned or driven from their homes. Even chiefs might be at risk. We came upon Chief Joshua Mongadi nervously minding his own business on a battered old deck-chair. No, he was not going to attend the meeting, And if we could be so kind, could we leave, as he was rather busy.

The meeting was over within twenty minutes: the Baleagas had to leave. The villagers melted back into the night as quickly as they had come, no doubt anxious to return home and bar their doors. As the last few lingered, we buttonholed David Sekgobela, the unofficial chairman of proceedings, an urban sophisticate who had recently returned from Johannesburg. He looked at me wrily when I suggested that we had just witnessed a gross injustice.

'And what if I stand up and talk them into letting these four stay here, and someone goes to their house and burns it down and kills them? Would that be any better?'

Maake, the detective, made no attempt to intervene in the drama. Instead he watched and listened. To do his job well required an understanding of witchcraft belief and also a conviction in the primacy of the law. He certainly had the former, but just as many a lapsed Christian hesitates to deny the existence of God, he seemed far from convinced in the textbook police world view. The problem, he suggested, as we headed away from Sekororo, was not one of ignorance but rather that South Africa's *nyangas* had lost their forefathers' powers and could no longer cope with the problem.

'I think today they do not have strong magic to stop the witches,' he explained. 'In East Africa they must still have strong magic. That is why you don't hear of witch-burnings there.'

♣♣♣♣

So can such beliefs be reconciled to the modern state? In a bid to resolve an issue that bedevils sub-Saharan Africa, South Africa appointed a commission to investigate witchcraft killings. The chairman, Professor Victor Ralushai, a celebrated anthropologist, knows all too well the potential of *sangomas* and *nyangas* for humbug or mistakes. During the Second World War his cousin, who was serving with the British army in North Africa, went missing, presumed dead. His family consulted a *sangoma*, who pointed out a neighbour as the 'witch'. The neighbour had to pay three cows as compensation, a vast sum in those days, until one day the 'dead' man returned from a prisoner-of-war camp, emaciated but very much alive. The falsely accused neighbour was given five cows in compensation, the *sangoma* was humiliated and the young Ralushai gained a lifelong scepticism about 'indigenous customs'.

Ralushai however is the last person to mock belief in witchcraft. My American colleague and I met him in March 1996, in an ultra-modern hotel in Venda, the northernmost of South Africa's tribal homelands, by repute the most superstitious part of the country. We had come from an interview with a *sangoma* who had recommended that his 'hunting dog medicine' was the best medicine for sniffing out witches, and were looking for a more sober view. Sitting by the hotel swimming pool, sipping coffee, we were in another world from the medieval drama of Sekororo. But the professor gently chided my obvious impatience with the reluctance of the regional authorities to condemn the belief.

'If you say witchcraft does not exist, you will be ignored in the villages,' he explained. 'The message of the missionaries merely strengthened the hand of the traditional churches. Once you educate people properly they will realize that it is not true, but that takes time. My aunt was a well-known traditional healer and late at night you would see well-known public figures visiting her house.'

The Ralushai Commission recommended tougher sentencing for lynch-mobs, tighter regulations for *sangomas* to outlaw out-and-out charlatans, and an extensive public education programme. But the report also came close to implicitly recognizing witchcraft, as it all but endorsed the argument that Shakespeare would not have introduced witches in *Macbeth* if they had not existed. Professor Koos van den Heever, an Afrikaner anthropologist, indicated later that he was convinced that he and Ralushai were the only members of the commission who did not believe in witchcraft.

The approach of the Ralushai Commission has a relevance throughout Africa. The colonial powers condemned indigenous beliefs as barbaric. But it will take more than Western disapproval to change a culture. While Christianity is finding more converts in Africa than in any other continent, most of these are not to the established Western churches but to African denominations that find no contradiction in a belief in Christ, the worship of ancestors and visits to *sangomas*.

Post-colonial governments tended to skirt around the issue of how to adapt policy and law to indigenous beliefs. Most retained the colonial prohibition on witchcraft. Some went a step further and adopted an aggressively modernist approach. Mozambique went so far as to incarcerate thousands of traditional healers for 're-education'. But behind the sombre trappings of modern politics, the suits and ties and the convention rooms, at times of trouble many African leaders fall back on an older set of values.

In Mobutu's last years, a troupe of marabouts (Muslim mystics) from Benin and Senegal were among his most respected counsellors. After they told him in 1991 that he would never be ousted if he lived on water, he moved his household to a luxury steamer, the *Camanyola*, named after one of his early military victories, and steamed up and down the Congo directing – or rather misdirecting – the state. Even as the rebels closed on his capital in 1997, *nyangas* threw bones and he invoked the spirits of his ancestors before every significant decision. Much to the frustration of Western diplomats trying to broker a peaceful end to the crisis, Mobutu's seers had only to whisper and he changed his plans.

Mobutu's last act in Kinshasa was rooted in African spiritualism. Shortly before flying out for the last time, he cremated the body of his old friend, the former Rwandan president, Juvenal Habyarimana. The corpse had been carried out of Rwanda by the Hutus in their flight into exile in 1994, and Mobutu had embalmed it as a talisman against the new Rwandan government. By denying them the chance of burying it in Kigali, the Rwandan capital, he hoped to cast a shadow over their hopes of founding a new nation.

Even Robert Mugabe of Zimbabwe, who took power with a flurry of modernizing laws designed to root out what he regarded as 'retrograde' practices, has been known to resort to traditional forms of advice. He was said to be mortified when an influential medium told him in 1997 that his style of government had upset the ancestors' spirits, a terrible offence for a well-brought-up African, just as it was for Romans in classical times. Traditionalists muttered that it was no coincidence when lightning struck a tree in his grounds just two days after a powerful blast of wind nearly caused his plane to crash in neighbouring Mozambique. It was reported in the *Sunday Standard* of March 1998 that he later met nine tribal chiefs with a reputation for spiritualism to ask their advice on how to stem the decline of his political fortunes – subsequent events suggested their counsel was to no avail, although they would no doubt argue he had left his consultation until far too late.

In my despatch on the dramas at Sekororo I described the villagers' purpose as 'horrific'. I was chided by my American colleague for being too ready to apply my own values. In hindsight he had a point. When you come from a society that likes to 'know' rather than 'believe', it is easy to ridicule belief in witchcraft as primitive twaddle. To Europeans it is reminiscent of the Middle Ages, when wretched old women were ducked in ponds to see if they floated – if they did, they were witches and so were burned. But tradition and superstition are integral to the world view all over sub-Saharan Africa, where life is unpredictable and political structures unstable. Moreover, witchcraft in Africa does not have the connotations of Satanism that it had in Europe in the Middle Ages. In Africa suspected witches are one-off suspects guilty of a particular 'crime' or natural phenomenon. Once a witch has been expunged, a community can resume its old pace. That does not make the 'expunging' any the less shocking but it is important to understand that witchcraft in remote areas is not seen as a manifestation of evil; it is part of the tapestry.

Many Africans who abhor the idea of ritual killings point out that established world religions have beliefs and rituals that would seem extraordinary to many an African tribesman. While the word 'witch-doctor', the standard Western translation for *sangoma*, is steeped in the idea of mumbo jumbo and black magic, the respectable mainstream of *sangomas* bridle at such an association. They see themselves as traditional doctors and soothsayers and argue they provide a vital supplement to conventional Western medicine, which has the thinnest of infrastructures in much of the continent.

Soon after taking power, the ANC embarked on the sensitive quest to marry Western with traditional medicine. Eskom, South Africa's state electricity corporation, became the first large employer to subscribe to Thamba, a health insurance scheme which covered visits to *sangomas* and *nyangas*. South Africa's Traditional Healers' Association, which has over 20,000 registered members, was wary of being regulated, and suspected at first that it might be an attempt to bring them into line. But the organization soon saw the financial merits of a scheme that allowed people to claim *sangomas*' fees on health insurance – and also potential lucrative spin-offs from the added publicity.

But it is not always as easy for Africa to reconcile two very different approaches to healing. What about the *sangomas* who claim they can cure Aids or even deny its existence? On paper no African government can afford to turn a blind eye to such bluster, and yet many do – with devastating results.

Professor Gordon Chavunduka, the Vice Chancellor of the University of Zimbabwe, personifies such contradictions. With a doctorate in medical sociology from the University of London, he is one of Zimbabwe's top academics; he is also a senior *nyanga*. When I met him, he headed Zimbabwe's association of traditional healers, which, he claimed, had 50,000 members. In his university office, with its gilt-framed picture of alumni in gowns and its view of a manicured campus lawn, he came across as a mirror image of his academic counterparts in Europe, until the conversation moved to the subject of witches.

'They exist, of course they do,' he said with the same steady conviction as the science teacher in Sekororo. 'I even decided to go out into the field as an academic to test my belief. They cause illness and death, forcing students to consult *sangomas* for the right counter-spells just before exams, and candidates to do the same before standing for parliament.'

Calmly but firmly, the professor denied there was a contradiction between his academic background and his beliefs. Rather, he said, people were fortunate to have a choice of how to be treated, even if this had, he admitted, had some unfortunate results, including a number of patients with grumbling appendixes who might have fared better, indeed might still have been alive, if they had gone straight to a medical doctor and not a *nyanga*. But he insisted that such mistakes were balanced by the *nyanga*'s spiritual role.

To enter such a debate is to invite charges of cultural supremacism even though such reasoning is abused all over Africa in support of barbaric customs, notably female circumcision, an agonizing ritual decried by all women who have the opportunity and bravery to speak out. But other beliefs fall into a murkier category. They do not conform to the ideals of a modern state and yet discarding them can be a painful process. No leader more acutely sums up the dichotomy than King Mswati III of Swaziland, the only African state still run according to the old-fashioned ways.

The king is a keen Dire Straits fan and yet he is a polygamist with the right to choose his wives from an annual parade. He has to wrestle with all the usual socio-economic problems of a late twentieth-century Third World state. He is not a Big Man in the conventional sense. He is neither brutish nor corrupt. He is generally liked even by his opponents. But he is the closest Africa gets to an absolute monarch, is hailed as a semi-divinity with rain-making powers, and his attempt to reconcile his two worlds goes to the heart of one of Africa's fundamental dilemmas at the end of the twentieth century.

When I heard from Mbabane, his capital, in July 1996 that there was a chance he would agree to a rare interview, I put other plans on hold and headed to the twin peaks of Sheba's Breasts Mountain. There in Swaziland's misty Ezulwini Valley (Valley of Heaven) the King of the Swazis, the Lion Which Devours, Guardian of the Sacred Shields, Sire of the Herd, or Mak as he was known to his friends at Sherborne, holds court. My only stop on the way was in a small South African town to buy a sun-dress for my photographer so she would be suitably dressed for the king.

♦♦♦♦

Negotiating an audience with the king had inevitably required a good deal of protocol. Five years before my visit, an American writer who was researching the world's monarchies learned his most important lesson about dealing with the Swazi court at the very end of his trip when he went out on the town to drown his frustrations at failing to secure a meeting with the king. 'Let the Swazis and English deceive each other with politeness and the Zulu and the Boer have it out with clubs,' he was told.[1] Subtlety is very much the Swazi way.

To understand the intricacies of the Swazi royal order I was advised to attend the *Mhlanga*, or Reed Dance, the annual southern spring pageant when the nation's maidens parade before the king. The British High Commissioner, John Doble, one of the last of the Buchanesque old-school diplomats, offered to escort me. He wore a kilt and sporran and brandished a Zulu stick. Not to be outdone, the commander of the royal regiment arrived wielding a golf club.

The ceremony had begun a week earlier in time-honoured form when the most respected Swazi matrons marshalled thousands of young women in regiments and marched them down to the Usutu river to pluck a reed. By the time we caught up with them, they were nearing their goal. In a flurry of head-dresses and bead-skirts, as many as ten thousand bare-breasted women were swaying past the royal family in a vast meadow outside the queen mother's palace. The climax came as the king danced elegantly out at the head of an élite band of warriors, feinting this way and that, to inspect the women.

The parade was a cross between Trooping the Colour, a mass Morris Dance and a Moony marriage. The *Mhlanga* remains the best first place for the king to choose a bride. At his first *Mhlanga* the bashful young Mswati is said to have picked a wife by looking at a video of the dancers. On a subsequent occasion, a girl at Swaziland's International School, one of the best-known schools in southern Africa, is said to have fled the country after catching his eye. By the time of my interview, the king had six wives in all – although they had not all been picked from the annual parade.

For thousands of young Swazi women this was the highlight of the calendar, just as the *Ncwala* ceremony was for young men every December, when thousands went into seclusion with the king before ripping apart a live bull with their bare hands. The ceremonies provide a chance to preen or prance and crucially to feel involved in the royal life. But for the growing modernist movement they are emblematic of all that is outdated and distasteful about tradition. Mario Masuku, the head of the People's Democratic Movement, the main opposition move-ment, scoffed when I asked if he had attended the ceremony. Traditional ceremonies were fine if they were cultural displays, he said, but their feudal ties should come to an end.

'Conservatives say we want to make the king a playdoll. That's not true. He is a unifying force. We need him here. It's just that tradition should be modernized and not manipulative.' And so the battle-lines are joined.

𝄞𝄞𝄞

The foreign minister went first on his hands and knees. Then followed the head of the army and the chief of police, a jovial pot-bellied man who had already joked with me about his hawk-eyed officers who had stopped me for speeding on my way to the interview. I brought up the rear, heeding their advice that as a non-Swazi I could stay on my feet.

The king was already seated in a printed cloth robe and open sandals, with feathers in his hair. George Lys, his British tutor and mentor, a former Gurkha officer, stood discreetly to one side in a light grey suit. Outside, the praise-singers rounded off their routine before dispersing among the crowds of courtiers and princes who were lining the veranda.

If ever a leader had good cause to mistrust his siblings it is King Mswati. His father, Sobhuza II, is reputed to have had hundreds of children including more than sixty legitimate sons. During his sixty-one years on the throne he was widely admired for his skill in steering his mountain kingdom between the Scylla of Marxist Mozambique, which had banned traditional beliefs, and the Charybdis of apartheid South Africa. But the lessons of his statecraft did not last long in the royal court after he died, in his eighties, in 1982.

Mswati was preferred to his brothers, as was the royal tradition, because of his youth and disposition. As the youngest of the brothers he was the least 'tainted' and so the obvious choice, as the heir to the throne has to be unmarried. Mswati was also one of Sobhuza's favourites in the old king's dying days. But although the older princes had long known they were not in the running for the throne, all had an interest in influencing the succession, as favoured members of the Dlamini dynasty have the run of the land, or at least a headstart in the juiciest deals. From the moment Sobhuza died, government of the country ground to a halt.

The course of Mswati's early years as king-in-waiting reads like a thrill-a-minute historical novel. As he was still a minor, Sobhuza's senior widow, Dzeliwe, took over as queen regent, but she rapidly offended hardcore traditionalists by not carrying out the old king's funeral rites in the correct way, appointing a favourite to act in her interests, and sending the young Mswati, or Makhosetiwe as he was then known, abroad to Sherborne for his education. Within months she had been toppled in a palace coup and replaced as regent by Queen Ntombi, Mswati's mother, whom the plotters wrongly thought would be easy to manipulate, and the heir was hastily brought back from Britain in the first of several interruptions to his studies.

The putsch provoked public demonstrations on behalf of the ousted 'Great She Elephant' – or so at least I gleaned in dribs and drabs during a confusing week trying to understand the Swazi court. Mswati was soon sent back to his foreign school, partly to keep him away from the skulduggery back home, and yet not even Sherborne was far enough. To the bewilderment of the Dorset police, a witch-doctor was found in the grounds, or so the rumours claimed, trying to bury a potion that was aimed at killing the king. It must have seemed a preposterous tale to the Sherborne staff but in Swaziland there were far stranger stories circulating of princes plotting to take power using special *muti* (medicine) with human body parts. All the while Mswati was flitting between his two very different worlds. During one half-term he accompanied an élite group of warriors on a trek to hunt down and kill a lion which had been specially imported from South Africa, to prove, as custom demanded, that he was greater than 'the one that devours man'.

The Swazis are sensitive about their traditions and bridle at the tendency of foreigners to view their kingdom as an anthropological theme park. Courtiers tartly suggest there is little difference between the royal lion hunt and the British royal family chasing foxes on horseback. Looking at King Mswati I found it easy to imagine him at Sherborne, where he was said to have been an able but unexceptional student, the exotic foreigner who played by the book and whom everyone liked but no one knew. Remarkably for an African leader he could hardly wait for the interview to start. Turning to me with a boyish smile that made him look younger than his twenty-eight years, he urged me to begin.

As I listened to him reminisce about his boyhood in the royal court I was irresistibly reminded of Evelyn Waugh's *Black Mischief*, which tells the tale of Seth, a young black ruler who returns from a public school education in England to take over a tiny African state and embarks on an energetic modernizing programme. His reforms soon come up against the potent forces of tribalism and tradition with catastrophic effects that ended in a coup, civil war, his overthrow and the daughter of the British envoy being served up as stew.

Such a scenario, albeit without the culinary climax, was not totally far-fetched when 'Mak' was summoned back from Sherborne at short notice without finishing his studies to be crowned as the world's youngest king in April 1986. School rules dictated that he had to wear school uniform at all times during term-time. On his flight home he changed into traditional dress but the appropriate sandals could not be found. Sherborne legend has it that he returned to his kingdom with feathers in his hair, painted robes on his back and sporting a pair of Dunlop Green Flash gymshoes.

Like Waugh's Seth, Mswati acted decisively on taking power. Within a month of his coronation he dissolved the supreme council, the Liqoqo, the shadowy body of advisors. He also rapidly dispensed with a number of the old guard. One of the most powerful princes, Bhekimpi, was charged with treason on the grounds that he had treated the king like a boy – an offence which in the prince's defence it must have been easy to commit given Mswati's tender years. The minister of health, Prince Phiwokwakhe, was fired for incompetence, a charge unheard of in the royal court. He had been in charge of family planning, a key state policy in the light of Swaziland's exploding population, which was growing at more than 3 per cent a year, and yet he had six wives and reputedly more than forty children. But it seems likely that his dismissal had more to do with palace politics than with his contribution to overpopulation.

Mswati was moving far more cautiously, however, by the time of my interview a decade after his coronation. When he took power, his kingdom was an island of stability. But by the mid-Nineties the southern African stereotypes had been reversed: South Africa, the regional big brother, had moved triumphantly to democracy; even Mozambique had emerged from its ruinous civil war and held multi-party elections; but

Swaziland was paralysed by mounting calls for democratic reforms. Thousands of striking workers brought the capital to a halt in 1996. Resorting to repressive colonial-era legislation, the police fought running battles with the demonstrators. By African standards the security forces were a model of restraint, but the use of tear-gas and batons was new to the Swazis. The old affectionate talk of Swaziland as a toytown was a distant dream. There was a whiff in the air of the house of Stuart in the 1630s – or of Europe in 1848.

Critics said Mswati had been seduced by the trappings of power and had no interest in the weighty matters of state. There were reports of a playboy lifestyle. His new palace was said to have a glass-bottomed swimming pool and a designated disco dance floor. Hostile rumours trickled from the court that he was an unwilling pupil at his morning lessons. Malicious tongues recalled a rally early in his reign when the king addressed striking teachers sounding suspiciously as if he was drunk, and abused them in a most un-Swazi fashion. The next time he addressed a public meeting he was a model of contrition. 'The last time I addressed you the sun was very hot,' he explained.[2] The nuance would not have been lost on his audience.

But in the king's defence it is easy to see why from time to time he might have wanted to retire to his palace to let his hair down. From the moment he returned from Sherborne he was smothered in protocol. He was at the head of a system which had somehow survived the twentieth century almost unchanged. His every move and decision was hedged and constrained. When the Prince of Wales visited, commentators suggested drily that the two men had a lot in common: both fronted institutions in need of reform and both were desperately uncertain how far to go.

⁂

Over two tempestuous centuries the Swazi kings have perfected the art of survival, an extraordinary achievement for such a tiny nation in one of the world's most troubled regions. Their record dates back to King Sobhuza I, one of the few regional rulers to survive the *mfecane*, the devastation wrought by Shaka's hordes. Sobhuza sensibly realized there was a time for courage and a time for prudence, so he ceded territory and retreated to the hills. As soon, however, as Shaka was dead, he set about winning his lost lands back. He is also said to have had a dream before he ever saw a white man in which he saw white-skinned people with hair 'like tassels of cattle' bringing a book and money. His interpretation was to accept the former but be wary of the latter. Consequently missionaries were welcomed but business-men were not.

Inspired by his example, the Dlaminis made flexibility their trademark. Subsequent generations saw off the Boers, the Zulus and the British and expanded the kingdom with a mixture of guile, warfare and charm. The only king to try a different tack had disastrous results. Mbandzeni, who ruled until 1889, effec-tively mortgaged the nation to concession-seekers who ended up with monopolies on anything from the then unbuilt railway refreshment rooms to minting money and, most iniquituous of all, the land.

Mswati's father, Sobhuza II, who oversaw independence from Britain in 1968, proved himself worthy of his forefather's name by taking on and ultimately defeating the concessionaires in the law courts. With his watchword 'I have no enemies' he cannily shored up the monarchy against the tide of reform. Even when he suspended the constitution in 1973 and banned politi-cal parties, his diplomacy ensured he avoided the opprobrium other leaders would have faced for such an authoritarian step.

Mswati, however, had far less scope for flexibility. Not only was the conflict between tradition and progress becoming increasingly heated, but as a young man he had no clout with the *labadzala*, the shadowy group of royal relatives and advisors for whom flexibility was merely a way of stalling for time. J.S.M. Matsebula, Sobhuza's private secretary and Swaziland's official historian, was once asked to explain who exactly the elders were. He replied: 'They are men and they are every-where.' Mswati's challenge was to accommodate their demands while staving off the dangers of a revolution.

Mswati may well indeed have been thinking of his counsellors' reaction when I asked him what were the most important lessons he had brought home with him from Sherborne. It was an innocent question intended to put him at his ease and I expected the hoary old line about public schools and a sense of fair play. Instead, after a brief pause, he replied, 'Flexibility.' I had little doubt his answer was in due course relayed to the cohorts of half-brothers who had been outside the king's audience chamber as I went in, strutting up and down like the peacocks which lined his lawn, competing with a group of American Peace Corps volunteers to bend his ear.

On my way to the palace I had driven past the centre of the capital, Mbabane, a bustling little town, whose facilities put to shame Africa's larger capitals to the north. Dark-suited executives bustled in and out of glistening glass-fronted offices. It seemed ridiculous to suppose that in such a sophisticated setting the king's brothers really could pose a threat. Then I recalled the words of a royal advisor who had talked to me over tea the previous weekend in his hilltop home.

'You must remember that at the back of his mind is the fate of his grandfather, King Bhunu . . .' Bhunu, I gathered, had made the mistake of falling foul of a royal clique. He died in 1899, after a mere ten years on the throne, of a mysterious 'snake-bite', paving the way for Sobhuza II, who no doubt the *labadzala* of the day assumed would be a more pliable chap.

Surrounded as he was by the *labadzala* of the late twentieth century, Mswati unsurprisingly spent much of my interview defending tradition, weighing every word even though he was clearly repeating a well-rehearsed speech.

'Tradition shows where you come from,' he said. 'In the past the *Mhlanga* would keep girls from getting early pregnancies. They get a chance to talk to one another. If you maintain your tradition you maintain your identity . . .' Multi-party democracy would of course be considered if the people wanted it, but it would not, indeed could not, be rushed. He was, he was at pains to impress upon me, far from being an absolute king.

'The king of Swaziland merely takes decisions. Even on paper

I'm not an absolute monarch. Change never stops,' he said. 'Something that is good for this year may not be good for next year. We know multi-partyism but it did not work well. If you do things overnight you make a mess. You must take time and do it right.'

The debate is no stranger to the West, where traditions have had centuries to adapt. But in Africa modernity has come almost overnight, bringing science and enlightenment but also confusion and fear. Now it is lapping at the doors of a last redoubt. The king insists that Swaziland's *tinkhundla* system of 'popular democracy', in which people discuss issues in regional assemblies, is fairer than the 'tyranny' of multi-partyism where a few demagogues can hold sway. *Tinkhundla* has parallels with Uganda, where a ban on party politics since the mid-Eighties has brought stability after years of chaos and an opportunity for much-needed economic reform. As with the Ashante kings in Ghana who traditionally were de-stooled by royal councils if they overstepped the mark, so, too, the Dlaminis insist they have checks on despotism: the queen mother has her own court with its own powers; the royal council acts as an inner cabinet. But these 'checks' are an integral part of the status quo.

Prince Masatsele, one of Mswati's elder brothers, a giant of a man with feathers in his hair and a nimble grasp of European history, took me to one side after my interview. He could see only chaos coming from multi-party reform. He jabbed a finger at my notebook as if to a serf: 'Modernity has always been mistaken for wisdom.'

Wearied by endless procrastinations, progressives dismiss such talk as stalling for time. For them, the Swazi system of holding elections without parties is an excuse for autocracy and is ripe for exploitation. According to tradition, the national assembly has sixty-five members, ten of whom are appointed by the king and the rest elected by popular vote. The body is supported by a senate of thirty members, twenty of whom are appointed by the king and ten nominated by the national assembly. The progressives insist the time has come for accountable and representative government.

'We are run like a family,' Jan Sithole, the secretary general of the Swazi Federation of Trade Unions, told me. 'Confrontation is not our first ticket, but we don't want to fool the world there is meaningful change. It is only cosmetic. And you must remember there is a difference between peace and silence. The problem is the cabals around the king. In change is their demise.'

Sithole has powerful support across the border among South Africa's trade union leaders, who are itching to flex their muscles in support of their 'oppressed comrades'. The risk, however, is that as the royal dyke gives, as it inevitably must, Swaziland's stability will also founder. The challenge is to finesse a smooth transition.

Privately the king recognizes the need for change. The difficulty is to find a peaceful way to back down. The humiliation would be unbearable if he was forced out by strikes and protests. He is after all endowed with fabled rain-making powers. He smiled when I asked him about kings and clouds.

'It's part and parcel of the culture of being a king. There are certain things that one can do if you believe in them. Sometimes when you do those things I think it is a matter of faith. If you have enough faith, those things will happen. It's the queen mother that does most of those things but sometimes she does it together with the king . . . and the rains do come.'

The foreign minister, the police chief and the head of the army were all listening intently. I cleared my throat and tried again: 'So do you yourself think you can make rain?' The king paused. 'If the Swazis believe that the king can do something then you must go along with this feeling.'

It was a deft answer. But the travails of a fellow 'rainmaker', the legendary 'rain queen' of Duiwelskloof (Valley of the Devil), suggest that Mswati has a fight on his hands if his authority is to survive.

⁂

There was a time when the 'Rain Queen' of the Modjadji Mountains was worshipped thousands of miles from her secluded home. The Modjadji dynasty arrived in the far north of what was to become South Africa over two centuries ago. Such was their reputation that even Shaka left her and her tiny Lovedu tribe well alone. Her crown lands encompassed hundreds of miles of misty valleys. As the cult grew in the nineteenth century, rumours of immortality and fair-skinned beauty spread. Her gender was no barrier in this most patriarchal of regions and she was seen as second only to the Zulu king in the roll call of regional royalty. White travellers paid tribute to her as they headed north in search of the fabled riches of Monomatapa, the ancient Zimbabwean kingdom whence the Modjadji were believed to have come. It was from this mysterious figure that Sir Henry Rider Haggard drew inspiration for the beautiful and immortal warrior queen 'She who must be obeyed' in his novel *She*.

Nelson Mandela himself is said to have come up against the queen's legendary hauteur when he visited Modjadji V on the campaign for the April 1994 election as a courtesy call to prove his 'traditional' credentials. His aides portrayed the visit as a triumph, but in Modjadji's mountain kraal 250 miles from Johannesburg people remember it rather differently. There the elders still speak a court patois. The queen appears in public only once or twice a year when it is time to beat the sacred drums to hasten or withhold rain. Her advisors recall that, far from welcoming the ANC leader, she turned her back on him and refused to endorse his campaign.

Rather than risk a repeat of Mandela's rebuff I heeded the advice of an anthropologist and, on my way to interview her, stopped at the local store to buy her presents, opting for a bouquet of flowers and a box of chocolates. They had only Black Magic. The assistant wrapped them up in bright paper and I hoped the queen would not take offence.

Victor Modjadji, a cousin and official from the local tribal authority, was waiting at the outer stockade of wooden staves. After taking off my shoes I followed him across the smooth red earth to the veranda of a colonial-style bungalow. The building overlooked twenty grass-roofed rondavels whose occupants were welcoming the new day at the slow and deliberate pace of rural Africa. Fittingly the sky was heavy with rain. As the sun broke through the clouds our guide reappeared and beckoned up the hill to another bungalow, the far side of a second palisade.

A dumpy old woman was squatting in the corner of the veranda. She was draped in a tartan blanket and wore a cheap flowery headscarf. I assumed she was the cleaner taking a break. It was only when our guide coughed that I realized we were in the presence of Modjadji.

I was not the first to make this mistake. Even her advisors conceded that Modjadji V did not take after her fictional forebear whom Rider Haggard, when lodged nearby as a young colonial officer, had described in his usual stirring tones: 'No man who had once seen "She" unveiled and heard the music of her voice and drunk in the bitter wisdom of her words would willingly give up the sight for a whole sea of joys.' Modjadji V was, I was told, the result of an ill-judged union between her mother and a commoner – but she certainly maintained the family tradition for elliptical replies. She answered my questions almost entirely in monosyllables, using her kinsman Victor to interpret even though she understands English.

'I don't remember a thing about his [Mandela's] visit. I don't know a thing about him,' she said. 'I just ask you white people if his government is doing all right.' There was not the hint of a smile. The only time she raised her eyes was when asked about the ANC whose revolutionary water policies were clearly not welcome in Modjadji. For one whose authority waned as rivers rose, the supply of water to hundreds of previously dry communities was a cause for concern. Still more troubling was a new 'irreverence' coursing through the nation's youth. She once chased a group of ANC youths away from her kraal with a whip.

'These boys don't want to listen. They just want to do their own thing,' she said disconsolately. 'I feel very sad about that. The youth can do anything and they will not get punished.'

In the local Masanalabo secondary school halfway down the

mountain, five of the brightest pupils were having a tutorial under a tree. They welcomed the chance of breaking off their studies to talk about the Rain Queen. Brimming with the fire of school-leavers, four of them were adamant that Modjadji was outdated, undemocratic and did not understand the changing order. Her teenage granddaughter Makobo, the next in line, would get short shrift if she tried to maintain the mystique.

But their attitude changed when asked how they would react if the Rain Queen approached them. Only one said he would stay seated. A trifle sheepishly, the others admitted they would kneel down and bow their heads to show respect.

And so, with gentle prompting, a more complex picture emerged. Their complaint was not with the cult but with the Rain Queen's high-handed ways. Modjadji had compromised her powers by praying in a church during a recent drought. She was also unpopular because she summoned locals for lectures on land tenure at strange hours. As for her granddaughter, she was suspect because she drank beer and went to discos, not what a Modjadji should do.

Their teacher deftly intervened. Tradition was, he suggested, part of their identity and they would in time come to terms with it. Parts would be rejected and parts would endure.

'Our tradition is built on taboos,' he said. 'There are some I agree with and some I disagree with. But if you research taboos, you will learn to love them because of tradition. It is in our veins.'

⩍⩍⩍⩍

King Mswati might do well to heed the teacher's advice on the need to let traditions come and go. Even in Swaziland tradition has shifted with the times. The Reed Dance had for several generations fallen into abeyance before Sobhuza II reintroduced it, on the model of an old Zulu custom, to stiffen the national spine. Swaziland needs a wily helmsman if it is to reach a solution. Mswati could do worse than travel to Pretoria to consult Nelson Mandela, who, by the end of his presidency, had assumed the mantle of world sage and whose style, whatever his mistakes, was the opposite of Big Man rule. By the end of my allotted time with the king I had run out of questions and I murmured I did not want to take up more of a busy man's day. He brushed my protestations aside and urged me to continue, as if he were desperate for a chance to escape from the formulas of his position, not to mention his factional court. So we sat chatting about his schooldays while his officers of state nodded their heads – and the *labadzala* and the American volunteers besieged the door.

9

Madiba Magic

Nelson Mandela – Playing the *Ubuntu* Card

Hemmed in by the drab streets of central Johannesburg, the Carlton Hotel was a dispiriting place. In its heyday it was one of the continent's premier watering holes. On his release from prison Nelson Mandela could be found in its Three Ships restaurant on many an evening, relaxing with friends or strategizing with colleagues before he lost his freedom again as president. He even celebrated his April 1994 election victory in the hotel ballroom with the stilted jive that he was to make his trademark, before leaving the floor to younger generations and retiring to bed as elderly gentlemen do.

But within a few years of that most exuberant of parties the hotel was dying. As white businesses fled to Johannesburg's northern suburbs, the city centre took on the turbulent tones of the Third World it had tried so long to keep at bay. One by one the Carlton's suites closed. Then came the news that the Three Ships was to serve its last meal. As I stood at the hotel entrance in December 1997, waiting for a lunch guest, the hawkers and autograph-hunters who used to wait for celebrities had long since followed them north to the multinational chains.

Lunch had been set for 12:15 for 12:30. At 12:14 on the dot a black limousine purred into sight, pausing to allow traffic to pass and then drew up in front of the hotel. The front passenger skipped to the side and opened the back door. A tall silver-haired figure manoeuvred his way on to the pavement almost colliding with a gaggle of school-children. As they hurried on their way chattering excitedly, one of them stopped as if to tie a shoe-lace, glanced at the elderly African in the brightly coloured shirt, looked away and then stared again. There had been no fanfare, no outriders, no flashing lights, no fenced-off streets. It couldn't be the world's most famous and best-loved politician, could it? And yet it was.

I could understand the girl's confusion. I had just come back from central Africa, where presidents close down their capitals for the slightest errand and keep you waiting as a mark of their power. With Mandela, however, it was a point of honour to make the opposite true. Indeed his office had called me in the middle of the morning to inform me he would be half an hour early. Mercifully for the stress levels of the hotel staff, he changed his mind at the last minute and made a detour via a relation before arriving bang on the time.

Smiling his famous dazzling beam, he summoned the school-girls. His bodyguard, long since inured to his whims, did a minuscule shrug to the presidential secretary as if to say 'here we go again', while Mandela wove his magic, asking the girls where they were from and where they went to school before concluding with a playful question about their ambitions.

'So what do you want to do when you grow up?' he asked. 'Do you want to be a politician?'

'Oh no,' one of them gasped. 'That is too much hard work!'

Mandela laughed as if it was the funniest thing he had heard all week. Then he turned to the girls' companions and delivered an impromptu homily on the importance of going to school before moving back to the doorway to greet the Carlton's manager with the warmth most of us reserve for a long-lost friend.

I was there in my capacity as head of South Africa's Foreign Correspondents' Association as he was due to address us over lunch. I had watched his charm at work many times before over the years. But his magnetism had lost none of its powers. He switched from cheeky family confidant, asking my wife how long it had taken her to persuade me to get married, to mischievous quipster, joking that he had just come from the

African Development Bank, where he had asked for the keys of the safe, to pillar of rectitude.

'I will defer to you, Mr Chairman, in everything,' he said when I asked when he wanted to speak. 'I am sure you know what is best. I am in your hands.'

Thus we gathered around him over lunch open-mouthed, like novices before a seer, utterly unable to pose a serious question as he indulged what his friends joke is his desire to go down in history as the grandfather of story-telling. He started with a Solomonic tale about how one Christmas he had been called on to mediate in a chicken dispute in his home village in the Transkei region. From time to time he lost the thread – and I had in fact heard the chicken story before – but as with all the best stories it was the telling of it that mattered. He closed with a lecture on the importance of Africans learning good time-keeping.

Mandela can be electric when he speaks off the cuff, but he is ponderous when delivering formal speeches, and so it came as no surprise that his address elicited nothing new, particularly since the ANC's triennial congress was three weeks away. But no one was disappointed. As he headed for the exit, a gaggle of journalists and waiters blocked his path to shake his hand. Halfway down the line he stopped in front of one of my female colleagues, a striking six-foot television producer. Ever the lady's man he looked her up and down with an approving glance.

'You must play sport. Do you play basketball?' he asked the astonished young woman. Startled to be flirted with by the world's most popular statesman, she spluttered that swimming was her only exercise. He did the closest thing there is to a presidential wink. Then he pottered on to the door with a broad smile.

♦♦♦♦

So what is his secret? Good manners play a large part. Mandela is a perfect synthesis of informality with form; and his especial brilliance is knowing when and where each applies. His values blend the stern precepts of the British missionaries who taught him in his early years in the Transkei with the *mores* of the proud Thembu chief in whose home he was raised. He is a model of courtly old-world charm, although he is also a stickler for protocol. As a young lawyer he was disappointed on meeting a leading white radical lawyer who was not wearing a tie. Fifty years later when he was introduced in the Bundestag to MPs from Germany's Green Party, he chided them for not wearing suits, asking them how they thought they would be taken seriously if they were dressed informally. He regularly remonstrated with reporters for asking him about his private life, saying it was not right to ask an old man such personal questions. Young guns in the ANC leadership soon learned that the genial grandfather figure who would always ask them about their families had more than a touch of a Victorian headmaster.

Six months into the new era, Whitney Houston, the black American singer who was an idol for black South Africans, was performing in Johannesburg over a weekend when the party's national executive was meeting in Cape Town. Several of the younger members were desperate to go, but so wary were they of incurring Mandela's disapproval by asking to miss part of the meeting that they slipped out on the Saturday evening, flew the two hours to Johannesburg in time for the second half of the concert and then flew straight back in time for the Sunday morning session. 'There we were, a bunch of former freedom fighters with years of imprisonment and activism behind us, and we suddenly felt like naughty children,' recalled Mannie Dipico, one of the rebels, who was premier of the Northern Cape province. 'We just knew it would be a big mistake to tell him.'

Mandela, however, tempers his propriety with a dislike of pomposity and a finely judged wit. He seldom loses sight of the humorous side of his change of fortune. He was once being interviewed in his office when the telephone rang. On picking up the receiver and listening to the receptionist, he paused and then turned to the interviewer.

'It's P.W.' he said in a stage whisper, meaning De Klerk's predecessor, P.W. Botha. When the Great Crocodile, as Botha was known in his heyday, came on the line to plead for Mandela to intervene on behalf of right-wing prisoners, Mandela chatted away in Afrikaans as if to an old friend.

While a believer in etiquette, Mandela could certainly never be accused of being staid. Early in his presidency he urged South Africans to address him by his clan name, 'Madiba'. He also did to South Africa's fashion what he had already done to its politics – he turned it upside down. Taking their cue from European royalty, post-colonial African leaders have tradition-ally had eclectic tastes. The old Big Man favourites were khaki fatigues, pantomime uniforms, Afro-chic or Savile Row. Man-dela, however, forged his own distinctive path, opting for jazzy flowing shirts, garish but always elegant and never an eyesore. 'Madiba', humorously known as 'Madiba Formal', even became an accepted dress code on invitations.

His old friend Bishop Tutu, the former Archbishop of Cape Town, was a lone critic, arguing that he preferred Mandela in a suit – prompting a classic Mandela retort: 'That's a bit rich coming from a man in a dress.' And yet Mandela never made the mistake of looking casual when an occasion called for respect. He wore one of his shirts to the summit of UN world leaders but a dark grey suit for his speech to a joint sitting of the two houses of parliament during his state visit to Britain in 1996. This was a forum he had long admired. One of the few surviving pre-Robben Island photographs of Mandela shows him glancing up at the sky outside Westminster in 1962, when he was roaming the world's capitals drumming up support for the 'struggle'.

Such was his impact during his state visit that one bedazzled British commentator went so far as to hail him as a very British African leader.[1] After the long years of greedy and cruel post-colonial presidents, Mandela was seen as a man whom Britain could understand and trust. He himself writes of his anglophilia, both at mission school and on his visit in 1962. There is indeed a touch of the old-fashioned country gentleman about him. Legend has it that one of his first questions on being freed was to ask whether the Australian cricketing genius Don Bradman was still alive. He loves his garden, reads Shakespeare – or at least did in prison, when he had the time – and goes for an early morning 'constitutional' each day.

But it was a huge mistake, not to say presumption, to assume Mandela was a Brit *manqué*. It is just that he knows what the Brits want to hear. He is a natural socializer, and although even his closest friends confide they are frozen from his inner feelings, he loves meeting people, particularly children and women. Wherever he goes he has a cheery 'Hello. How are you?' His skill is to to dredge out a connection, however tenuous, to put interlocutors at their ease. His eyes rolled when I interviewed him in 1994 and introduced myself as the correspondent of the *Daily Telegraph*.

'Your paper interviewed me before,' he said. 'In August.' It was then December and my mind raced: it had not been me; had someone else come out from my paper and interviewed him? After a suitable pause, Mandela continued in his usual deliberate manner: 'August 21st . . . 1964.'

It transpires that the *Telegraph* has no record of the interview. Indeed *Telegraph* journalists of the era do not recall a 'Mr Newman', the name Mandela gave the reporter in his autobiography, ever working for the newspaper. It could be that a South African security agent masqueraded as a correspondent to try to elicit some information, or that a local newspaper sold the story to the *Telegraph*, or that Mandela's memory was faulty. Whatever the truth of the matter, the man whom I grew up knowing as the name of a dozen student common rooms had won me over before the interview had even begun.

Mandela was at his most brilliant when charming the Afrikaner. The dourest of Nationalists melted at his approach, beguiled by his mixture of blokishness and brio. He was after all an amalgam after their hearts. He dispensed with the British desire for the 'done thing' but had a respect for authority and age. He appealed to Afrikaners' rustic hankerings. Soon after his release from prison he confided that more than anything he had missed the fresh smell of the first summer rains on the veld after the dry winter months. He also felt they had an affinity through their common heritage, African and Afrikaner, oppressed and oppressor, and latterly ruler and ruled.

At the start of his presidency he was a one-man cure for Afrikaners' 'new' South African blues. I lost count of the number of right-wingers I met who were converted by a brief encounter with the 'old man'. Lieutenant Attie Wessels, a dour weather-beaten police officer in the remote Northern Cape town of Griquastad, was standing at a road-block when Mandela broke away from an official tour and accosted him.

'He shook my hand and said he'd try to pay me more,' Wessels recalled moments later. 'I'll be telling my children about this until the day I die.'

Mandela's most famous reconciliatory pose came in the 1995 Rugby World Cup when he embraced the cause of the Springboks, the national rugby side. For so long they had been a symbol of white muscular defiance. By sporting a Springbok cap and jersey at the final he sent a signal to the *volk* that all that they cherished was safe in the 'new' South Africa, and created an image that will endure in the collective white memory far longer than the sight of Mandela taking the salute at his inauguration. Officials later revealed, to no one's surprise, that it was a personal decision.

The success of his Springbok support set in motion an extraordinary chain of events which led some critics to suggest he had taken his crusade too far. He hosted a lunch for Percy Yutar, the prosecutor who had argued long and hard for the death sentence in the Rivonia trial, and had aired his disappointment when Mandela was only jailed for life. He invited the widows and wives of Nationalist former heads of state and black liberation leaders to tea at his residence in Pretoria. Then, as the apex of his reconciliatory mission, he paid a call on Betsy Verwoerd, the widow of the architect of grand apartheid, Dr Hendrik Verwoerd.

The frail ninety-four-year-old had declared she was too weak to take up his invitation to tea with the wives and widows but would be at home if he was in the neighbourhood. She can never have expected he would take up her offer. Her husband, who was assassinated in 1966, refined the apartheid edifice and introduced the legislation that led to the banning of the ANC and Mandela's imprisonment. Verwoerd was reputed to have prided himself on never having shaken a black man's hand. And yet there was his widow, wrinkled like a dried-up fruit, offering Mandela coffee and *koeksusters* (treacly Afrikaner cakes) and glancing up at him for approval as she read out a statement in a quavering voice.

The sight of Mandela leaning over and helping her to read her message was a striking symbol of how South Africa had moved forward. Mrs Verwoerd was one of a handful of diehard separatists living in Orania, a whites-only settlement in one of the remotest parts of the country. Mandela was making the point that he could and would go anywhere in South Africa. Critics, however, argued that his trip was a gimmick and that he would do better focusing on uplifting the poor. At an impromptu press conference on the Verwoerds' *stoep*, a black journalist pointedly asked Mandela how a community which barred blacks fitted into the new South Africa. A testy Mandela replied that his reconciliatory drive cost South Africa only a few moments of his time and yet helped to bind the fragile fledgling nation together and had saved it from war.

🏃🏃🏃🏃

Anyone who spent more than a few weeks in Mandela's South Africa will know the question which no one has satisfactorily answered – how can he have emerged from prison so lacking in bitterness, or rather, as many suspect, so good at disguising it?

Just like De Klerk fielding the question about his decision to unban the ANC, Mandela has developed a pat answer. Disappointing as it is to believers in the Mandela myth, he is the first to reject the Christian echoes, talk of saintly attributes, and parallels with Gandhi. For Mandela humanitarianism came a distant second to strategy. Reconciliation was a policy with specific aims which he identified in prison and then re-emphasized early in his presidency: reaching a settlement, avoiding civil war and shaping the country's future.

The foundation of his reconciliatory vision can be found in his early career. As a young man he was in the Africanist wing of the ANC Youth League, which argued that blacks should fight white rule on their own, without the support of Asians or whites. 'While I was not prepared to hurl the white man into the sea, I would have been perfectly happy if he had climbed aboard his steamships and left the continent of his own volition,' he later recalled.[2] But later, after contact with white Communists and ANC members, he came to believe that the ANC's doctrine of non-racialism was the only way forward for South Africa. As he rose through the ranks of the ANC in the Fifties he had bitter arguments with the Africanists who eventually broke off to form the Pan Africanist Congress.

Raymond Mhlaba, an ANC stalwart who was sentenced with Mandela in 1964 and served almost as long, told me that soon after they arrived on Robben Island they sat down and assessed that apartheid could not work for ever. It did not take long, Mhlaba said, to learn to lay aside their anger at the petty prejudices of whites and focus their energies on defeating the system. Confident that eventually they were bound to be released, they started preparing for power and particularly how to handle whites.

'I knew that people expected me to harbour anger towards whites,' Mandela said when recalling the morning after his release. 'But I had none. In prison my anger towards whites decreased, but my hatred for the system grew.'[3] South Africans had good reason to expect him to be angry. When he went into prison he had a reputation for spirited leadership, as immortalized in his defiant performance in the dock in the Rivonia trial when he was on trial for treason facing a possible death sentence and yet refused to tone down his criticism of apartheid. But he was also known for his impulsiveness. His decision to launch the ANC into the armed struggle in 1961 went against the instincts of many of his colleagues, including the then leader,

Chief Albert Luthuli, who was shortly to receive the Nobel Peace Prize for his efforts to effect peaceful change. It also gave the authorities the excuse they needed to clamp down on opponents.

Mandela's subsequent – and brief – career as an underground revolutionary was also marked by rashness. He had followed Fidel Castro's revolution in Cuba and hoped that the conditions were right for a similar rolling uprising in South Africa, an assumption that flew in the face of logic given the strength of the white government. Baroness Orczy's Sir Percy Blakeney, the 'Scarlet Pimpernel' of the French Revolution, would have snorted with derision at the idea of Mandela being a 'Black Pimpernel', his nickname when he was on the run from 1961 until his arrest the following year. He flouted the most basic rules of insurgency, carrying incriminating documents and notes on his person as he toured the country visiting known members of the ANC. Accounts suggest the ANC was riddled with informers and that the authorities just bided their time before picking up its leaders. Indeed the biggest difficulty the government faced seems to have been in getting a conviction, so incompetent were the police in preparing their case. But the police's shortcomings were offset by the ANC's, for which the party leadership, including Mandela, has to take much of the blame. By 1965, the year after he was imprisoned for life, the ANC was a spent force in South Africa with all its leaders exiled or in prison. Eleven years would pass until the anti-apartheid movement would strike a serious blow in South Africa with the schoolchildren's uprising in Soweto in 1976 – and that was an internal protest which owed nothing to the ANC.

Mandela's misjudgements, however, have to be seen in context. It is easy in hindsight to argue that liberal politics had still not run their course, and that by pursuing a policy of civil disobedience the ANC might have won some concessions. But by 1961 the ANC had been waging a non-violent protest for nearly forty years and had made no progress. The government did not reply to Mandela's letters calling for dialogue. The Sharpeville massacre of March 1960 when white police shot dead sixty-nine black protesters showed how far the government was willing to go in defence of white rule.

One mainly white school of thought would have it that prison was the making of Mandela. After his release Nationalists liked to argue that in the rest of Africa he would have been executed for his crimes and that they were owed a debt of gratitude for preserving him intact. Certainly there was a hypocrisy in the way the world treated Mandela: blacks mistreating blacks was not as bad as whites mistreating blacks. Had Mandela been in prison anywhere else in Africa it is a fair assumption that he would not have been half as well known.

Mandela himself readily admits that he was able to mature behind bars. The chapters of his autobiography detailing his prison years read in places like a philosophical handbook on leadership. Time and again he writes how he thought that such an attitude or action was, or was not, the right thing for a leader to do. He had time to analyse South Africa and he learned to turn his anger towards apartheid and away from its beneficiaries. He was also able to watch as his contemporaries floundered in the rest of Africa and grew to realize that seducing South Africa's whites was critical to the nation's chances. Samora Machel, Mozambique's independence leader who was killed in a mysterious plane crash on the South African border in 1986 and whose widow, Graca, was to marry Mandela twelve years later, reflected during his presidency that Mozambique had been crippled by the flight of the Portuguese colonists.

Mandela is also gracious enough to suggest that his warders played a part in his development. While most were brutish and racist, a few isolated acts of kindness reinforced his conviction that there was humanity behind apartheid's uncompromising veneer. One of his jailers, James Gregory, was even asked to his inauguration as a guest of honour. Gregory said that after the ceremony Kobie Coetsee, the Minister of Justice, who had brokered the secret talks between Mandela and P.W. Botha, introduced him to a judge as 'the man who took the hatred for the white man out of Nelson Mandela.'[4]

But the Nationalists' argument that prison indirectly did him a good service is scant consolation. He had every reason to emerge embittered and enraged. So packed and colourful has been his post-imprisonment career – and so warm and embracing has been his smile – that it is easy to forget he was released well into his eighth decade. His emergence as a visionary and reconciliatory statesman has nothing to do with the Nationalists who initially did all they could to break him. One of the most striking aspects of his autobiography is the way the four years of transition from white rule are tacked on to the end almost as an epilogue. He devotes 200 pages to his imprisonment and barely sixty to the bloody and fraught time between his release and taking office. During his first eighteen years in prison on the few visits from his wife Winnie, he could not even hold hands with her and had to communicate through a glass screen. He was not allowed to attend the funeral of his mother, or that of his eldest son, who was killed in a car accident. All this was against a background of relentless baiting by warders and, on the bigger canvas of South Africa, of increasingly ruthless repression.

Conditions in prison improved in the last few years when the Nationalists were grooming him for release. He had his own cottage in the grounds of Victor Verster prison outside Cape Town where he could receive visitors and make telephone calls. But no one knew how he would react to freedom. For twenty-seven years he had been deep-frozen. His words had been proscribed. There was just one photograph of his life in captivity. When his warders took him on walks in Cape Town to acclimatize him to life in freedom, he met several people but no one recognized him. He was more a symbol of a people's hope – and repression – than a reality.

Certainly when he made his famous first steps of freedom in February 1990 his status as an international icon owed a lot to ANC marketing. The 'Free Mandela' campaign was one of the most effective decisions of the ANC in all its years in exile. By personalizing the 'struggle' the organization made it easier for the world to understand, as was reflected by the success of the Wembley 'Free Mandela' concert marking his seventieth birthday.

But there is far, far more to Mandela than marketing and charm. He was from his early years in politics an intuitive leader. While he led as he played draughts in prison, in a 'slow and deliberate'[5] manner, crucially he could throw off the straitjacket of inflexibility, most audaciously in 1986, when he decided to open talks with P.W. Botha without consulting his colleagues. He knew many in the ANC would have been deeply suspicious of such a move and also that it would have taken months to get the party's approval, so he pressed ahead. It is for such flashes of individualism and bravery that he can lay claim to being a truly great politician.

Try as journalists did throughout his presidency, it was next to impossible to cleave the private from the public persona. Outside the immediate political arena his guard seldom drops. But just occasionally his mouth folds into an uncompromising grimace, belying the platitudes he feels obliged to vouchsafe, and hinting at his old passion and an anger that in the interests of reconciliation he has hidden away.

The first time I saw Mandela close at hand was at the official party for his seventy-fifth birthday in, of course, the Carlton Hotel. Surrounded by white businessmen, who made up the bulk of the guest list, he was beaming away, nodding his head thoughtfully as if he had long since forgotten their long history of profiting from apartheid. But as I watched from the shadows, a look of utter sadness transformed his face.

***

For the outside world Mandela has become known as the living embodiment of reconciliation. But it may be more accurate to describe him as the personification of *ubuntu*, the mystical African ethos which loosely translates as 'humanity' but means so much more. An old Nguni saying gets as close to its essence as anything: '*Ubuntu ungumuntu ngabanye abantu*' – 'People are people through other people.' To be branded as lacking *ubuntu* is, in many parts of Africa, the ultimate insult, implying a betrayal of identity and Africa itself.

Ubuntu became something of a catchphrase for South

Africa's whites in the post-apartheid era. It was adopted by copy-writers in advertising firms and became part of the sophisticates' argot. To feel *ubuntu* was to be part of the new era and by extension to be with-it and cool. Invoking it drifted perilously close to the old romanticized dreams of purple sunsets and noble natives. Inevitably this devalued it in the eyes of many blacks, for whom it became a symbol of whites trying – and in their eyes often failing – to understand what it means to be African.

But the debasement of the word *ubuntu* has not undermined its essence. *Ubuntu* is more than a wistful Africanist musing. In its most tangible form it is to be found in the community spirit which relieves the bleakest of tableaux all over the continent, and in the tradition of extended families and hospitality. Africans working in the cities invariably remit most of their earnings to support their relations in their home villages. On a philosophical and sentimental level it is an aspiration which is hankered after around the African hearth. It reflects how Africa in its dreams would love to be. Africans proudly attest it as a powerful moral corrective to the West's cult of the individual, which they brand as selfish and cold.

Unfortunately, however, in *ubuntu*'s strength lies its weakness. It is a beguiling ideal but its culture of tolerance is easily abused. Too often in Africa it has become an excuse for subservience or tyranny or both.

Such was the desire for a new beginning in Liberia after seven years of brutal war that Charles Taylor, the most notorious warlord, was greeted at election rallies in 1997 with the cry: 'He killed my father. He killed my mother. He get my vote.' Taylor's lust for power had prolonged the civil war for six years after the overthrow of the dictator, Doe, and yet he was elected with a massive majority. His victory reflected Liberians' war-weariness and their desire for a 'strongman', not to mention their liking for the T-shirts and biros which Taylor's campaign organizers showered on the crowds at his rallies, but it also reflected a popular desire to look forward, stemming from the realization that the past was so appalling that there was no point in looking back.

The celebration of the group over the individual implicit in *ubuntu*, poses a couched threat to basic freedoms of speech and assembly. Moi, Mobutu and countless other Big Men have over the years endlessly resorted to versions of *ubuntu* as a defence on the lines that the West does not understand their African-ness. *Ubuntu*'s defenders counter that Moi and co. misused the hallowed principle, but the fact remains that for many Africans as well as outsiders the continent is more often synonymous with chaos and discord than with cosy *ubuntu*. The West may be 'selfish' and 'cold' in comparison with Africa, but in running a society all but the most ardent Africanists would have to concede it has been more successful.

For much of his presidency Mandela represented the best of *ubuntu*. When he was on song, it felt as if Africa at last had a leader who stood for all that was good about the continent. As a corrective to the cynicism of Western politics, he tore up the old rule book of government. When he walked into world summits, his fellow heads of state seemed tawdry and insignificant. His aura was all the more potent in a society which had long been run as the opposite of *ubuntu*. But *ubuntu* was not enough for the day-to-day running of a state.

👫👫

From Mandela's first day of freedom it was clear that much, indeed too much, was to be expected of him by both South Africans and the rest of the world. His age, experience and moral stature set him so far above his colleagues that he became the ultimate arbiter. Only he could hold the radical black youths in check. Only he could reassure whites that they would be led by a man they could trust. When disgruntled former ANC guerrillas wanted to show their dissatisfaction with the integration process into the white-led army, they marched to Mandela's residence late at night, insisting they would not go until he had addressed them. White right-wingers said they would trust only 'Mister Mandela'. Striking refuse workers outside my Johannesburg office said they would desist only if 'Madiba' addressed them.

Mandela clearly rather liked the idea of cutting through the bureaucracy of government to tackle problems. He telephoned a British businessman who had been frustrated by officialdom in his attempts to get a work permit. He contacted the relatives of victims of high-profile murders to commiserate with them. Time and again he proved he alone had the moral authority to calm large crowds, most strikingly in Katlehong, a crowded township south-east of Johannesburg, in the wake of three days of bitter fighting between the security forces, the ANC and the Inkatha Freedom Party in the countdown to the April 1994 election. Packed into a tiny stadium, the crowd of about 10,000 ANC supporters were baying for blood. A lesser leader would have been tempted by populism. Mandela instead gave a withering criticism of ANC vigilantes.

'We should put our own house in order. If you have no discipline you are not freedom fighters and we do not want you in our organization. If you are going to kill innocent people and old men you don't belong in the ANC. I am your leader . . . If you don't want me, tell me to go and rest. As long as I am your leader I will tell you when you are wrong . . . Your task is reconciliation.' Remarkably, the shouting died away and we all, journalists, 'peace monitors' and demonstrators, looked at our feet like chastised school-children.

It was a speech worthy of Pericles, the Athenian statesman. There were indeed parallels in the way the two men were regarded by their electors. Thucydides said of Pericles' relationship with the Athenians: 'It was he who led them, rather than they who led him, and, since he never sought power from any wrong motive, he was under no necessity of flattering them: in fact he was so highly respected that he was able to speak angrily to them and to contradict them.' The same applied to Mandela, although he would have denied it vehemently. Loyal party man, he always pays lip-service to the ANC's collective tradition.

But in the running of the government Mandela was no Pericles. His dazzle sustained South Africa through the inevitable post-election hang-over. His mere presence in the Union Buildings, Pretoria's imposing sandstone government headquarters, was enough to reassure doubters in the outside world. But his 'magic' was not always enough for the rigorous demands and Machiavellian requirements of high office. As South Africans were to discover, even a demi-god has flaws, particularly when exposed to the close scrutiny of the press.

One of the most erratic objects of his presidency was his foreign policy. Some of his early undiplomatic gaffes, such as his declaration of support for the IRA's 'struggle against colonialism' in 1990, shortly before a visit to London, could be excused by his Rip Van Winklesque re-emergence into the real world. But he had less excuse as president when he gained a reputation for making off-the-cuff foreign policy. He stunned American officials when one day in Cape Town out of the blue he criticized the American aid programme as 'peanuts'. John Major was startled when he was telephoned by Mandela following the execution of the Nigerian writer Ken Saro-Wiwa and eight other activists and asked outright to impose an oil embargo on the Nigerian junta.

His insistence on remaining loyal to the ANC's old friends from the struggle era was deeply irritating to the West. When he flew to Libya to see Colonel Gaddafi in 1997, and hosted Fidel Castro in 1998, there was talk of his frittering away his moral authority. Domestic critics also complained that many of his ties were linked to the need to fill the ANC's depleted coffers following its expensive 1994 election campaign.

To be fair to Mandela, in an age when expediency takes precedence in politics his sense of loyalty is to be admired. He did not limit his affections to his old friends. When President Clinton was enmeshed in the scandal of his affair with the White House intern Monica Lewinsky, Mandela gave him unequivocal support, calling him a great man and a friend of Africa. He also remarkably championed the search for a permanent exile for Mobutu and was talking of providing a home in South Africa when the Zairean dictator died, ending the dilemma.

South Africans were rather proud of Madiba's iconoclastic approach, which was seen as embodying a new national identity and patriotism. 'We are not going to be type-cast,' he was saying. His forthright style certainly sent an invigorating blast through the world's foreign ministries. He defended his 'open doors' approach vigorously against criticism, arguing that he had learned from dealing with the Nationalists that you had to be prepared to talk to anyone, however unsavoury their reputation. He was also determined not to be seen as the patsy of the West. Rather he wanted to be a bridge between the Third and First Worlds, a role he played brilliantly when he helped to broker a deal over the Libyan suspects of the Lockerbie bombing.

Nonetheless, South African and Western diplomats were right when they muttered that idealism was not enough in international relations. For years Africa had been badly in need of a statesman with unimpeachable credentials to take the lead and steer it out of the abyss. Mandela tactfully argued it was not right to assert himself too swiftly, because of South Africa's history of destabilization in the continent, and because of the weighty matters that needed his attention at home. But many of Africa's leaders understand only one thing, power, and proved less amenable than South Africa to his touch. As the years passed his caution prompted criticism that he was failing his responsibilities to the rest of the continent.

For years African leaders had been past masters at using the rallying cry of 'African solutions for African problems' as an excuse to have their own way. They soon realized that they could run rings round Mandela. His first humiliation came in 1995, when he thought that by talking to Nigeria's military despot, General Abacha, he could guide the West African rogue nation back into the world's embrace. He wholly underestimated Abacha. Even as Mandela a prepared to brief a Commonwealth meeting of heads of state on the Nigerian problem, it was announced that the writer Ken Saro-Wiwa and eight other activists had been executed.

The bubble of expectation over South Africa's role in the continent finally burst in 1997 with the negotiations for the handover of power from Mobutu. The talks took place off the Atlantic coast on the *Outeniqua*, a South African naval ship, in an ingenious bid to find a neutral venue for Mobutu and Kabila. But Mandela was left empty-handed as both men played for time, broke their pledges and paid the barest of lip-services to his authority.

An American official attending a press conference on the *Outeniqua* muttered to a colleague 'Who is this clown?' as one of Mandela's advisors delivered a muddled resumé of the state of play. Mandela would not have been unduly upset to hear of the American's disdain. Like many South Africans he despised America for its 'imperialism' and 'arrogance'. But there was a sense that South African officials were out of their depth.

In another blow to his prestige, Mandela's call for peace talks on the Congo in 1998 was ignored by the key players. Paying no attention to Mandela's position as head of the regional grouping, the South African Development Community, Zimbabwe, Namibia and Angola sent troops to shore up Kabila against a rebellion from the east. For Mugabe it was a golden opportunity to snub the man he felt had usurped his position as regional leader. In the Eighties Mugabe had been southern Africa's senior statesman. At the meeting of the Non-Aligned Movement in Durban in August Mandela had to do an embarrassing U-turn and he announced his support for the intervention.

In a final setback that was heavy with irony, when Mandela did decide to intervene in Africa's bloody politics by sending troops to shore up the government of the mountain kingdom of Lesotho, he besmirched both his government's and the South African army's records. Lesotho, a tiny landlocked state in the heart of South Africa, with a population of just two million and an economy a fraction of the size of its giant neighbour, should have been little more than a policing operation. Instead it hastened the very descent into anarchy the South Africans argued they were trying to prevent. The sight of white officers commanding armoured vehicles sent out all the wrong signals with the echoes of apartheid's incursions into Angola. It took two days to take control of the capital, Maseru, by which time the city centre was a looted shambles and twelve South Africans and dozens of BaSotho had been killed.

The repercussions of the Lesotho debacle were depressing for the rest of Africa, at least for those dreaming of a new era. Not only did it once again highlight the difficulty of enforcing order in the continent, it also entrenched a suspicion in South Africa of foreign entanglements, suggesting that hopes that it might be able to nudge, bully and guide the continent towards democracy were hopelessly over-ambitious. The lesson of Lesotho was clear: South Africa was far from ready to fill the shoes of the retreating West.

The ANC bridled at the hypocrisy of the world's expectations of Mandela and the idea that he had failed just because his 'magic' had been unable to resolve the mess which had defeated – and partly been created by – so many more powerful states. But there was no such excuse for the blots on Mandela's domestic record. Once again his reputation was diminished by an excess of loyalty.

In five years of government he never sacked a cabinet minister for poor performance even though there was no shortage of candidates. The one casualty, Pallo Jordan, the Minister of Post, Telecommunications and Broadcasting, was known for his independence of thought and was said to have poor relations with Mr Mbeki, Mandela's deputy and effective prime minister. It was these two factors which were believed to have counted against him. After an outcry in the press he was reinstated in another cabinet post, but the lesson was clear for all who wanted to prosper in politics.

The more opponents targeted weak links in the cabinet the more defensive Mandela became. Loyalty took precedence over ability. The past appeared to count for more than the present. His foreign minister, Alfred Nzo, was a time-serving stalwart who had been voted out of office as the ANC's secretary general in 1991 in a show of dissatisfaction with his record. But he was an old ANC hand with decades of service to the ANC to his credit, so he kept his job as foreign minister. His uninspiring style soon earned for himself the nickname 'Nzzzzo'. I once waited in a Johannesburg car park with him for forty minutes after lunch as his official driver and car had disappeared. This was the foreign minister of the most powerful country on the continent and yet his time was apparently so unpressured that he was happy to chat in a car park in the middle of an afternoon.

The support of his old comrade Nzo could be explained as sentimental, but there was no such quasi-justification for Mandela's exoneration of incompetence. One of the biggest political scandals of his administration concerned an Aids education play. Commissioned by the Health Ministry, the playwright, a prominent member of the new 'afrostocracy', was allocated more than two million pounds of European Union aid money. In a society lacking the most basic medical health care it was a crass misuse of money. But Mandela backed his minister, Dr Nkosazana Zuma, without a whisper of disapproval. He even leaned on the parliamentary health committee to soften its criticism. When journalists continued to probe the scandal, Mandela suggested the furore was an attempt by the white-owned press to discredit a black minister.

The display of loyalty was very much in keeping with the centralizing ethos of the ANC. Politicians in the most developed democracies bridle when criticized by the press. But there was also a personal element to his stance. His stubborn streak was no secret to members of the ANC. It was as if right at the end of his career he had let down his guard to reveal the autocratic tendencies he had imbibed in the chief's household where he was raised.

In a continent with a record of intolerance like Africa's the waiving of the principle of accountability set a worrying precedent, although the most prominent case of Mandela's loyalty was also the most excusable or at least the most human.

♦♦♦♦

We had at least to admire her gall. Her voice was hesitant and her stance unassuming and yet she commanded the attention of everyone in the packed court. Her skin glowed. She looked a decade younger than her sixty-three years. For two days Winnie Mandela had sat in Johannesburg's High Court as her husband had gone through the agony of parading their personal life in a bid to end their marriage once and for all. They entered the courtroom at opposite ends and sat only a few feet from each other but never exchanged a glance. She kept her face down on the first day as he took the stand and haltingly described how he had become one of the world's best-known cuckolds.

'Ever since I came back from jail not once has she ever entered the room whilst I was awake,' he said. 'I said that man and wife normally discuss their most intimate and personal problems in the bedroom. I told her there are so many issues, many of them sensitive, I would like to discuss with you, but she always refused. She is the type of person who fears confrontation. I was the loneliest man during the period I stayed with her.'

Now, halfway through the second day, she had dismissed her counsel and the denouement was nigh. The time had come for Winnie to speak. It was like watching a Greek tragedy. The crowd in the gallery was the chorus; they filled the adjournments with agonized commentaries. The set, the benches of Johannesburg Supreme Court, was suitably simple and remained unchanged in every scene. The protagonists were no mere mortals. They were the most famous couple in the land. The journalists in the press bench were the audience. We knew how the drama would end, with the granting of a divorce, and yet first we had to go through a heart-churning series of scenes culminating in Winnie's transparently bogus attempt to plead for more time to prepare her case.

When Winnie married Mandela in 1958, in the briefest of interludes between the trials, bannings and imprisonments which blighted forty years of his life, her father warned her she was marrying a man who was already wed to the 'struggle' and that their marriage would be under constant strain. He closed by saying she would have no choice but to follow him and that if he was a witch, she would have to become one too – a prediction that her critics would argue came true.

In the early years of the Mandela marriage it is hard not to feel sympathy for Winnie. When they met in the early Fifties he was sixteen years her senior with three children from his previous marriage. As a marked man he could seldom spend two nights under the same roof. She was a headstrong twenty-two-year-old who had already made a name for herself in Soweto as a social worker, and yet he was prone to lecture her as if she was a political *cadre*.

Mandela says it caused him great pain when he was in prison to think of his children growing up without him. Time and again in his autobiography he writes of his guilt at his absence and ponders the politician's hoary dilemma over how to divide one's time between family and 'cause'. In his case the argument was particularly acute. Winnie suffered appallingly for her connection with South Africa's foremost political prisoner. The security police raided her house night after night in the grim pre-dawn hours. She endured repeated stints of solitary confinement. In 1977 she was banished to a remote rural township, 300 miles from Johannesburg, where she lived on and off for seven years until she broke her banning order and returned to Soweto.

For the outside world she was the indefatigable martyr whom everyone wanted to hear. In the dog days of the anti-apartheid movement in the early Seventies she was almost alone in refusing to lie down. She would shout at the policemen as they came to arrest her and even resist them. A local newspaper coined the nickname 'Mother of the Nation'. Desperate to do their bit against apartheid, foreign donors showered money on her. Visiting delegations and journalists made the trek down to Brandfort to pay court.

But the heady brew of politics and the impregnability of her position as Mandela's wife seem to have had an intoxicating effect. She had been known for her impulsiveness in her childhood and had a reputation at school as a bully. As a student in Soweto she is said to have earned nicknames like 'The Amazon Queen' and 'Lady Tarzan'. While Mandela was free, her spirit was in check. But once he was on Robben Island it became increasingly difficult for anyone in the anti-apartheid movement to control her. She developed a personality cult, spent all the money and, more dangerous still, nurtured the idea that she was above the law.

Her sympathizers see her as a tragic figure brought low by circumstances beyond her control. Certainly the anti-apartheid movement inadvertently hastened her downfall. As with foreign aid to the Big Men leaders, much of the funding she received required no accounting. British aid helped to pay for her lavish mansion in one of the upmarket areas of Soweto. A police search of her house revealed uncashed cheques lying around in boxes. The South African security police did their best to weaken, brutalize and corrupt her. But the argument that in a normal society she would never have faced such temptation is an old and discredited defence. It is also an insult to the thousands of black South Africans who suffered appallingly, like Albertina Sisulu, the wife of Mandela's close friend Walter, but did not descend into the swamp.

Winnie's precipitous slide into infamy accelerated in the mid-Eighties, when she moonlighted in Soweto as a *mafiosi capo*. In public she was the doughty face of resistance. In private she ran from her backyard the infamous 'Mandela United Football Club', a group of activists and hoodlums who terrorized the neighbourhood. The veil briefly lifted in 1988, when children from a school that had been attacked by her 'club' burned down her house. But her reputation started to suffer serious damage only in January 1990 with the discovery on a Soweto rubbish dump of the mutilated body of Stompie Moeketsi, a fourteen-year old activist who had last been seen in her backyard.

The 'Stompie' case led to the unravelling of a lurid tapestry of murder and assault which enveloped the 'club' – or at least it led to the unravelling of some of the threads. The club coach, Jerry Richardson, was convicted of murdering Stompie. Winnie herself was convicted of kidnapping him and three others and also of being an accessory to brutal assaults they suffered in her house. She was sentenced to six years in prison after the judge gave an excoriating assessment of her nature, describing her as a 'calm, composed, deliberate and unblushing liar'. The sentence was suspended on appeal and later commuted to a fine. Other club members were convicted of a series of crimes including murder and assault, and there was a string of outstanding cases of unsolved disappearances linked to Winnie and her club.

And yet, far from keeping a low profile while she waited for the result of her appeal, she embarked on a spending spree largely at the ANC's expense. She had to resign as head of the ANC's welfare department in 1991 after it emerged that £80,000 had disappeared from its account. Much of it is believed to have been frittered away with her deputy and lover, the young lawyer Dali Mpofu, with whom she had flown to America on Concorde the year after Mandela's release.

Mandela was the one man who could have criticized Winnie with impunity. But instead, torn by his love and possibly guilt, he backed and even promoted her. His loyalty was easy to understand. They were passionately in love before he went to prison and her memory helped to sustain him during the bleak periods that assailed even as strong-willed a prisoner as Mandela. He realized they were growing apart during their long separation but when he emerged from prison he was desperate to believe in her. He continued to support her in the face of heated opposition from senior officials in the ANC. The careers of several high-fliers who had dared to say the unsayable and criticize her over Stompie came to an abrupt halt after his release from prison. On the day of her sentencing he declared: 'My faith in her has been fully vindicated.' By the time he came to appreciate her flaws it was far too late.

And so the pattern of scandal, sidelining and then recovery was set. Winnie was elected to parliament for the ANC despite the ANC's pieties about a new moral order. She won a place in Mandela's government as deputy minister of arts, science and culture. She lasted less than a year in his government after a succession of financial and political scandals, including attempted illegal diamond-buying and abuse of government funds and ministerial influence. But Mandela fired her very much as a last resort only after persistent attacks on his style of leadership and after she flouted his authority by flying to West Africa against his instructions. In 1997 she was back as head of the ANC's women's league as an irrepressible counterweight to South Africa's hopes of entrenching a belief in the sovereignty of the law.

All the while she proved herself a brilliant self-publicist. The more the white-dominated establishment criticized her, the easier she found it to play the race card and present herself as a victim of a racist campaign. Her defence of the common man in the townships was laughable in the light of her corrupt and extravagant lifestyle. Court papers in the divorce hearing suggested she spent £1,700 a month on clothes, £350 on cosmetics and over £2,000 on entertaining, massive sums in South Africa. But her politics were canny. The 'Black Evita', as she was dubbed by one satirist, gave the impression that while others talked, she 'did', arranging for running water and electricity to reach impoverished settlements. She was seen at all the right township funerals lending an ear to grievances and disappointment with the new order. For millions of poor blacks she was a heroine.

I followed her to a remote township in the KaNgwane homeland, on the edge of the Kruger National Park, shortly before the April 1994 election. She was the first and only big name in the ANC to campaign there. As her helicopter touched down, scores of people charged through the dust cloud to pay their respects. She was led to the podium as if she was a visiting queen.

'If any of the promises I have made are not recognized when the ANC is in government, please come and fetch me,' she said to roars of support. 'I will lead you against my own government' – a threat which many whites and even some in the ANC fear could yet return to haunt South Africa.

Her opponents' best opportunity to discredit her came in December 1997 at a special hearing of the Truth Commission into the activities of her football club. Her critics hoped that the sight of the relatives of dead and missing activists who had last been seen in her company might turn the tide against her. In the commission's final report the 'club' was linked to at least eighteen killings and Winnie was considered 'politically and morally accountable' for these and other gross human rights abuses committed by the club. Many of the details emerged in heart-rending testimony at the hearing. But the process back-fired badly. Winnie had astutely judged that the sight of her being quizzed by a panel of mainly white jurors would play in her favour among her supporters watching the proceedings in the townships live on television. For that very reason, it is suspected, she had specifically requested a public hearing. While outrage at her audacity reached new levels in the media, and lawyers derided her performance as contemptible, she coolly dismissed the allegations as lies or claimed her memory failed her.

The hearing temporarily checked her career. She was due to stand as deputy president of the ANC at its congress ten days later, but, in a moment of high drama, on the day of the vote Winnie withdrew her nomination. The ANC leadership appreciated that her triumph would send all the wrong signals to the outside world. Many of them also had misgivings about her record. Delegates later told me that the word had gone round that she was not to be backed. Winnie, it seemed, had read the runes.

Mandela gave the Truth Commission hearing a wide berth in marked contrast to his stance at Winnie's kidnap trial six years earlier when he stood by her with a set face through day after day of embarrassing testimony. He had broken the shackles of his old relationship. He had a new love, Graca Machel, the widow of the former Mozambican president. To the delight of South Africans they behaved like teenagers on their first date, holding hands and shyly deflecting questions. No one could resent his new-found happiness; it had taken a long time in coming.

But Winnie was clearly far from finished. Through her name and her history she will be the keeper of the Mandela flame long after he has left politics. After her divorce she rekindled her maiden name and styled herself Madikizela-Mandela. But there is little doubt she will brandish the Mandela part to its maximum advantage. She may even return to government.

There is a strong tradition in African politics of feisty women defying the establishment. In Zimbabwe it was a woman MP, Margaret Dongo, who was the first to break ranks from the ruling party and challenge Mugabe. The cynical calculation in ANC circles is that Winnie will be needed in the years ahead to maintain public support.

A few hours after Winnie's testimony to the Truth Commission I sat in a shebeen (unlicensed bar) in Soweto discussing her performance with a band of late-night drinkers. Some had lived in her neighbourhood during the worst abuses of her 'football club' and were grudgingly prepared to admit that she had done wrong. But the consensus was that the past was the past, whatever she had done should be forgotten, and that 'whites' were guilty of a concerted campaign to bring her down. The racist jibes against Indians with which she had peppered her final remarks had struck an especially popular note.

'So what about the pain she caused the "old man"?' I asked the assembled company. 'Could you vote for her ahead of him?' The more sober heads prevailed: Mandela came first. But it was a close call.

♦♦♦♦

One Friday morning, in March 1996, nearly halfway through Mandela's presidency, South Africans awoke to news in Johannesburg's *Mail & Guardian* of an extraordinary and hugely controversial new project. Danie de Jager, one of the principal state artists under white rule, who designed the statue of Verwoerd that overlooks his grave, was tipped to build a gigantic sculpture of one of Mandela's hands. The proposed 108-foot-high bronze of a hand breaking through prison bars was billed as the largest bronze cast in the world. It was to cost about eight million pounds. Compounding the controversy, the principal backers were businessmen who had made their fortune by selling quack medicines and skin-lightening creams to blacks.

The plan was shelved in a storm of protest but the saga bolstered critics who suggested that Mandela's hero worship had gone too far and that it was blinding South Africans to reality. After so many bleak years it was always going to be hard for South Africans to see Mandela objectively, and after the disappointments of the post-Cold War 'New World Order' the rest of the world too was desperate for a story of hope. Indeed the more Mandela tried to play down hero worship the more it was thrust upon him. By the late Nineties his personality cult was assuming embarrassing proportions. Street-sellers in Johannesburg sold rolls of cloth emblazoned with Mandela's face. Journalists couched criticisms in delicate terms. A few days before his state visit to Britain I found myself on his lawn outside his Johannesburg home shaking my head ruefully with a group of British colleagues. We had just had an hour with Mandela and such had been our hero worship that we had failed to hit home with a single probing question.

Bishop Desmond Tutu was almost alone in daring to criticize him. A few months into the ANC's first term in office he chided MPs for voting themselves high salaries and stepping on to the 'gravy train'. His attack prompted an irritated outburst from Mandela, who suggested the cleric should stay out of politics. Tutu was too seasoned a campaigner and too old a friend of Mandela's to take offence – or indeed take cover.

'He [Mandela] is a very substantial pebble on the beach, but not the only pebble,' he told me in an interview to mark his retirement as Archbishop of Cape Town. 'It's very dangerous for everyone to put him on a pedestal and for him to be seen as unassailable. He's got faults.'

Mandela did his bit to minimize the dangers of the cult. He was genuinely concerned by the implications of the assumption that he was indispensable. With the financial markets jittering every time he caught a cold, his exasperated staff booked him into a Johannesburg clinic for a three-day health check to prove he was fit and well. He regularly berated South Africans for putting him on a pedestal and begged them to treat him as an ordinary man. 'Like other leaders I have stumbled,' he wrote in a Johannesburg newspaper. 'I cannot claim to sparkle alone on a glorified perch.'

He loved to stress his ordinariness. He banned naming streets

after him and he travelled almost incognito. One of his neighbours in Houghton was on his way home when he saw a group
of black men waiting outside his door. Convinced there was
something afoot, he drove past the gate several times and rang
the police. It was only later that he realized that Mandela had
come to pay an unsolicited call.

But Mandela's self-deprecating ways only served to magnify
his legend, as he probably knew. For a puritan who goes for
dawn walks, eschews alcohol bar the odd glass of sweet wine,
and when possible sticks to traditional African food, he developed a surprising fondness for the glitzy and glamorous. The
second half of his presidency was a round of photocalls with
visiting pop stars and celebrities. When photographs of Mandela
with the Spice Girls, Whitney Houston, Bjorn Borg and many
others were published round the world, they served as a
reminder of South Africa's 'miracle' and a welcome boost to its
international image. But it was hard to escape the conclusion
that the seduction of the rich and famous had more to do with
the indulgence of an old man than with realpolitik.

He was moreover too much the politician to ignore the
practical advantages of his icon status. De Klerk was probably
right when he suggested in his autobiography that one of
Mandela's failings was his tactic of 'papering over problems with
charm and promises, without taking effective remedial action.'
When his government was accused of being in the pocket of Sol
Kerzner, the millionaire casino and hotel owner, he wrongfooted his critics by admitting that he, and he alone, had known
of a donation from him. His admission raised more questions
than it answered, but somehow they were never posed and the
scandal died. A few lone voices muttered that while everyone
bowed at Mandela's 'shrine', South Africa was slipping into
disarray.

ⵜⵜⵜⵜ

In one of Mandela's favourite anecdotes he recalls a visit to the
Bahamas in 1994 when he was accosted by a couple who
seemed to recognize him. 'Aren't you Nelson Mandela?' the

man asked. 'I'm often confused with that chap,' Mandela replied. Clearly unconvinced, the couple muttered to themselves, until, determined to pin him down, the woman asked: 'What are you famous for?'

Just as De Klerk cut a dusty figure by the end of his political career, so too Mandela's lustre inevitably tarnished. There was a buzz to Mandela's South Africa in its early days. 'Rainbowism', the dream of a vibrant, multi-cultural united society, which was first coined by Bishop Tutu, was brilliantly marketed by the 'old man'. He appreciated that South Africans, particularly whites, needed a vision. But his was not really a Golden Age. Historians may conclude that his presidency ended not a moment too soon.

The criminal violence that blighted society left South Africans of all races close to despair. Johannesburg was known as the world's murder capital. Lynch-mob justice, which began in the townships under apartheid as a primitive way of dealing with suspected informers, remained a part of daily life. After a brief honeymoon, race, too, returned to its pivotal position in South African life. Even Mandela's patience started to run out by the end of his term. In his final speech to the ANC as its president he launched a swingeing attack on white reluctance to embrace the new order, peppered with paranoic talk of conspiracies by unnamed forces to undermine the government. In the last year as state president he dismissed white emigrants with a trenchant 'good riddance'.

But Mandela's faults do not destroy the legend; rather they help to explain it by showing glimpses of the human beneath the hype. He was clearly far from a saint and yet nonetheless he was able to take a saintly approach towards his old enemies. Remarkably for a politician, he was ready to admit his faults. After appealing to lower the voting age to fourteen-year-olds he later conceded that it showed how wrong he could be. He was also able to rise above the political maul. When the Truth Commission published its final report, ANC officials were outraged by the criticism of their record. Mandela distanced himself from their anger, pointed out that the commission had been intended to be impartial, and rebuked the party's bid to stop the publication of the report.

He was not unique. Andrei Sakharov might have provided the same role for Russia had he lived to see the end of the Soviet Union. But the comparison only serves to emphasize Mandela's remarkable qualities. Mandela provided the spiritual and emotional glue for the new society which De Klerk with his ideological baggage and dry pragmatism could never have provided and without which the post-apartheid settlement might never have happened. He was a pop star-cum-philosopher and he became the distillation of South Africa's and indeed the world's hopes, partly because people were in need of a Messiah, partly because he was deliberately fashioning himself after their wishes, partly because of the world's desperation for South Africa to succeed, but also because he was who he was.

His most enduring legacy to South Africa, however, was that he knew when to go. Africa's history is littered with rulers who lingered. A cautionary tale for South Africa lies across the Limpopo River in neighbouring Zimbabwe. When Mugabe took office in 1980 after the bloody war of independence, he was hailed for his reconciliatory approach to whites; he thanked Ian Smith for handing over intact 'this jewel of Africa'. Two decades later he was running an autocratic and corrupt regime, beset by street protests, with only a token façade of democracy.

Mandela, however, made clear that South Africa was to be different. He signalled from the outset that he intended to serve only one term and he reinforced the message by slowing his schedule, spending more time on ceremonial, and allowing his successor to take over the daily running of government. It was up to the 'new' generation of African leaders to take up the challenge.

10

Small Men

The 'New' Leaders – Or More of the Same?

An architectural blend of science fantasy and Pharaonic sentiment, Ghana's Independence Square towers over the Atlantic
coast as a giant stone talisman of freedom. From the stands you
can see cargo ships retracing the course of the slavers which
headed off across the ocean with their grim cargoes two centuries before. The stadium was built back in the days of Kwame
Nkrumah, who showered money on grandiose projects, even
giving £50 million to help neighbouring Guinea to buy independence. As I joined tens of thousands of Ghanaians taking
advantage of the cool dawn air to secure a good seat ahead of a
mid-morning rally, older citizens chattered that they had not
seen a gathering like it since Nkrumah first roused the continent
with his immortal cry: 'Freedom. Freedom. Africa.'

But the Africanist visionary would have been distraught if he
had been alive to witness the scene. His people were gathering
not for one of the Third World heroes for whom the stadium
was built but for the leader of the reviled imperialist West,
President Clinton, who had picked Accra as the first stop-off on
his much-trumpeted African tour.

The requirements of Clinton's vast entourage had stretched
Ghana's infrastructure and patience to the limit. The Americans
had insisted on bringing their own generator to compensate for
Accra's erratic electricity. When the White House discovered
one of the city's principal hotels was owned by Libyans they
reneged on months of planning and decided not to stop off for

the night. But the Ghanaians did not mind. Under the personal supervision of 'J.J.' Rawlings, their president, a swashbuckling former fighter pilot, they sealed sewers, blocked off roads and gave signposts a new coat of paint, preparing a boisterous welcome as West Africans do so well.

The Ashanti kings were among the last to arrive. Ferried under extravagant gilded palanquins they perched on giant ceremonial stools just as their predecessors had at the end of the last century when they kept the British at bay – or indeed the previous century when they sold rival tribesmen into slavery. A black American Secret Service agent in Wall Street shirt and braces ran up and down in front of my stand dripping with sweat as he vainly tried to marshall the crowd, much to the amusement of the spectators, who joked that if that was what America did for you they were relieved their ancestors had been left behind.

'What is wrong with the brother?' one of my neighbours shouted.

'It does not matter,' said another. 'He is a relative from overseas. He is welcome.'

The Clintons' ten-day six-nation trip of Africa in March 1998 was the most comprehensive tour of the continent ever taken by a sitting American president and was promoted by the White House as the start of a new era in the continent. The resonance of those claims was reinforced by the parallels of his visit with another symbolic twentieth-century African tour by a leading Western statesman. In 1960 Harold Macmillan travelled through the continent paving the way for the end of colonial rule. Indeed he first uttered his legendary 'wind of change' phrase on the opening leg of his tour at a banquet in Accra, but the remark was made off the cuff and was not recorded by the accompanying press pack. It became famous only when he repeated it before the shocked MPs in South Africa's whites-only parliament.

To optimists the Clintons' visit represented a tiny hope that, second time round, Africa's liberation dreams might still have a chance. 'One hundred years from now your grandchildren and mine will look back and say this was the beginning of an African Renaissance,' he told the crowd in Independence Square. 'By coming and going a bird builds a nest. We will come and go and do all we can to help you build a new Africa.' Such was the crowd's excitement that when he went on a walkabout draped in a glorious orange, purple and gold *kente* cloth, he was nearly knocked over. Looking distinctly flustered, he was forced to tell the crowd to move back.

It was impossible not to be moved. Since leading Africa into independence in 1957, Ghana had spiralled into chaos. The coup which ousted Nkrumah nine years later when he was on a trip to China merely set in motion a series of incompetent and corrupt governments and more military coups. By the early Eighties Ghana was a symbol of African decay. And yet now in recognition of Rawlings' reformist record it was being touted as a seed for the continent's rebirth.

In an attempt to add weight to his vision, as Clinton toured the continent he hailed Rawlings, Yoweri Museveni of Uganda and Thabo Mbeki of South Africa as three beacons of hope of the new era, shining in the West, the East and the South. It is no coincidence that all three were born in the mid-Forties. Raised amid the excitement of the Fifties, they reached adulthood in the euphoria of the early Sixties only to watch the dream of new Africa collapse into chaos. All three are seen as pragmatists with an abhorrence of Big Man excess and a desire for a fresh start for the continent.

Accra was abuzz with the talk of new beginnings as Clinton left, but as I sat down to write my despatch, a more sober realism prevailed. It shows quite how desperate the rest of the world is for good news from Africa – and how low expectations have become – that Rawlings, a man who inaugurated his government by lining several of his predecessors up on the road out of Accra and shooting them, and Museveni, who is embroiled in three vicious wars, are hailed as the continent's brightest hopes.

✦✦✦

Rawlings certainly has the dynamism to lead Africa into the new millennium. The most colourful of the three 'new' leaders, he has been Africa's 'angry young man' ever since he realized that, shortly after he was born, his father, a Scots chemist, abandoned his mother and returned to Glasgow. At school he is said to have joined gangs only if he could be their leader. Still simmering, he joined the air force and was recognized as the best pilot of his year. He was not promoted above flight lieutenant as his superiors were said to distrust his habit of talking to the lower ranks. But the generals no doubt regretted their snobbishness on 4 June 1979 when Rawlings seized power at the head of a group of young populist revolutionaries committed to grass-roots socialism and eradicating corruption, with the slogan: 'Let the blood flow.'

Within a fortnight he executed two generals, including a previous head of state, on the main road from the capital. Two weeks later, six more commanders were shot, including another two former heads of state. Remarkably for a dictator, Rawlings stepped down after only 112 days in power. But as the civilian political class returned to their old ways, he led another coup on New Year's Eve 1981 and this time he stayed.

Initially the story seemed all too familiar. Critics were imprisoned and in a few notorious cases disappeared. But unlike the Big Men, Rawlings never lost sight of his ideals: he was, by West African standards, uncorrupt, avoided fancy titles, hated hero worship, and did what he thought was best for the poor. When it was explained to him in the mid-eighties that unless he embraced free-market reforms the remnants of the economy would disappear, he allowed his head to rule his heart and submitted to the World Bank. Over the next decade Ghana recorded a steady average 5 per cent growth. It came from a low base but it was a marked improvement after a decade in which wages had sunk by almost a third.

Rawlings remained at heart an old-fashioned Marxist. He loathed the businessmen whose sharp practices he associated with all that was rotten with the early independence years. When the Berlin Wall came down, he said elliptically that he hoped reforms in the East would be reciprocated by reforms in the West. In August 1992 in an interview with the *Financial Times* he described the World Bank's economic reform programme as 'economic blah blah blah'. But he applied the 'medicine' with the determination that only a benign dictator could get away with. Not even Rawlings' closest ally would call him a natural democrat. He is a man of action, not consensus, who would rather fly a fighter plane than chair a political caucus. In his early years in power he did much of his governing assisted by only a tiny cabal. He is famously impatient of the civilian political classes. In October just before the 1992 elections he told one interviewer from *The Times* that he was 'the only person who can rule this country.' During a cabinet meeting in 1996 he is said to have knocked his vice-president down and kicked him as he lay squirming on the ground. But unlike the generals who have ruled neighbouring Nigeria for most of its post-independence years, he has moved towards multi-party democracy, acknowledging that if it encourages Western investment then it is in Ghana's interest.

In the campaign for his first elections in 1992, he undid much of the good work of his economic reforms by a spate of populist overspending. 'As head of state he was referee, linesman and player in the transitional process,' wrote one commentator in the *New African*. 'Frightened like little children, his civilian challengers did as he told them. Jump – they jumped. Sit – they sat!' But the 1996 election was fairer and more hotly contested. His challenger won 40 per cent of the vote. Eighteen months later Rawlings nominated his deputy to succeed him as party leader, scotching speculation that his ambitious wife, Nana, an Ashanti princess, would replace him.

The hope is that his record can act as a guide for the regional giant, Nigeria, to recover from the excesses of its own coup culture. With more than 100 million people and a long literate tradition Nigeria should be the 'Lion of Africa', nudging the rest of the continent forward. But instead it has become an international byword for trickery and drugs. The sudden death of General Abacha in 1998 ended the most corrupt and vicious in a series of post-independence governments. His successor, General Abdulsalami Abubakar, did much to unravel Abacha's corrupt apparatus of state, encouraging Wole Soyinka, the literary scourge of Big Men, and other dissidents to return, before stepping down at long-awaited elections in 1999.

But the election of General Olusegun Obasanjo, a former military ruler, was only the first step towards recovery. The danger with 'strong men' is that they seldom let go. Moreover, civilian rule does not offer automatic salvation. Travelling through Africa it is depressing how often you have to conclude that the 'real test' will come only 'at the next election'. Civilian governments in both Nigeria and Ghana have almost as bad a record as the military. Ghana's progress towards political and economic freedom is one of the more encouraging stories in Africa in the last decade. But Rawlings is a young leader, particularly by African standards, and he might find it difficult to keep to his promise of staying out of politics after the 2001 election, particularly if the country drifts. Still more sobering is the stark fact that even if Ghana's economy continues to grow at 5 per cent a year, it will take thirty years to reach the same standard of living they enjoyed in 1970, an equation that is grimly familiar to the people of Uganda.

🕴🕴🕴🕴

In the closing years of the millennium Yoweri Museveni became something of a cult figure among Africa analysts trying to wrestle with the conundrum of democracy, progress and rights. Museveni was the pragmatist who transformed Uganda from a shambles into a thriving concern. He spoke the reformist language of the West without kowtowing to Washington. He was the 'Bismarck of Africa', his panegyrists claimed, whose aim was to overthrow tyrants. At last, the world said, central Africa has a leader to follow and admire. With his mixture of peasant and free-market economics and his blend of coalition and autocracy rooted in traditional African government Museveni is an intriguing and original leader. But it is far from clear whether he is the template of a new Africa or just a staging post, and whether without him Uganda will plunge back into anarchy once again.

Born, as he loved to remind his admirers, into an illiterate peasant family, from his student days Museveni is said to have displayed the fiery independence of thought that would stand him in good stead in later life. When Julius Nyerere, Tanzania's independence president, made a speech at his university at Dar es Salaam in 1969, the young Museveni publicly attacked his policies, an astonishingly bold move given that Mwalimu, (teacher), as Nyerere was known, was then revered throughout the continent even though his *ujamaa* home-grown Marxism policy was turning Tanzania into a giant collective farm, destroying the vibrant peasant agriculture which could have fed much of East Africa.

'Dar' was the place to study in Africa in the Sixties and Museveni made some vital political contacts. His generation of students included John Garang, the Sudanese rebel leader, and Paul Kagame, the vice-president and *eminence grise* of Rwanda after the genocide. Laurent Kabila also passed through Dar at the time, although he appears to have spent more time drinking and womanizing than planning for the future. Just as many of Margaret Thatcher's cabinet colleagues had studied together at Cambridge University, so years after his graduation Museveni worked with his old student friends to forge a cohesive central African bloc. But before that was possible he had to fight a long and gruelling battle to wrest control of Uganda from two of Africa's more egregious tyrants.

When Idi Amin took power in 1971 in a coup, he was initially welcomed in the West. Milton Obote, whom he ousted, had a sinister record. Indeed MI6 and Mossad are believed to have connived in Amin's takeover; a highly regarded former NCO in the King's African Rifles and Uganda's heavyweight boxing champion, he had often declared his devotion to the queen and empire. But he soon fell out of favour in the West as he expelled the prosperous Asian middle class, and his death squads slaughtered tens of thousands of rival tribesmen and suspected opponents. African leaders remained supportive long after the horrors of his regime were exposed: the Conqueror of the British Empire, as he styled himself, was appointed head of the OAU in 1975 when his reign of terror was at its height. But he finally outraged even his African neighbours and was overthrown in 1979 by a force of Ugandan rebels, including the young Museveni, backed by Tanzanian soldiers who pillaged their way to Kampala.

In a depressing postscript Obote had hardly been restored to power in his devastated capital before he set about trumping Amin's atrocities. Returning to the bush with, as legend has it, just twenty-seven men, Museveni forged one of Africa's most renowned guerrilla armies and led them to victory five years later. Shortly after he took power, a British diplomat met him outside Kampala and was startled to find the battle-hardened guerrilla was a studious, quick-witted man. 'His eye for detail was remarkable,' the diplomat recalled. 'He had just taken over the country and he was going through a report on an alleged incident of racism by a British officer charged with training the Ugandan army, point by point, without missing a thing.' Museveni's style has been impressing the West ever since, although not without misgivings on both sides.

Museveni is a firm believer in the argument that Africa is not ready for multi-party democracy. But he has not used this as a pretext for a single-party state. Instead he set up a 'no party' state, divesting authority to a network of village revolutionary councils which were formed during his long fight in the bush. He bases his vision on the parable about 'sowing the mustard seed' in St Matthew's gospel. According to the parable, 'The kingdom of heaven is like a mustard seed, which a man took and planted in his field. Though it is the smallest of all your seeds, yet when it grows it is the largest of garden plants and becomes a tree, so that the birds of the air come and perch in its branches.'

Museveni argues that before the 'mustard seed' of democracy and freedom can be sown, Uganda first has to be cleared of 'the rocks and weeds' of the corrupt former system. He fends off the inevitable criticism that this is a guise for dictatorship by attesting the grievous record of African political parties polarizing down tribal lines, and by arguing that Uganda is still pre-industrial, and hence needs a peasant-based system.

'Western democracies criticise our system of government but we ignore them,' he wrote in his autobiography *Sowing the Mustard Seed*. 'Their opinion is not our concern. I consider it arrogant that the whole world must be managed in the same way. The substance of democracy is essentially the same – governance by the population, but the forms must be different, depending on the situations.'

His is a striking vision, independent, self-assured and rational. What is more, it is not just talk. The economy has grown between 5 and 10 per cent annually since 1990. Kampala has bounced back from the grim days of the Eighties. By the late Nineties it was one of the most efficient capitals north of the Limpopo, a testimony to massive investment by Washington, where Museveni is regarded as America's most important regional ally. He won further credit by inviting back the Asians whom Amin had expelled. Businessmen applaud his no-nonsense calls for Africans to take responsibility for their own destiny, and also his belief in privatization, which he once called 'fantastic, a magic solution to the problem of inefficiency'.

Moreover he cannot be bothered with looking for the old scapegoats. He startled South African MPs in parliament in Cape Town when he told them that blaming colonialism is 'like a drunken man blaming someone who steals his hat'. On the same visit to South Africa he reinforced his reputation as his own man when he castigated the 'you scratch my back and I'll scratch yours' habits of African leaders. In June 1997, in an interview with the Johannesburg *Sunday Independent*, he described the OAU as a 'trade union of criminals' and laughed when asked about his record in toppling tyrants. 'Fighting black dictators is not a recommended activity in Africa. You are supposed to accept black dictators because they hide under the cloak of sovereignty. So if anyone fights them he must do it clandestinely as much as possible.'

But Museveni is no stooge. He believed in working with the

West but on his own terms, and he does not hesitate to make clear when he feels their prescriptions are wrong. He has tackled Aids in the same direct fashion. In the mid-Nineties as Aids claimed tens of thousands of lives a year in Africa, most African leaders were too embarrassed to acknowledge it, but not Museveni. In the Eighties Uganda was the worst hit country in the world. While Museveni had no compunction in calling it a 'white man's' disease, he broke the 'taboo' and instituted an education programme that has led to the only recorded decline in African infection rates.

I hitched a lift one evening from Kampala to the Rwandan border and, struck by the Aids awareness roadside billboards encouraging abstinence, fidelity and condoms, sat up through the night talking to my driver. Accustomed to a social conservatism that straddles every strata of African society, I was astonished by his frankness. He discussed his and his family's sexual habits with an ease that eludes many in the West. When I commented on his candour he replied simply: 'I have lost a brother and three of my closest friends.'

The West hopes that Rawlings' Ghana and Museveni's Uganda offer a blueprint for other post-Big Man states: economic reform administered by a stable if authoritarian government – in short, the elusive enlightened dictator. East Africa in the late Eighties and early Nineties had a flowering of such leaders, for whom democracy and human rights were less important than self-sufficiency, economic reform and peace.

'There are some seeds of a new Africa,' Museveni said in an interview with the *Chicago Tribune* in March 1998, shortly before Mr Clinton's visit. 'The changes aren't everywhere and I would not want to call Uganda a model. But certainly there are some issues that are relevant to the whole of black Africa which we are addressing, and one of those is the most efficient way of producing wealth.'

No one, however, should be starry-eyed. Like Rawlings, Museveni is a controversial role model. His regime raises the age-old dilemma of autocracy – when does the freedom to buy a banana in peace cease to justify the lack of the right to elect a leader? His achievements are impressive only in the context of the chaos and anarchy that prevailed elsewhere. Uganda's economic growth rate, while one of Africa's success stories, started from a tiny base. Notwithstanding his triumphs on the battlefield, Uganda is beset by the ravages of three rebel guerrilla armies backed by Museveni's old enemies in Khartoum, the Sudanese capital. His answer was to meet force with force, leading to atrocities which even his staunchest international backers found hard to excuse.

Like Bismarck, his single-minded ways have made him many enemies and may have sowed the seeds of his downfall. He over-reached himself when he fostered a rebellion against his old protégé, Kabila, before he had lined up the rest of the region on his side. His hubris plunged central Africa into further chaos and shattered his dream of forging a central African commercial bloc from the Indian to the Atlantic Ocean. Moreover, while better than Mobutu's Zaire and Abacha's Nigeria, Museveni's Uganda is far from pure. His brother, Major-General Salim Saleh, one of Uganda's wealthiest businessmen, had to resign from his post as a senior government advisor after admitting his role in an illegal deal to buy secretly 49 per cent of the country's largest bank. The scandal followed the drafting of a confidential World Bank report that exposed high-level graft of public and donor funds.

Museveni, the archetypal 'new' African leader, does not wear a leopard-skin hat. But, as history has proven so many times, the theory of an enlightened dictator is hard to sustain.

⁂

The striking exception to the rest of Africa – or so the world fervently hopes – will be South Africa under Thabo Mbeki. He has been groomed for high office almost from birth. His father, Govan Mbeki, was one of the ANC frontrunners of Mandela's generation. Indeed he clashed with the 'Old Man' on policy many times on Robben Island. Nearly ten years after his release I travelled to the Mbeki township home in Port Elizabeth seeking insights into the mind of Mandela's heir apparent.

Mbeki senior, then in his early eighties, was too wily a politician to discuss his son, but his quick mind, and the shelves brimming with political histories and philosophy, left little doubt that Thabo was raised in a rigorous intellectual environment.

Thabo Mbeki was steeped in politics from his earliest years. Attending his first rally aged ten and joining the party four years later he was sent into exile in 1963, shortly before the authorities effectively closed down the ANC. Twenty-seven years were to pass before his return in 1990, exposing him to the realities of world economics and politics. One of his contemporaries at Sussex University, where he studied economics in the Sixties, recalled to me how even then, in the darkest days of the anti-apartheid struggle, he was known on the campus as a future leader of South Africa. She also recalled how his charisma made him one of the most sought-after consorts, a quality which stood him in good stead later when he was charged with wooing white business.

After representing the ANC all over Africa in the early Seventies he was appointed political secretary to Oliver Tambo, the party leader, in 1975 and soon showed signs of his master's political pragmatism. He discreetly distanced himself from the Communist Party, the ANC's ally, several years before the Berlin Wall came down, although he was careful never to make a formal renunciation of the party line. In the late Eighties he became the ANC's unofficial foreign minister, a position to which his easy-going manner, conservative dress sense and suave charm made him ideally suited. He was the obvious choice to head ANC delegations at secret talks with the Afrikaner establishment and, still more sensitively, with apartheid intelligence officers.

On his return to South Africa after 1990 his omni-present pipe and his penchant for suits entrenched his reputation among whites as the kindly face of the ANC. He was called in to mollify the white right wing and came up with a skilful face-saving formula to allow them a forum to debate the possibility of a white homeland. Visitors invariably come away from one-on-one meetings impressed by the sharpness of his mind and his grasp of South Africa's problems. Mbeki has a gentle and reflective demeanour which will endear him to the foreign leaders and financiers whose support he and South Africa will need. He is an expert conciliator. He is also an economic moderate. He helped to steer the ANC away from its traditional statist policies, presiding over the formation of the Growth, Employment and Redistribution macro-economic strategy. As I left his residence at Pretoria after an interview, Julian Ogilvie Thompson, the chairman of Anglo American, the mining con-glomerate that dominated South Africa's economy, was arriving for one of Mbeki's regular kitchen meetings with top financiers.

As soon as he was confirmed as Mandela's deputy, his popularity started to wane among whites. Partly this was because his vision of the future was starker than Mandela's. While Mandela called for reconciliation, Mbeki's rallying cry is transformation. He fell from grace, he suggested in a interview, because he dared to air unmentionables.

'The creation of a non-racial society is a painful process. I say – very foolishly – things that I shouldn't. I say, "Look at the press – should we not be involved in its deracialization?" Then a debate begins about what is wrong and what is right and people form opinions, and so your nice deputy president ceases to be a nice deputy president. When we begin to grapple with the real issues, when you pass beyond the Gloria! Hallelujah! What a lovely thing we've done! then the problems begin. You cannot have reconciliation without transformation.'

As he assumed more of the day-to-day responsibilities for running the state, however, so more diverse misgivings emerged. When he stood in for Mandela at a South Africa v. Brazil football match in Soweto he was ten minutes late. It was the biggest game in months and the ground was packed. But the opening ceremony and the kick-off were delayed until Mbeki arrived, prompting angry mutters from the mainly black crowd: Mandela would never have made such an elementary mistake. It was a trivial incident, more to do with style than substance, but it strengthened the perception that Mbeki is more at home in a cabal than on a podium and that he has a disdain for the popular touches that voters like – and need in a jittery society like South Africa.

Mbeki's golden-boy image was tarnished more seriously by his controversial attitude towards the press. The white liberal newspapers which had targeted apartheid were subject to a regular sniping from the new black intellectual élite attached to his office. The ANC's resentment that the press was still domi-nated by white journalists was understandable. But calls for a 'patriotic' media had disturbing echoes of Mugabe's Zimbabwe. When Mbeki rebuked the press for covering only 17 per cent of Mandela's five-hour closing speech as ANC president he was opening himself to ridicule. His complaint had added piquancy given that the speech, which was heavily critical of white attitudes, was widely believed to have been drafted by Mbeki's office, furthering the impression that despite his long years in exile he did not understand the role of a free press – and that he was still consumed by the paranoias of the 'struggle'.

His aides countered that he was the victim of a white anti-ANC campaign. He disarmingly contends it is one of the drawbacks of succeeding an international idol that whatever you do will be seen as a let-down. But the most direct attack on Mbeki could not be shrugged off by his office as 'racism' as it came from none other than Bishop Tutu, South Africa's favour-ite son after Mandela. Incensed because Mbeki rejected criti-cisms of the ANC in the Truth Commission's final report, the bishop warned the ANC against becoming the country's 'new oppressors'. The report condemned the ANC for the bombing of civilian targets, the execution and torture of dissidents and suspected informers and the 'necklace' killing of blacks who opposed its tactics against apartheid. The report made clear that the ANC's abuses were a sideshow compared to the crimes committed by the white security forces, and a clear distinction was drawn between the 'legitimate' struggle against white rule and the 'injustice' of apartheid. But in a significant lapse of judgement Mbeki rejected the criticism and tried to get the report blocked by a court injunction. Tutu did not need to consider his response. 'Our struggle was against tin gods, or those who thought themselves to be little gods,' he said. 'We didn't struggle to remove them in order to replace them with others of a different compexion.'

And so the enigma remains. Part of the rationale for Mbeki's more controversial pronouncements was to secure his position among the ANC's rank and file; it was important that he proved he was not the patsy of the whites. But he does have an autocratic streak. His diplomatic veneer masked a steel forged in the years of clandestine exile politics. One by one in the mid-Nineties potential rivals or challengers to his position as heir apparent fell by the wayside. An acquaintance from his years in Britain recalled that his friends at Sussex University used to joke that one day they would be lost in Africa and they would have the choice of going before 'Chief Wanga Banga' or Thabo Mbeki – and, so the joke went, they would all opt for the chief. After his challenge of the Truth Commission he still has to prove he is to go down as the man who entrenched South Africa's hard-won democracy, rather than the man who set in motion a gradual decline.

Even if he does succeed, it is clear that he will have little time or money to devote to the rest of the continent. Mbeki is a committed 'Renaissance' man. He delivered a lyrical address to parliament to mark the adoption of the final post-apartheid constitution, eulogizing his African roots and outlining his vision of a new Africa. He peppered subsequent speeches with talk of the Renaissance as it became closely linked to his domestic agenda and his calls for whites to accept that they had a price to pay for the years of domination.

But with 100,000 illegal immigrants trying to cross into South Africa each year in search of a new life, Mbeki may find himself more preoccupied with keeping the rest of the continent out than with bonding with his African fellows. His government has an unenviable task. The social and economic pressures can only intensify as, despite the party's pledges of jobs for all, employment at the end of Mandela's presidency was at its lowest level in sixteen years. As Mandela's presidency drew to a close it was noticeable that Mbeki's 'Renaissance' evangalism slackened. It was as if he had finally recognized that even with an economy nearly three times as big as the combined economy of the thirteen fellow members of the Southern African Development Community, South Africa was hard-pressed to tackle its own problems, let alone the continent's.

In the opening address to a conference, in Johannesburg in September 1998, on the 'Renaissance' he cautioned there was no way people could speak of a rebirth given Africa's endemic corruption. He also bemoaned the businessmen who came 'with bags full of money' from countries 'beyond our shores and participated in the process of purchasing our souls so that they win tenders and contracts or gain special favours to improve their bottom lines'. It seemed that his advisors were belatedly appreciating what a challenge they faced.

⋀⋀⋀

Appropriately enough it was Nelson Mandela who first talked of an 'African Renaissance'. He was addressing an OAU summit of heads of state a month after his inauguration, in June 1994, and he was infused with hope that Africa was at last on the threshold of a new era. Opening with Rome's defeat of Carthage 'in the distant days of antiquity' and the censor Cato's vindictive '*delenda est Carthago*', he led his audience through a litany of African suffering and subjugation, climaxing in the twentieth century with Africans as 'the outstanding example of the beneficiaries of charity' and as 'the permanent victims of famine, destructive conflicts and the pestilences of the natural world'. He acknowledged that many in his audience had failed their people. But he concluded resoundingly that Africa's time had come.

> Africa cries out for a new birth; Carthage awaits the restoration of its glory. If freedom was the crown which the fighters of liberation sought to place on the head of mother Africa, let the upliftment, the happiness, prosperity and comfort of her children be the jewel of the crown . . .
>
> We must face the matter squarely that where there is something wrong in how we govern ourselves, it must be

said that the fault is not in our stars but in ourselves that we are ill-governed. Rwanda stands as a stern and severe rebuke to all of us for having failed to address these matters . . . [But] we know that we have it in ourselves, as Africans, to change all this. We must assert our will to do so. We must say that there is no obstacle big enough to stop us from bringing about an African Renaissance.

The very talk of a revival is a step forward from the Seventies and Eighties when it would have been seen as a joke. Africans have been looking in vain for a new vision since the collapse of their independence hopes. But as the twentieth century draws to a close, the Renaissance is more aspiration than reality. Grinding poverty, corrupt leadership and abuse of power remain the norm. According to the 1998 United Nations Human Development Index, the world's fifteen poorest countries were in Africa. As the report was released, more than a quarter of sub-Saharan Africa's forty-two countries were at war. Africa in the twenty-first century will not be a pretty sight.

For South Africa's black élite, the ideological engine room of the African Renaissance, this is racist defeatism. They point to the bloody political upheavals that accompanied and followed the Renaissance in Europe and point out that it was hailed only in retrospect. 'What of the Wars of the Roses?' they cry. 'What of the fighting and factionalism between Italian city states? What of the monks who led the intellectual revolution that preceded the Renaissance? They must have felt perilously isolated, surrounded as they were by illiteracy, barbarism and abuse of power.'

Their analogy is valid, but unfortunately South Africa's idealism often seems motivated more by black South Africans' desire to throw off the legacy of white rule than by an understanding of the problems facing the rest of the continent. Most black South Africans are as ignorant of the continent as their white counterparts. While travelling through Africa I met a number of black South Africans on their first trip north of the Limpopo whose excitement at having escaped from the prism of a race-based society had rapidly turned to bewilderment and shock at the disorder they found.

Professor Malegapuru Makgoba, one of South Africa's most eminent black academics, organized a conference to discuss the Renaissance. His enthusiasm could not be faulted, but the conference swiftly became mired in the old debates over African culture and identity. The professor floundered when asked to pinpoint how South Africa should become more African. He ended by talking of his frustration at not being able to buy an African meal when he was travelling abroad, and contrasting his experience with the lot of the Chinese and French being able to eat their own food wherever they go.

When Pierre Sané, the Secretary General of Amnesty International, toured South Africa ahead of the fiftieth anniversary of the UN's Charter of Human Rights in 1998, he ridiculed the idea of a new dawn. It was not that he did not want to see a rebirth. It was just that unfounded optimism is as dangerous for Africa as knee-jerk pessimism.

'Renaissances have been promised by African leaders since independence,' he said. 'In the Sixties we heard of Renaissance. In the Eighties with the moves to democratization we heard of it. The reality of Renaissance to the ordinary people will come [only] when human rights are a reality . . . and when the right to food and access to health care is a reality. As long as those are not the case it will remain what it is, just talk.'

The truth is there have been too many failed promises and dreams in the last hundred years. At the end of the twentieth century Africa is facing a desperate struggle not to fall off the world map; effectively most of the continent has ceased to feature in the world economy. There are changes. Africa is not the dark hole that it sometimes seems from afar. It has an energy and spirit which defy the worst disasters. But there is a big difference between rejecting the cults and corruption of the old order and a genuine rebirth. Africa is not as it was in the free-for-all days of Cecil Rhodes, but he would have understood perfectly how to operate in the Africa that is entering the new millennium. Rawlings and Museveni are unquestionably an improvement on the Big Men, but they lead relatively small countries. If Rawlings can inspire Nigeria to follow down his reformist path and Museveni can first stay on course himself and then invigorate the region, then parts of Africa may be on course for a recovery. But they are big ifs.

Among the more trenchant commentators on Africa since independence is Indar, an Asian businessman in V.S. Naipaul's *A Bend in the River*, working in East Africa at the end of the colonial era. His crude maxim remains as sadly apposite now as in the Seventies when the book was written.

'To be in Africa you have to be strong.'

Notes

1. The King of Kleptocracy

Most of this chapter is based on interviews conducted by the author in Zaire between October 1996 and May 1997, the last seven months of Mobutu's rule.

1. Thomas Pakenham, *The Scramble for Africa*, London, Weidenfeld & Nicholson, 1991, p. 678.

2. George Ayittey, *Africa Betrayed*, New York, St Martin's Press, 1993, p. 257.

3. Ayittey, *Africa Betrayed*, p. 257.

4. Blaine Harden, *Africa – Despatches From a Fragile Continent*, New York, Houghton Mifflin, 1991, p. 49.

5. Crawford Young and Thomas Turner, *The Rise and Decline of the Zairian State*, Madison, Wisconsin, University of Wisconsin Press, 1985, p. 169.

6. *Newsweek*, 14 April 1997, article by Jorge G. Castaneda, author of *Companero: The Life and Death of Che Guevara*, New York, Knopf, 1997.

7. Ayittey, *Africa Betrayed*, p. 259.

2. The Last Days of a North London Doctor

Most of the material in this chapter is taken from visits to Malawi and Zambia in 1995.

Notes

1. Philip Short, *Banda*, London and Boston, Routledge and Kegan Paul, 1974, p. 250.

2. Short, *Banda*, p. 92.

3. Ayittey, *Africa Betrayed*, p. 26.

4. Short, *Banda*, p. 260.

4. The Cold War Crooner

The Nigerian interviews took place in October 1995.

1. Ryszard Kapuściński, *Another Day of Life*, New York, Harcourt Brace Janovich, 1987, p. vii.

2. Fred Bridgland, *Jonas Savimbi: A Key to Africa*, London, Mainstream Publishing, 1986, p. 30.

3. Kapuściński, *Another Day*, p. 18.

4. Ayittey, *Africa Betrayed*, p. 319.

5. Bridgland, *Jonas Savimbi*, p. 60.

6. Judith Matloff, *Fragments of a Forgotten War*, London, Penguin, 1997, p. 75.

5. The Last White Patriarch

The material in this chapter is based on interviews held between 1993 and 1998.

1. Willem de Klerk, *F.W. De Klerk: The Man in His Time*, Johannesburg, Jonathan Ball, 1991, p. 140.

2. F.W. De Klerk, *The Last Trek: A New Beginning*, London, Macmillan, 1998, p. 264.

3. F.W. De Klerk, *The Last Trek*, p. 40.

4. F.W. De Klerk, *The Last Trek*, p. 393.

5. Professor Hermann Giliomee, *Surrender Without Defeat; Afrikaners and the South African Miracle*, South African Institute of Race Relations, Spotlight. Johannesburg, November 1997.

7. A Very Zulu Chief

1. Ayittey, *Africa Betrayed*, p. 37.

2. Henry Francis Fynn, *The Diary of Henry Francis Fynn*, Pietermaritzburg, Shuter and Shooter, 1986, p. 71.

8. From Sherbourne to Swaziland

1. Edward Fox, *Obscure Kingdoms*, London, Hamish Hamilton, 1993, p. 178.

2. Fox, *Obscure Kingdoms*, p. 160.

9. Madibe Magic

1. Steven Glover, *The Daily Telegraph*, 12 July 1996.

2. Martin Meredith, *Nelson Mandela: A Biography*, London, Hamish Hamilton, 1997, p. 67.

3. Nelson Mandela, *Long Walk to Freedom*, Macdonald Purnell, 1994, p. 559.

4. James Gregory, *Goodbye Bafana: The Man who took the Hatred out of Nelson Mandela*, Headline, 1995, p. 6.

5. Mandela, *Long Walk to Freedom*, p. 440.

Bibliography

Ayittey, George, *Africa Betrayed*, New York, St Martin's Press, 1992

Boynton, Graham, *Last Days in Cloud Cuckooland*, Johannesburg, Jonathan Ball, 1997

Bredin, Miles, *Blood on the Tracks: a rail journey from Angola to Mozambique*, London, Picador, 1994

Bridgland, Fred, *Jonas Savimbi: A Key to Africa*, London, Mainstream Publishing, 1986

— *Katiza's Journey*, London, Macmillan, 1997

Buthelezi, Mangosuthu, *My Vision of the Future*, London, Weidenfeld & Nicholson, 1990

Cassidy, Michael, *A Witness for Ever*, London, Hodder & Stoughton, 1995

Castaneda, Jorge G., *Companero: The Life and Death of Che Guevara*, New York, Knopf, 1997

Crocker, Chester, *High Noon in Southern Africa: Making Peace in a Rough Neighborhood*, New York, W.W. Norton, 1992

Davidson, Basil, *The Black Man's Burden*, London, James Currey, 1992

De Klerk, F.W., *The Last Trek – A New Beginning*, London, Macmillan, 1999

De Klerk, Willem, *F.W. De Klerk: The Man in His Time*, Johannesburg, Jonathan Ball, 1991

Fox, Edward, *Obscure Kingdoms*, London, Hamish Hamilton, 1993

Fynn, Henry Francis, *The Diary of Henry Francis Fynn*, Pietermaritzburg, Shuter and Shooter, 1986

Gilbey, Emma, *The Lady: The Life and Times of Winnie Mandela*, London, Vintage, 1994

Giliomee, Professor Hermann, *Surrender Without Defeat: Afrikaners and the South African Miracle*, South African Institute of Race Relations, Spotlight, November 1997

Gourevitch, Philip, *We Wish to Inform You That Tomorrow We Will Be Killed with Our Families: Stories From Rwanda*, London, Picador, 1999

Harden, Blaine, *Africa – Dispatches From a Fragile Continent*, New York, Houghton Mifflin, 1991

Kapuscinski, Ryszard, *Another Day of Life*, New York, Harcourt Brace Janovich, 1987

Kemp, Arthur, *Victory or Violence: The Story of AWB*, Johannesburg, Forma Publishers, 1990

Krige, E. and J., *The Realm of a Rain Queen*, Juta Publishers, 1980

Lamb, David, *The Africans: Encounters from the Sudan to the Cape*, London, Mandarin, 1990

Leach, Graham, *The Afrikaners*, London, Macmillan, 1989

Maclean, Veronica, *Crowned Heads*, London, Hodder & Stoughton, 1992

Mandela, Nelson, *Long Walk to Freedom*, Macdonald Purnell, 1994

Matloff, Judith, *Fragments of a Forgotten War*, London, Penguin, 1997

Matsebula, J.S.M., *A History of Swaziland*, 3rd edn, Cape Town, Longman, 1988

Meredith, Martin, *Nelson Mandela: A Biography*, London, Hamish Hamilton, 1997

Morris, Donald, *The Washing of the Spears*, London, Jonathan Cape, 1966

Morton, Andrew, *Moi: The Making of an African Statesman*, London, Michael O'Mara Books, 1998

Munnion, Christopher, *Banana Sunday*, Johannesburg, William Waterman, 1993

Museveni, Yoweri, *Sowing the Mustard Seed*, London, Macmillan, 1997

Naipaul, V.S., *A Bend in the River*, London, Penguin, 1980

Pakenham, Thomas, *The Scramble for Africa*, London, Weidenfeld & Nicholson, 1991

Short, Philip, *Banda*, London, Routledge and Kegan Paul, 1974

Sparks, Allistair, *The Mind of South Africa*, London, Heinemann, 1990

— *Tomorrow is Another Country*, Johannesburg, Struik Book Publishers, 1994

Van Onselen, Charles, *The Seed is Mine*, Cape Town, David Philip, 1996

Waldmeir, Patti, *Anatomy of a Miracle*, London, Viking, 1997

Young, Crawford, and Turner, Thomas, *The Rise and Decline of the Zairian State*, Madison, Wisconsin, University of Wisconsin Press, 1985

Index

Index

Index

Index

Afrikaners
Afrikaner Weerstandsbeweging
165, 168–78
battle of Bop 171–8
exit from South Africa 127–31,
190
post apartheid 140–61
trekboers 127–9
Volksfront 171–2, 176
Ystergarde 165, 178
apartheid 65, 130, 145–6, 205
black/white relations 136–61
Grand Apartheid 198
bombing campaign 177
Bophuthatswana homeland 171–3
battle of Bop 171–4
diamonds 125
economic programme 55
human rights abuses 143
Immorality Act 135
Inkatha Freedom Party 143, 144
feud with ANC 199–200, 207,
258
land reform 216
mercenaries banned 189
minerals 121
murders 151, 155
National Party 146–8
Ossewabrandwag 168–9
Pan Africanist Congress 130
Police Cultural Group 168
political ethics 39
post apartheid 88, 130–31, 170,
216, 274
pre-colonial history 194–5
'Rainbowism' 273
Rand Afrikaans University 159
Rivonia trial 249
Sharpeville massacre 252
support of Angola 100, 112, 164
traditional leaders 197–219
tribal homelands 170–73, 198
Truth and Reconciliation
Commission 143–7, 268–70,
273–4, 288
United Democratic Front 198
white collar crime 39

witchcraft killings 224
Xhosa connection 88
Zululand 191, 197
KwaZulu 198–203, 207,
217–18
Shaka Day 214
Zulu nationalism 199–200, 213
Zulu wars 162–3
Southern African Development
Community 290
Soviet Union 109
in Angola 109, 113
Soyinka, Wole 3, 280
Spice Girls 272
Spicer, Lieutenant-Colonel Tim 188
Stanbrook, Clive 42, 51–2
Steyn, Douw 172
Stockwell, Graham 37, 39
Strasser, Valentine 184
Strijdom, Hans 134
Swaziland 220–42

Tambo, Oliver 88, 286
Taylor, Charles 256
Tembo, John 53–4
Terre Blanche, Etienne 167
Terre'Blanche, Eugene 6, 166,
178–80, 190
battle of Bop 171–8
Jong Afrikanerharte 167
libel case 168
oratory 166
racist attacks by supporters 168
Weerstandsbeweging 165, 168–76
Ystergarde 165, 178
Thambwe, Alexis 24, 36
Too, Mark 75–6
tribalism in Africa 69–71, 80–89
Tshisekedi, Etienne 35
Tutsi people 30, 81–3, 87, 181
Tutu, Bishop Desmond 247, 271, 288
'Rainbowism' 273

Uganda 30, 281–5
Aids 284
ban on party politics 237
United Nations aid 121